THE
BRIAR
PATCH

MURRAY KEMPTON

THE BRIAR PATCH

**THE PEOPLE OF THE STATE OF NEW YORK
V. LUMUMBA SHAKUR ET AL.**

E. P. DUTTON CO., INC.   NEW YORK 1973

for Mike and Jeannie Kempton

"All the people wore armbands in honor of us."

345.73

K326

89468

aug 1974

Published simultaneously in Canada by
Clarke, Irwin & Company Limited,
Toronto and Vancouver

SBN: 0–525–07089–3
Library of Congress Catalog Card Number: 73–190698

Some Acknowledgments

It was Albert Murray, that good and wise man, who reminded me of Uncle Remus, our most precious piece of stolen goods, and directed me towards my title. Jason Epstein set me on this project and Harold Scharlatt saw it through. Many of those who helped me are mentioned in the chronicle with due affection. I owe immeasurable thanks to dozens of others, most especially Bruce and Naomi Bliven, William F. Buckley, Roger Wilkins, Stanley Brezenoff, Robert Silvers and Barbara Epstein. These events took a very long time made shorter by the company of Margot Adler, Jackie Friedrich, Martin Kenner, Peter Zimroth, Ruth Silber, J. C. Bull and Iris Moore. My wife, Beverly, and my son, Christopher, were the joy they have always been and will always be.

I

At five o'clock in the morning of April 2nd, 1969, Sergeant George C. Abraham, of the Special Services Division of the New York City Police Department, knocked at the door of Apartment 4D at 460 West 126th Street. When the voice of a woman inquired who was there, he answered that he was a social worker come to investigate the application of Richard and Iris Moore for public assistance.

At the same moment, Patrolman John Regan was standing outside an apartment at 469 West 163rd Street occupied by Michael Tabor and Rosalind Bennett and was explaining through the door that he had come there in response to a noise complaint. Detective Francis Dalton was outside Apartment 9, 112 West 117th Street, the home of Lumumba and Afeni Shakur, having put on his bulletproof vest, and ignited a rag; and he and the four police officers with him were loudly crying "Fire." Detective James McDonnell was at 336 East 8th Street, where Robert Collier lived with his wife and child and two homeless Puerto Rican boys he was giving shelter from the streets. There had been no answer to the patrolman's knock and Detective McDonnell was setting to work with a crowbar before Robert Collier asked, "What are you doing? Who is there?" Detective McDonnell announced himself an arresting officer; and Robert Collier opened the door for him.

Sergeant Abraham, Detectives Dalton and McDonnell, and Patrolman Regan had gathered with a hundred or so other policemen in a jury room of the Criminal Courts Building two hours before, to be briefed by Inspector William Knapp and Captain Michael Willis of their department's Special Services Division and then dispatched for the simultaneous capture of nineteen of twenty-one persons—"many of them Black Panthers"—who had been indicted for conspiracy to murder police officers and to bomb five department stores.

The arresting parties went forth with each five-man detail provided with one shotgun, two bulletproof vests, and a black officer, it being the function of that last piece of equipment to recite, in the style and timbre of address most soothingly familiar to his quarry, whatever pretext for peaceful entry his commander might devise.

Lieutenant Arthur Deutsch was commander of the detail that Patrolman Regan thus served as native bearer. Arthur Deutsch had been a policeman for sixteen years, the most recent of them in charge of the squad that investigates burglaries in Manhattan North; and this experience of going out each day with a teacup to empty an ocean had left him without illusion that he was astride any white charger as he sat in the car bearing him toward the confrontation with Michael Tabor. The main occupation of his thoughts seems rather to have been the mysterious ways of superiors who would provide only two protective vests for five policemen assigned to subjugate a criminal that Inspector Knapp had called "armed and dangerous" and that Captain Willis had reported to have sworn that he would never be taken alive.

Later Lieutenant Deutsch could not remember that Captain

Willis had made reference to any threat so dire; but he would be reminded of it by Detective Joseph Coffey, who was the district attorney's representative on the expedition and whose angry blue eyes suggested that here was a spirit that would quicken when the briefings touched levels of high romance, while Lieutenant Deutsch's melancholy brown ones suggested that here was a spirit that would only tune out. Detective Coffey was plainly thrilled; Lieutenant Deutsch merely said, again and again, that everybody should take care of himself.

The spurious noise complaint failed to persuade the apartment's occupants to open the door peacefully; and, finally, Lieutenant Deutsch had to proclaim—in a voice whose volume he certainly thought unbecoming to the hour—that he was a police officer with a warrant to arrest Michael Tabor. Detective Coffey then kicked open the door and pushed in, having disdained the bulletproof vest as too cumbersome, followed by Lieutenant Deutsch, who, being the sort of captain whom *noblesse* obliges, declined to wear a vest and deprive some subordinate of its protection.

Detective Coffey would testify later that he had held a gun to Michael Tabor's head and said, "If you move, I'll blow your brains out."

Michael Tabor would testify that Detective Coffey had also shouted: "I've got you, you black bastard. You Panthers say you like to shoot policemen—well, let's see you try now." The shared hyperbole of these recollections may be credited to the accident of natural selection that had put these particular two actors on this scene together—Joseph Coffey the policeman furthest enough gone to indiscretion and Michael Tabor the Panther best equipped in majesty of bearing and cadence to express every degree of the hatred lying between one's clan and the other's.

When they met on trial in October of 1970, Michael Tabor would be serving as his own defense counsel and he would ask Detective Coffey, "Do you feel it's your patriotic duty and obligation to assist in elimination of the Black Panther Party and its members?"

And Joseph Coffey would proudly answer, "It's my duty to common decency, sir."

And, in that same spirit, on the morning of the arrest, he set passionately forth to tear from the walls of Michael Tabor's abode the posters of Malcolm X, of Huey P. Newton, and of Bobby Seale, and even of John Carlos rendering the black power salute at those 1968 Olympic games. All totems, Detective Coffey would later affirm, seemed to him consequential evidence of conspiracy, arson, and attempted murder. Lieutenant Deutsch seems to have watched this display in silence—members of the district attorney's squad, like Coffey, subjects to be treated delicately in a structure where you are never sure which stranger can hurt you. Still his bearing as witness did suggest unspoken thoughts about those stoopings below institutional dignity a policeman indulges when he shows a civilian how he really feels. Since any such outbreak implies that the civilian has gotten to you, might even have alarmed you, and is thus on your own footing and beyond your management.

Arthur Deutsch might have taken the posters, but he would have done it decorously and unhurriedly and with the care a footpad brings to the removal of property whose value to him depends on its not being damaged. His normal round was, after all, the investigation of burglaries; and policemen on special squads seem after a while remarkably to resemble the criminal type they are charged to pursue. When the department has to suspend a degenerate, it is usually from the vice squad; and, if one of its own turns out to be an addict, he is generally on the narcotics squad.

To come upon members of a burglary squad gathering evidence is to witness the contained and silent movements associated with burglars on the prowl.

Arthur Deutsch was a line officer in a department whose commanders are immune to mayors and can be broken only when lieutenants like himself unite against them. He carried the double assurance of the professional whose institution is more powerful than any force outside it and whose grade is as powerful as any within it. Rage of the kind that impelled De-

4

tective Coffey to manifest his contempt for the affronters of common decency had to seem to him close to paranoia; his own assessment of the Panthers must have been very like the judgment of another veteran law officer when he looked across the chasm of class snobbishness at the paltry assemblage of armament the searching parties would bring back and observed, "Don't these people understand that you can't run a revolution on welfare?"

And Sergeant George Abraham, knocking on Richard Moore's door thirty-seven blocks to the south, could feel assured of what Lieutenant Deutsch could only assume: his Department of Special Services knew more about these old subjects of its curiosity and sudden new objects of its authority to crash upon civilians by night than most of them knew about each other. George Abraham was a policeman of the bureau rather than the streets. He was a man of files and paper; and he had not often been used to those insecure moments when the street policeman comes into the dark of close and crowded places to take the suspect who may be armed. But any unease about being unfamiliar with his immediate circumstance could be calmed by the knowledge of being so familiar with all the circumstances surrounding these persons. For there was not much about the Harlem Panthers that George Abraham would have thought unpredictable; at least five agents of the Bureau of Special Services had been members of the party almost from the day in April of 1968 when it first came to New York.

And Sergeant Abraham was the only historian the subsequent events had so far had, being both librarian and exegesist of the documents and the observations provided the police department by these hidden watchmen. The Negro who rises with the least struggle is still the one who happens into the craft of telling whites about blacks. The big Negroes who were first enlisted into the New York City Police Department were there to beat up the little ones. Even into the sixties, those who advanced made their way four parts thanks to the alarm to every one part reflecting the conscience of their superiors. Just as the lieutenant who was appointed a deputy inspector

5

and commander of the Harlem Division owed his eminence to the need to appease the black militants, Sergeant Abraham could credit his own promotions to a no less lively need to contain them; and the most tangible achievement of the Black Panther Party in New York could well have been the chance it gave a recruit patrolman named Ralph White to rise to the rank of detective third grade barely a year after he had been assigned to spy upon it.

So then, Sergeant Abraham could feel assured of knowing not just the schemes of these persons, more real at least to his official self than they may have been to them, but indeed their very intimacies. It was the knowledge that Richard Moore had lately been married—and above his station—to Iris Bull, the daughter of Newark strivers, and had applied for public welfare that had suggested to George Abraham the disguise of an investigator of such claim. And to ease him over any insecurities he might have about coming upon ground entirely unknown, he was carrying a sketch of the apartment's layout provided him by Detective Eugene Roberts who had dined there with the Moores as a Panther just a few weeks before.

Sergeant Abraham knew Richard Moore as Dharuba, more saucy boy than disciplined criminal, once sentenced to from three to five years for a street fight and serving all five for repeated refusals to restrain the impulse to talk back to his keepers, having a nature whose Badness drew much of its strength from the presence of an audience.

Abraham knew that Lumumba Shakur had, until lately, two wives, a privilege of his Moslem tenets, and had only just cast forth one to cleave to the other alone. He knew that Michael Tabor had been an addict-burglar who had lost touch with his parole officer since his redemption through *The Autobiography of Malcolm X.*

No intimacy seemed outside his knowledge: he knew that Alex McKiever, one of those named in the indictment, had recently requested a discharge from the Panther Party's guerilla team because he wanted to marry and get a job and that he could therefore be found asleep at the apartment of his betrothed. He even knew that the wife of Ali Bey Hassan, another of the night's targets, had transiently strayed with Ralph White, a special services agent on underground assignment, because it is one duty of the bureau's servants to report any evidence that they have earned the trust of any subject person.

And he knew that Robert Collier had once been convicted for conspiring to bomb the Statue of Liberty, a fragment of history that could only fortify his sense of entire control over such people, since whatever coherence and purpose had ever gone into this scheme had been the contribution of Raymond Wood, a Bureau of Special Services detective. The bureau had paid for the dynamite and the rental of the car that transported it. Throughout the affair, Patrolman Wood had been the driver while Collier had only been a passenger but dimly aware of the destination. And Sergeant Abraham knew that, since his parole, Collier had been conspicious less for his peripheral and at most avuncular association with the Black Panther Party than for his struggle to establish himself in community youth work on the Lower East Side, an activity whose troubled progress was especially familiar to the sergeant, since one of his functions was to maintain the files his department relied upon to discourage any public or private agency from subsidizing some program where so debased a criminal might affect the posture of a social servant.

Sergeant Abraham was, of course, most dependent upon the Panthers, since he could hardly seem as useful to his superiors as he did unless he could keep their morbid susceptibilities attuned to the terrifying portent of such persons. But his private self could hardly have taken them as seriously as his official self required him to; and, if the minute when a policeman stands with gun drawn outside a stranger's door is especially one belonging to a policeman's private self, George Abraham had the comfort of knowing that he advanced to meet one of those strangers over whose movements he had long ago gained the advantage of learning even before they became movements. Even in this uncertain moment of their changed relationship, he had come to confront less the armed enemy than one more instrument of improvements in his career.

Sergeant Abraham knocked and, upon inquiry from within, announced himself as a welfare inspector. Back came the voice of Richard Moore, asking if he was out of his goddamned mind, it was five in the morning, and let him come back after one in the afternoon.

"I said I had to get in at this time," Sergeant Abraham would later testify, "and that, if he wouldn't let me in, I would bring a police officer with me. The male voice said, 'You better get out of here, and if you bring back a cop—' and I heard a revolver clicking behind the door."

Then, subtleties having been so inadequate, George Abraham proclaimed himself a policeman with a warrant for Richard Moore leading a heavily armed detachment which, one way or another, intended to come in. Richard Moore then opened the door and allowed himself to be carried away. Later that day, in detention, he would tell a policeman that no one could have taken him thus unresisting if all his guns had not been disassembled for cleaning; and an assistant district attorney would set down as potentially valuable evidence of Richard Moore's desperate nature this poor invention to explain away the shame of having shown such common sense.

The professional decorum of Richard Moore's capture seems to have been more typical of the night's doings than the passion injected by Detective Coffey into Michael Tabor's arrest. Detective McDonnell could even suggest the intrusion of a mounting civility between the parties to the taking of Robert Collier:

"I felt as though the man was a gentleman. . . . From the time we walked into the apartment he respected us. He abided with any request we had given him. . . . And the biggest factor involved was the fact that he was able to calm his wife down, because she was running frantically through the rooms, and we were very concerned about this [because the detective had been] informed by my superior officers that they believed

8

that there was a loaded rifle in the apartment and to take extreme precautions."

And, just as Mrs. Collier grew quiet, Detective McDonnell heard a stirring in another room and went to find there lying on a mattress the two Puerto Rican boys Collier had salvaged from the street. Beside their feet he found a shopping bag full of small pieces of brass pipe; and, as Detective McDonnell cast over this lot, he came upon three with holes in them that his training suggested might be the makings of pipe bombs. With the warning about the rifle still vivid in his mind, McDonnell had earlier said that Collier must know what he was looking for and that he wouldn't leave until he got it; and Collier had answered that he would give the detectives whatever they wanted "so you won't rip the place up," and had gone into his bathroom to return with a red can containing enough gunpowder to fill a talcum box. Detective McDonnell made the requisite leap and charged Collier with possession of an explosive substance and the waifs with possession of the pipes Collier's gunpowder could in theory have armed.

By the time all three suspects had reached their detention cells, McDonnell later remembered, Collier's major concern had been the trouble that had befallen the two boys. The detective recalled him asking, "Why are you picking on these kids when you know the pipes are mine?"

"I said, 'I am sorry. I will have to let the court decide that.' "

"He then said to me, 'You know it. I told you they were mine . . . and you went ahead and you arrested the boys anyway.' "

He had made himself the victim of his own generous nature. For those three pipes, whose clouded title Robert Collier had so conveniently taken upon himself, would constitute almost the whole complement of explosives that the district attorney of New York County would offer as its most compelling evidence of a plot to bomb five department stores the very day of the arrest. Assistant District Attorney Phillips would look upon them and declare, "If I'd known that Collier had those things

9

ready at hand, I'd have been really scared about how imminent this business was." And, for months to come, he would carry one of those pipes to court with him, to hold it up and remind all present of the horror visited upon a Chicago department store by "a bomb just like this" and to wave away whatever fugitive doubts a judge might entertain about holding the prisoners under bail of $100,000 each.

Altogether, ten persons had been arrested where they were sleeping that morning; along with Tabor, the Shakurs, Moore, and Collier, the police brought to their pens John J. Casson a.k.a. Ali Bey Hassan; Alex McKiever a.k.a. Abayama Katara, and Eddie Joseph a.k.a. Jamal, both high school students; Walter Johnson a.k.a. Baba Odinga; and Joan Bird, a nursing student at the Bronx Community College.

Besides these bodies, the police detachments had carried away with them five .38 caliber pistols, two military rifles, and three shotguns—a whole arsenal only slightly larger than the table of equipment issued to any one of their own raiding parties; along with a pair of handcuffs from Michael Tabor's; a spear and bow and arrow taken from the wall and a canister that might be usable for signal smoke found in the kitchen of the Shakurs'; a sword cane from Ali Bey Hassan's; some aerosol cans and an old alarm clock mounted for timing explosives from Eddie Joseph's; and reams of paper including a map of the Bronx with the locations of railroad stations marked in pencil and a manual called "Urban Guerilla Warfare" found at Moore's.

Nathaniel Burns a.k.a. Sekou Odinga had jumped thirty-five feet to the ground from the window of his Brooklyn lodging when the police knocked at his door. He would make his way to Algeria to find Larry Mack and Thomas Berry a.k.a. Mshina already there before him.

There had been no need to search for Richard Harris and Donald Weems a.k.a. Kuwasi Balagoon, who were already secure in jail in Newark where they had been arrested for robbery.

No one was found after the police broke in the doors of the

10

last known dwelling places of Lee Roper a.k.a. Shaba Om; Clark Squire, the computer analyst; Curtis Powell, the research chemist; and, most alarming escapee of all, William King a.k.a. Kwando Kinshasa, once a marine sergeant and now a subway toll changer, captain of the Panther guerilla team, and author of "Urban Guerilla Warfare," the mimeographed handbook for the terrorist of the imagination, one copy of which Sergeant Abraham had seized from Richard Moore. Abraham had, of course, read "Urban Guerilla Warfare" long ago, while it could be suspected that Moore had only meant to get around to it soon, having as he did a nature distinctly less habituated to sedentary responsibilities than the sergeant's.

That afternoon, his father brought Lonnie Epps, a high school student, to police headquarters; the chemist Powell and the computer analyst Squire yielded themselves over for dishonorable discharge from the middle class; and Powell's captors could add to the district attorney's stock of evidence one bottle of hydrochloric and another of nitric acid and a volume called *High Explosives and Propellants*.

By the next morning, Lee Berry was the last of the lot unaccounted for either as a prisoner or as a known fugitive. Berry was a patient at the Manhattan Veterans Hospital, under treatment for the epilepsy that had finally proved too much for him in Korea. His mother telephoned to say that the police had come inquiring for his brother and himself. Berry called the police to say where he was; and they promptly entered the hospital with the full complement of armor that had been appointed for the arrest of his armed and dangerous accomplices in the briefing of the morning of the day before, ordered the supervising physician to discharge the patient as "a murderer, an arsonist, and a Black Panther," and took him to the Tombs and the solitary confinement where he would shortly grow too sick to stand trial with the others.

Twelve hours after the arrests, Lee Roper had wandered into the Harlem office of the Black Panther Party still unaware that he was a wanted fugitive from a criminal indictment. The first person to greet him was Dolores Patterson, who had been with

11

Ali Bey Hassan when the police had broken in upon them that morning.

"What you doing here, brother?" Dolores Patterson asked Roper. "Don't you know you're indicted?"

"Fuck it," Lee Roper answered. "If they want me, let them come get me." Someone else present seems to have observed that, if they didn't have him by now, there was no sense hanging around to get picked up.

"Maybe you're right," Lee Roper decided. "Let me out of here." He paused to ask Carl Woods, a Panther more faithful than most to the common office chores, if he might borrow money for a taxi.

"Don't you think I ought to come with you?" Carl Woods wondered. And Roper answered, no, he didn't want to get Woods involved and took the money and somehow managed to link up with William King in Columbus, Ohio, where the FBI would find them in November. By then, the police had captured eighteen of the twenty-one suspects they sought.

He need not have included among his manifold worries any particular concern that he could possibly get Carl Woods in trouble. When next they saw one another, he would be listening to Carl Woods, now known to be Patrolman Carlos Ashwood of the Special Services Division, give evidence for the people against him and all the others for crimes supposed to have arisen from hatred and moral indifference of the sort that has abandoned all compunction toward its object.

II

The march of the journalists to an audience with Frank S. Hogan passes down a corridor lined with portraits of departed district attorneys of New York, first as city and then as county, beginning with Protestants charged to contain the Irish hoodlums of their time, moving past Irishmen commissioned to overcome the Jewish and Italian gangsters of theirs, and ending in the presence of Mr. Hogan himself, who has become the last refinement of all this history and could, if vanity were his weakness, claim, after thirty-two years in his chair, to have had a longer and larger part in it than any man who came before him.

The district attorney's invitation to the journalists had been for eleven o'clock in the morning of April 2nd, precisely six hours after Sergeant Abraham had knocked on Richard Moore's door; and it signaled the end of the improvisational and the restoration of the ceremonial. Mr. Hogan's press conferences are state occasions; he is unique among prosecutors for neither intruding nor letting himself be intruded upon. Neither pride nor ambition would ever move Mr. Hogan thus to array the journalists; he responds only to his concept of obligation to persons he trusts not to bother him because they know that he will not bother them unless it is worth their time. His appearances are so rare and the sophistication of his judgment so revered that his pronouncements are taken not as allegations but as definitions of the crime, not the commencement of its history but its completion; and any questions from his auditors are founded not on doubts about the narrative but on anxiety to approach Mr. Hogan's mastery of each detail.

In this case, as is his custom with all clangorous ones, the district attorney read to his audience from the indictment of twenty-one persons who, as members of the Black Panther Party, had used "its paramilitary structure and discipline in pursuit . . . of an overall plan to harass and destroy those elements of society which the defendants regarded as part of the 'power structure.'" Twelve had been arrested, two were already in jail on earlier charges, and seven at that moment were still missing.

Together, the indictment declared, they had executed dynamite attacks on four police stations in the fall of 1968 and the winter of 1969 and had thereafter planned to bomb a commuter railroad's Queens right-of-way, the Bronx Botanical Gardens, and the shopping crowds in five department stores on the day after the one on which they had been taken.

Mr. Hogan elaborated upon the indictment in only two details: he identified Macy's, Alexander's, Bloomingdale's, Abercrombie & Fitch, and Korvette's as the targets and "tomorrow" as the planned date for the assault upon them; when combined with his public thanks to the grand jury that had labored until one that morning to avert this peril, these small, skilled touches served both to suggest its imminence and to elevate the social standing of the persons and the property that would have suffered as its objects; and the district attorney's quiet tones had created a public image of these defendants that no strain after hue and cry could have made any worse.

14

The moment when they were intruded upon had passed for all time; they had already become and would henceforth remain the intruders. While the journalists were listening to the indictment, the defense lawyers were searching for it fruitlessly in the office of the clerk of the Supreme Court of New York County. Mr. Hogan had the only fair copy; and the clerks had not yet refined their own beyond its state as a rough and working draft. Priorities in these matters rest on subtle notions of need and capacity: it was assumed that the journalists could not wait and that the defendants had nothing else to do.

Their lawyers did not carry any weight that could depress in their favor what balance there could ever be between the clerk's sense of his own convenience and his attention to the complainant outsider. William Kunstler is the only member of the radical bar whose entry upon the stage might suggest to a New York civil servant that to affront him could bring clamors that, in turn, might produce inquiries from one's commanders the next day; and Mr. Kunstler was elsewhere that day, and his firm had no one to send except Arthur Turco, a junior associate.

Few choices are fortunate, and Mr. Turco was the unhappiest choice of all—an Italian street boy not sensible enough to affect to be a *mafioso* but wantonly distracted enough to call himself a white Panther. He had a reputation as a stocker of guns, and so open an appearance as a conspirator indistinguishable from the others that when Afeni Shakur entered the courtroom he would enfold her so shamelessly as to start in all proper observers intimations not just of plots but of unthinkable intimacies between them. Mr. Turco was already distrusted even by radicals as a creature so wild that he must be a police agent, to be suffered if at all only as proof and penalty of the blunders Mr. Kunstler had made inevitable when he dedicated himself to the pursuit of the authentic.

Mr. Turco was accompanied by Gerald Lefcourt, who had represented Lumumba Shakur in prior engagements with criminal prosecutors but who was otherwise acquainted with few of the defendants and would at once incur the assistant district attorney's suspicion that he had been drawn there by no summons more formal than the emanations of the morning news broadcast. Mr. Lefcourt was engaging while Mr. Turco seemed everything else but; even so, he could not persuade the clerks that he was someone not merely attractive but dangerous when disdained; and Mr. Lefcourt's graces had to be laid aside in deference to Mr. Turco's way of doing things, since he was the junior and Mr. Turco the surrogate for Mr. Kunstler, who was presumably, in this cause, as in all despaired-of ones, the senior counsel. Mr. Turco's way of doing things was to attack each official objective as the black militants are wont to do, with that underscored truculence which confesses its absolute dispossession of any power at all. The clerks soon enough assumed that his demand to see any document in their keeping had no authority at all and dismissed them both to wander listlessly until they came to a room on the fourth floor where they found their clients, tried to approach them, and were ordered to leave by the officers of the city's Department of Corrections. There was nothing for them to do thereafter but wait—lawyers denied detailed knowledge of the charges against their clients or, for that matter, even enough knowledge of their clients—until two in the afternoon when the defendants would all be arraigned by Assistant District Attorney Phillips before Supreme Court Justice Charles Marks. Mr. Phillips had been delayed by Mr. Hogan's press conference and Justice Marks by the need to rest after having been awake into the morning while waiting until the grand jury would order the arrests and he could approve the warrants.

The excesses of the morning had produced in both judge and prosecutor an inflammation of those parts where each was most susceptible—loss of sleep having made Judge Marks more peevish than usual and the sound of his great chief reciting Mr. Phillips' own allegations as demonstrated axioms having made the assistant district attorney's sense of self as embodied authority more passionate than ever. Together they fell upon Mr. Turco and Mr. Lefcourt like armed householders upon trespassers.

Mr. Phillips, fixed in the conviction that while there might,

16

in some theory or other, exist some excuse for these defendants, there could be no excuse for anyone who might come to their side, insisted that these two young strangers had intruded with so little warrant that he could see on their faces that they did not even know the persons they claimed as their clients.

He had aimed at a spot where Mr. Lefcourt, for one, could hardly feel armored; but he had the transient luck to have Lumumba Shakur brought forth as first to be arraigned and their mutual recognition for the moment quieted Mr. Phillips. His credentials thus tenuously established, Mr. Lefcourt could step upon the ground of argument that Shakur, as stable citizen impoverished by prior bail commitments, deserved consideration for a low bond.

Lefcourt asked first whether Justice Marks might grant him two minutes with Shakur to make his background less remotely tangible in his lawyer's memory; Justice Marks turned at once to Mr. Phillips; and, when he came back, the request went unanswered and remained forgotten. Mr. Lefcourt could only go forward from no more than his dim recollection that Shakur was director of the Ellsmere Tenants Council, a poverty agent, and married and the father of three children. The job and the marriage had both been dissolved since last they met.

Mr. Phillips, on the other hand, was master of every fact that might bring anyone discredit; he merely abstained from immediate challenge to Mr. Lefcourt's portrait of Lumumba Shakur's domestic constancy until it was his turn with Afeni Shakur and he could destroy them both.

"This is a defendant," he affirmed in the meanwhile, "who does not work for the tenants group, is not presently employed by the tenants group, and has a long criminal record. . . . He was arrested in Connecticut where he was going to do a bank robbery. He is under investigation for shooting any number of police officers. . . . This is a defendant who, after committing crimes and being arrested, goes back and continues to commit crimes. . . . It would be a menace to the community and a menace to society to admit this man to bail; and therefore we request that no bail be set."

17

And Mr. Phillips looked scornfully at Mr. Lefcourt across the stocky figure of Shakur, bearded, bespectacled, and bemused, his weight larger than theirs together. He knew more, he bulked larger; he seemed the familiar and they the strangers to their own affairs. His way of life must have been that of the boy unlikely to have taken easily to paper and the man struggling with paper until paper, that stubborn enemy, became at last his servant and the only fuel needed by his imagination; and now it could assert its triumph over inferior ways of life, whether they belong to young lawyers born to enough property to indulge their weakness for adolescent romance or whether they belong to defendants like this object of Mr. Lefcourt's sentimental fancy.

Mr. Lefcourt ran his fingers through his shamelessly abundant hair and protested that Mr. Phillips could not have known so much more than he himself did except from police agents within the Black Panther Party.

"The Connecticut case [Shakur] is on bail for," he concluded. "This is a pending matter. It is not a matter of investigation. It is already in the courts."

"He went to Connecticut with a sawed-off shotgun under his coat to rob a bank," Mr. Phillips interposed.

And then, for the first time, Mr. Lefcourt, wandering in the dark, began to touch and feel some suggestion that Mr. Phillips did not know everything after all, or that even if he did, he might be that opponent, otherwise without weakness, who could not resist making surmises that were more than he could have known.

"Of course, he is not charged with that in Connecticut," he replied. "It is just a malicious absurd statement by the district attorney."

None of these wrangles distracted Justice Marks from thoughts of himself and of all that he had endured:

"I am the judge who was here at twelve thirty this morning to receive the indictment in this case. I was requested by the district attorney to hold myself available at home so that the indictment could be returned before us this morning, as it was

18

alleged before the grand jury, as I understand, that certain acts might be performed today and, if they were performed, it might result in the deaths of many hundreds of people in certain large department stores. Now, under these circumstances, giving every benefit of doubt to the defendant . . . and [given] the seriousness of the charge and the background of the defendant, the bail is fixed by this court at one hundred thousand dollars."

"I am the judge who was here at twelve thirty this morning": the mind of Justice Marks had been so filled with the inconvenience these persons had caused him as to drive his concern for their rights as defendants into that corner deserving only a cursory nod. Charles Marks had been a criminal courts judge for thirty-two years, arriving and departing every day with step growing slower and thus fancied more stately year by year, gravely saluted by policemen, sitting among the window boxes on the thirteenth floor on those slow spring mornings when one must almost have had to push oneself to go downstairs and confront the refuse of last night's pens, and coming at last near the age of retirement; and that experience had meant to him the achievement of every hope of glory at no expense of effort to develop the means of grace. For it is the special curiosity of the correction process that its officers look all day upon specimens attesting that America is a failure and then go home at night, more often than not, with the renewed conviction of their selves as embodied evidence that America is a success.

Mr. Lefcourt pled that the bail was "obscenely unconstitutional . . . and might as well be a million dollars or five million" and Justice Marks snapped that he wanted to hear no more about it; and the defendant Shakur was led away to be replaced by the defendant Richard Moore and successively by each of the others, temporarily automatons, with faces that conveyed no more to the spectators than to their judge, heads down much of the time, replies almost submissive, and eyes with the last expression of pleading any courtroom would see in them again until they would sit behind their lawyers during the summations, leaning forward in unison, praying to and almost trusting in the jury. They were pushed by security guards —not from cruelty but because there were more guards than the well of the courtroom had room for—and they were bawled at by clerks who had so faithfully caught their tone from Justice Marks as to visit his bad temper upon the lawyers along with the defendants, until Mr. Lefcourt was moved to protest his treatment and the clerk dismissed him:

"Maybe he would like to exchange twenty-two years' experience for his experience."

Mr. Phillips continued to reaffirm his suspicions that Mr. Turco and Mr. Lefcourt, far from being chosen counsel, were mere intruders unknown to most of the clients they claimed were theirs. It was a suspicion not without supporting evidence; at one point, asked to name his counsel, the defendant Walter Johnson could only point to Mr. Turco, who could only rally himself with bold assertion:

"As far as not knowing our clients, your Honor, we have represented every one of them in an action, your Honor."

"I take it a *criminal* action," Justice Marks answered.

During one interval between the interchange of bodies, Mr. Turco asked the court to permit him and Mr. Lefcourt to confer with their clients after the arraignment; and Justice Marks ordered his clerk:

"Tell the Corrections Department to keep them here two hours after the conclusion of these hearings."

But as the process approached its end, Mr. Turco rose to report that the attendant corrections officers had told him that they could permit no delay to accommodate counsel because their orders were to take each prisoner to his appointed house of detention as soon as the arraignment procedure was accomplished.

"I am not the one to decide that," Justice Marks replied. "The Department of Corrections has complete control once they go out that door. I can only request it and I am not telling them what they should do on the question of security."

The defendants, still not having talked to their lawyers, were then carried off to seven different jails where Corrections

20

Commissioner George McGrath ordered each held in solitary confinement since, he later explained, the district attorney had defined them all for him as "dangerous, obdurate, and untrustworthy prisoners." The arraignment of the epileptic Lee Berry the next day would be a thing of urgency so desperate that there was not even time to inform his lawyers.

Lonnie Epps was also arraigned the next day, by which time Mr. Kunstler had appeared with plumes of rhetoric more flamboyant and therefore more affronting to Justice Marks than any Mr. Lefcourt had yet attained the years to dare; and the passages between them quickly rose from the grumpy and contemptuous tone Justice Marks had employed with the young lawyers to a slanging match between equals:

MR. KUNSTLER: We represent the Black Panther Party.

JUSTICE MARKS: I didn't know they were indicted. . . . Is that a political party or what? I never heard of it.

MR. KUNSTLER: It is a political party of young black men and women dedicated to a ten-point program.

JUSTICE MARKS: Have they got a certificate filed with the secretary of state as a political party?

MR. KUNSTLER: They are a national party, your Honor. They have run candidates.

JUSTICE MARKS: If the facts alleged in this indictment are true—of course I don't understand it—if these facts are true, I say, I don't know why they should be carrying guns and ammunition and all that stuff.

MR. KUNSTLER: That is a question Martin Luther King might answer, your Honor, if he could speak.

JUSTICE MARKS: Well, I wish you would follow the dictates of Martin Luther King and they wouldn't have this.

Justice Marks had agreed to review the $100,000 bails on April 11th, and the defense attorneys struggled to prepare themselves with the necessary affidavits—attestations of jobs and stability of existence that might persuade the court that these defendants were enough in tune with everyday life to be

21

worthy risks for bail. Given the condition and repute of the parties, this project was, of course, hopeless; but the defense went bravely at it only to discover that the papers they laid before Justice Marks interested him only to the extent that he could find something in the background of their subjects that might discredit them while he dismissed with suspicion or indifference anything that might do them credit.

Mr. Lefcourt introduced the affidavit of Michael Tabor.

JUSTICE MARKS: Just a minute. You have his occupation: an artist for the Black Panther Party. What kind of job is that? Is he getting paid for it? Or what kind of artist work does he do? I happen to have members of my family who are very high up in the field of art in the city of New York and I never heard of him, Michael Tabor.

Mr. Lefcourt certified that Lumumba Shakur had been employed for five years by the Ellsmere Tenants Council.

JUSTICE MARKS: What are his wages? You didn't put his wages.

MR. LEFCOURT: The exact wages I don't know. We know it is very small, and we know——

JUSTICE MARKS: What do you call "very small"?

MR. LEFCOURT: Your Honor, subsistence wages. I am not sure of the figures. And I don't think whether he earns forty dollars or thirty dollars or ninety dollars should really matter on the question of whether he should have a hundred thousand dollars bail.

JUSTICE MARKS: It does. He has three children. Is he getting relief from the city of New York to take care of his wife and three children? Because, if he is getting subsistence wages —around forty dollars a week—I understand in the city of New York that is not enough to pay for food, rent, and clothing, not even for an individual.

MR. LEFCOURT: Your Honor, his wife is one of the other defendants, and was working as well——

JUSTICE MARKS: What does she earn?

MR. LEFCOURT: Afeni Shakur?

MR. PHILLIPS: That is not his wife, the mother of his three children. He doesn't work for the Ellsmere Tenants Council.

JUSTICE MARKS: Just a minute, when I want you to answer, I'll ask you, Mr. Phillips. . . . Are they legally married or so-called "common-law," which has been eliminated in the state of New York for over thirty years? There is no such legal statement as "common-law wife" in the state of New York.

MR. LEFCOURT: They live together, your Honor.

JUSTICE MARKS: They live together. Then it's an illegal combination, living together. That is in violation of the laws of the state of New York. And, as to Walter Johnson——

MR. LEFCOURT: Your Honor, as to Walter Johnson, the thing I would like to add is that he was supporting his mother by the occupation listed in the affidavit, and he also has no prior record.

JUSTICE MARKS: What was his salary as a grocery clerk in the Harlem area that he is able to support his mother?

MR. LEFCOURT: Let's assume it was minimum wage.

JUSTICE MARKS: I see.

These lives were so alien to Justice Marks' that their mere description, even by their own counsel, seemed to him prejudicial to their chances for a fair trial. He said it was his duty to seal what had been offered to him as certification of good character; and, when Mr. Lefcourt protested that District Attorney Hogan's press conference had contained remarks most damaging to the defendants and that no judge had ordered them sealed, Justice Marks replied: "If you have any quarrel with the district attorney's office, that is for him to answer. I am not answering. The district attorney needs no defense from me."

Thereafter, Mr. Lefcourt could only travel in search of some court that might order reduction of bail from the level appointed by Justice Marks, grasping at judges in the Bronx and Queens and at the court of appeals in Albany or the federal court in Foley Square; and always, Mr. Phillips met them with Robert Collier's piece of pipe, which, whatever its inade-

23

quacies as device for *attentat,* was a most formidable weapon for his purposes.

"These defendants are not ordinary run-of-the-mill criminals. They are terrorists," he had cried out on May 1st in Justice Irwin Davidson's Bronx County courtroom, where defense counsel had come aground in their search for someone who might lighten the bails appointed by Justice Marks. It was Mr. Phillips' way, when the fit was upon him, to think first how disreputable the subject was and, only afterward, how dangerous:

"Lumumba Shakur is also portrayed by these lawyers as a man who has a family and is interested in the community. Before he was arrested, Shakur threw his wife and children out of his home. . . . So this Shakur is not really a conscientious family man as presented here." And then the afterthought: "Shakur has a criminal record that is absolutely shocking."

With time, the considerable zest Mr. Phillips brought to heightening his pitch before judges who knew little about the indictment began to be cast over with faint embarrassment; and he was almost engagingly relieved the next day at being able to forswear such flights when he came before Justice John M. Murtagh, a trusted familiar:

"Your Honor, because the press is represented here, I don't want to go into any inflammatory description of the evidence in this case. I did so before Judge Davidson. I will ask that the record before Judge Davidson be presented to your Honor."

By June, these weary rounds having trailed off, Mr. Phillips could exult that seventeen judges had heard and refused to heed the importunities of the defense. He had, throughout these passages, cut a figure quite outsize as against the proportions of the challenge, for these routine victories had been accompanied by an expenditure of passion in advocacy quite beyond his tactical needs. Defense counsel had entered upon these wanderings largely because, having no real expectation of refuge anywhere, it could only go everywhere, sustained perhaps by the instinct that, since it had no other way to attain familiarity with clients essentially cut off and by themselves, it

24

might gain some measure of trust from them by talking the way these defendants would have if their boldness had not been temporarily diminished by the shock of being isolated and helpless. The way to such a difficult communion was to assert in court after court that the indictment was a conspiracy to crush the aspirations of young black people, devised by a Republican attorney general, enlisting Democratic district attorneys, implemented by sitting judges; and this definition of matters isolated the defense even more than ever, since it demanded that judges believe the worst about the system which had made them judges.

Pretty much everyone accepts Justice Holmes' observation that judges reflect the felt necessities of their time. Still he might have been more precise if he had described them as creatures of the felt necessities of the time just before the one when they sit. In New York, men advance slowly to be judges and through steadfast fidelity to the managers of political parties they are rewarded for acceptance of our institutions and are naturally resentful of those who traduce them. Few judges are inclined to look behind the assertions of a district attorney who has held his office longer than they have theirs, who treats them with courtesy unaccompanied by hauteur, and whose description of the case at hand they have grown used to hearing accepted by most juries and even, for that matter, by many lawyers for the defense.

Fewer judges still are anxious to suspect the motives of other judges. It is far easier for an appellate court to put right the misjudgments of the brother below than it is to rebuke him for having lost his temper. Mr. Hogan's reputation made it unlikely that any of Justice Marks' colleagues would find it bad judgment in him to have set the $100,000 bail recommended by the district attorney; and if the record suggested that Justice Marks had introduced into that ceremony an atmosphere which could well seem undignified to most judges and even deplorable to some, what notice any of them gave this offense had to be overwhelmed by the excuse of its provocation. One fundament of the decorum of our courts is that defense attorneys accept the imbalance which dictates that they may be cited for contempt if they dare talk about the district attorney in terms approaching the language he inflicts upon their clients. Mr. Phillips, carried away, was attacking twenty-one strangers; Mr. Kunstler, carried away, was attacking whole institutions. The accommodations that produce tranquillity are endangered whenever counsel for the defense sounds the way his clients feel; and here were lawyers whose very briefs breathed sentiments perilously close to the utterances of the Black Panther Party itself. If revolutionary conspiracy is a crime, then how can the attorney who talks as though he approves it seem to a judge much different from a lawyer who approves armed robbery? When a lawyer asserts that his client is the victim of society, he can be forgiven for resorting to an honorable, if shopworn, word if by society he means that abstraction whose crimes belong to history; but, whenever he makes it clear that by society he means certainly the prosecutor and inferentially the presiding judge, he has impermissibly intruded into the present tense and upon the present scene.

Supreme Court Justice John M. Murtagh was never more clearly the voice of every judge than he was in June of 1969, when he had taken over the custody of the case he would maintain throughout the next two years and felt at once impelled to remind defense counsel of the proper bounds of advocacy:

"As a lawyer, I suggest that you have every obligation to defend the rights of the accused, but you have an equal obligation not to insult the court or to insult society."

Still, while Mr. Phillips summoned up and cast forth the burning arrows of what he had come—most curiously for a quasi-judicial officer—to be proud of as his talent for the inflammatory, the reflection arose that his universal success in these uneven combats might work some injury to the defendants at the cost of rather greater damage to himself. He was accomplishing nothing more than the destruction of reputations that barely existed and of presumptions of innocence

26

already dismissed by a public which had immediately assumed that the district attorney would not have indicted these persons if he were not certain of proving their guilt. They would likely have remained in prison if he had done no more than unobtrusively growl in the courts where he so loudly barked. But, wherever Mr. Phillips had traveled, the clangor of his definition of events had been approved until his assurance that no sensible person could question it grew harder and more brittle; and there fled from him those considerations of the element of reasonable doubt which, if they need not engage a prosecutor's sense of justice, are necessary to the caution and solicitude required for his approach to a jury. Mr. Phillips, from so much asserting without challenge, had commenced to forget that the matter of proving remained.

In any case, his passionate and occasionally malign flights were less effectively cruel to their objects than were the indifferent habits of city institutions that were not ·so much committed.to punishing these prisoners as to containing their inconvenience. In May, Mr. Hogan had sat down with Justice Saul Streit, administrator of the criminal courts, and confronted a calendar in its customary condition of coagulation. The district attorney had observed that, since the length and complication of the Panther trial could only make matters worse, it would be most sensible to select a single judge to see the whole business through. Mr. Hogan's choice was Justice Murtagh, who was thereupon appointed to the burden.

No significant bystander seems to have been to any degree distressed that Mr. Hogan had appointed the judge who would preside over a case that the prosecutor's office had already described as the most critical in its charge for the coming term, incompatible though such a process seems with any image of what Justice Murtagh unvaryingly calls "the American system of justice," knowledge of which these defendants might have acquired if they had listened to their civics teachers instead of the Streets. But Mr. Hogan rather frequently picks his judges; and this case was one where he felt so certain of the result that

27

he felt less need for a judge who might assist the hanging than for one who could manage with equanimity the ceremonies leading up to it.

Justice Murtagh was the son of a fire battalion chief; like many New York judges, he had gone to one of the municipal colleges; but, unlike most of them, he had progressed from there to Harvard Law School and had been graduated to a downtown law firm with the name Choate in it. He had inherited much of the bravery and the garrison mentality of the Catholics who established the police and fire departments of New York as their citadel and he had acquired some of the stuffiness of his first Protestant employers. This mingling of contradictions had left him with as much trust in the outsider as an Irish policeman and as much flourish as a Presbyterian lawyer.

Scandal had touched his career only once and under circumstances leaving no real scar upon his reputation. He was once New York City's commissioner of investigation and seems to have brought a moral zeal sterner than customary to an office where policy often sits beside probity as restraining influence. The only stain on his record was a failure soon enough to take seriously the evidence that the flower of the police department had entered the employment of Harry Gross, a Brooklyn bookie. Afterward, Commissioner Murtagh was indicted for misfeasance; but the appellate division had dismissed the charge even before he was formally arrested. The informed understood that political spite had been the real source of this embarrassment and that Commissioner Murtagh was honest to the point of being victim of his own innocence; he had asked the department's line officers whether they were corrupt, they had told him that they were not, and that declaration had sufficed for someone incapable of believing that a policeman could lie to him.

The sworn, if occasionally bent, witness of police officers is a prime support for prosecutors in their criminal trials; and Justice Murtagh's undamaged faith in the word of anyone in uniform contributed to the respect that Mr. Hogan had found increasing across the nineteen years of the judge's ascent from chief magistrate to justice of the state Supreme Court. But his manner was more to the point than the set of his beliefs, however useful. Mr. Hogan was worried mainly about ceremony; he was less afraid of the defendants than he was of Mr. Kunstler, who was certain to be not only contumacious but noisily accompanied by that cluster of the alienated young who had taken to following him about as they might an entertainer, feeding and loudly approving those effronteries so deplored by everyone who remembered how respectable he had been before he was seized by his present possession. Justice Murtagh seemed an ideal choice as wall against Mr. Kunstler's sallies. He had considerable bottom power; and he looked more like a judge than most of his colleagues, the shifty devices used for elevating them having left too few of them looking at all like judges.

Justice Murtagh, with his white hair precisely parted, his hard blue eyes and the sudden smile he turned upon those few favored customers of his, the jurors, looked indeed like that judge whose authority was unchallenged above all others, the Irish saloonkeeper, proud of his house and master over all the uncertainties any adversary proceeding might produce. His manner was stately and so was his speech; he was the author of books, and had even composed an introduction to a work of the renegade Kunstler, when they were both bound together in comity. The defendant Michael Tabor would remember having read *Cast the First Stone*, Judge Murtagh's plea for the prostitute as victim, during one of his terms in prison and pronounced it "right on." His literary exercises had marked the justice's every utterance with a most formal cast, homiletic in style and peculiarly stiff in dress. Things were never plain but always "manifest"; the conduct of defense counsel and the acoustics of his courtroom were never bad but always "left something to be desired." Justice Murtagh was a man of great pride in his periods and considerable deliberation in their pronouncement; and his effect, if not often solicitous, was definitely suppressive and altogether made him an irresistible convenience for a dis-

29

trict attorney and an administrative judge faced with the prospective inconvenience of Mr. Kunstler.

But then Mr. Kunstler, having been laid as cross upon this strong back, was suddenly lifted. His duties as chief of defense in the conspiracy trial of the Chicago Seven called him away, and he had to give up this case. His place as counsel, in default of any elder, fell upon Mr. Lefcourt.

Mr. Lefcourt had briefly been a staff attorney for the Legal Aid Society, the appointed representative of New York's criminal poor, and had been separated for his inability to adjust to a system that relies upon the district attorney for most of the kindness its clients can hope for and must therefore be so dependent on his goodwill that it is an assumption of the criminal courts that no director of Legal Aid can be selected without the approval of Mr. Hogan, whose position as society's gatekeeper against intrusive outsiders thus includes the power of helping to choose not just some of the judges who will try the indigents who are most often his adversaries but even the overseer of the lawyers who defend them.

"I felt like a hangman," Mr. Lefcourt had said upon his departure from Legal Aid, which would likely have been voluntary soon enough if not sooner requested. He had then set up the Law Commune with his sister-in-law, Carol, and with William Crain, another expellee from Legal Aid, whose maladjustment to its conventions had been so openly contemptuous that his memory in that family was bitter where Mr. Lefcourt's was no worse than regretful. It was remembered of Mr. Crain's apprenticeship that when a colleague had advised him to adhere more deferentially to the society's acceptance of its place as a second-class institution in the cause of tenth-class clients, Mr. Crain was said to have replied that anyone who thought him overzealous in court now need only wait until his probation period was over.

The Law Commune was governed by the principles of mutual aid; and Mr. Lefcourt, who has a modest inherited income, took there a salary lower than the share allotted its legal secretaries; its clients were drawn from the radical young,

30

a community spirited enough to provide any lawyer who served its members with the courtroom experience of years within months. But, despite the intensity of his education, Mr. Lefcourt was only twenty-seven years old; and, in the talk where Mr. Kunstler had said that the whole load must now fall upon him, he drew the impression that Mr. Kunstler had almost wanted to say that no counsel adequately senior was left and that it might be better all around to consider pleading the defendants guilty.

Still this was one of those times when a young man feels naked and consequently more sensitive than he need be in suspecting signals from his elders. Once, later on, Mr. Lefcourt went to a wedding where his hosts, less conscious of the notoriety of the stage he occupied than they ought to have been, introduced him to the chief judge of the New York State Court of Appeals; and Mr. Lefcourt confronted a visage that mingled so much repulsion with so much embarrassment as to make him almost sickeningly understand how alone he was.

He thought he might have been less lonely if he had the support of deepening acquaintance with his clients, although he may have exaggerated the power of inspiration that was left them in their temporarily crushed and fragmented state. On the day they were arrested, George McGrath, the city's commissioner of corrections, had read their indictment and approved this directive for their future confinement:

"The inmates listed herein are charged with conspiracy as a result of an attempt to 'blow up' various institutions of the City. There is reason to believe that they are extremely dangerous . . .

"Therefore these inmates shall be treated as close custody cases at all times while in the respective institutions. While transferred to and from courts or other outside agencies as may be required, they shall be handled as special cases and extra precautions shall be taken. THEY SHALL BE KEPT SEPARATE AND APART AT ALL TIMES."

In the execution of this order, they were sequestered in seven different jails, and, in the first five months after their indictment, counsel for the defense was allowed to confer with them as a group for only three hours. When Mr. Kunstler protested in June that these conditions made it impossible for him to prepare a defense, the district attorney replied:

"I have assisted the defense on two occasions in holding joint conferences with all their clients at a separately located place. Those meetings for the convenience of defense lawyers are expensive for the Corrections Department."

For, since the defendant's claim of right is intangible and the institution's claim to comfort is concrete, the institution had won every argument between them. Just as it had suited the district attorney's convenience to select the judge who would try these persons, it suited the convenience of the Department of Corrections to accept the district attorney's description of their character. As late as December, McGrath could still assert that his treatment of these prisoners was "not based on the premise that they are guilty as charged . . . but rather is intended to ensure the greatest likelihood of success in maintaining the order and discipline of the given institution" and he would later be suffused with self-pity when a federal judge failed to see a difference until then clear to all responsible parties.

These were, Commissioner McGrath would himself tell the court, "dangerous, obdurate, and untrustworthy prisoners" and his written affidavit supported this judgment with one proven enormity: "The plaintiff [Lumumba Shakur] was disciplined on July 8, 1969, for possession of a ball-point pen and a Black Panther newspaper."

It would be November before Justice Murtagh could be moved to order the Corrections Department to permit their lawyers to meet with the defendants together as a group for one hour once a week. For most of the summer then, most of these persons whose defense was his charge were little more than shadows to Mr. Lefcourt; and it was a natural response to the needs of his spirit that he should fix upon Richard Moore as their Representative Hero. The figure of Dharuba evoked whatever trace Mr. Lefcourt retained of the white envy of the

32

black style, the white inadequacy in the face of the black commitment, the guilt of the revolutionary lawyer still to a degree bound by form and procedures when he looks upon the revolutionary prisoner still unbound in the worst confinements. Mr. Lefcourt would wait in the antechamber of the Tombs, then shudder past guards who watched his every motion as he passed those numberless doors, each one of which was noisily shut after him—an experience that could be endured a thousand times without wiping away the recurrent sense in any visitor from the middle class that he too was a prisoner. And then, bowed as under arrest, the lawyer would come to the window and look upon the client in his glass cage, superbly arrogant, supremely the spirit of the unconquered. Mr. Lefcourt and Dharuba shared youth and gaiety, but what Mr. Lefcourt could not know was that Dharuba suffered from a feeling of dues unpaid even larger than his own. The street was Dharuba's prison, and jail, dreadful though it was, almost the only place where he could live free of the difference between what he said and what he did, and certainly the only one where he could feel himself the authentic possessor of the moral superiority of the oppressed. He had been transformed into the ideal model for the gay and brave endurance of solitude; but what he had to say was rather less inspiring than his presence. For, in Mr. Phillips, Dharubu had at last found someone who believed that he was just as bad as he wanted to think himself. For the first time the exaggeration of his indictment had given official support to the exaggerations of his boasts; and he cherished that testimonial too much to suggest to Mr. Lefcourt that he was not as guilty as Mr. Phillips said he was. He had become the revolutionary preacher, deeply pessimistic whenever he talked about the actual and wildly hopeful whenever he talked about the visionary. "You haven't got a chance," he told Mr. Lefcourt. "We already got a ticket on this railroad. They gonna give us forever. The court will never free us. Only the people will free us."

Taken in sum, then, even Mr. Lefcourt's Representative Hero was a mixed tonic; he could leave Richard Moore in one part elevated by the spectacle of how nobly troubles worse than his could be borne but in another part turned down once again to the reflection that everywhere he looked—at the judge who disdained him, the district attorney who bullied him, and even the client who inspired him—he was being told that his were troubles too large for him to overcome.

Mr. Kunstler's necessary peregrinations even before he finally had to surrender the case altogether had left Mr. Lefcourt to supervise what day-to-day management it had that summer; and, by fall, with the great captain departed and various outriders having dropped to the side of the road, he had his defense team: his sister-in-law, Mrs. Carol Lefcourt; Mr. Crain; Robert Bloom, a young lawyer, who wanted to think he was building a viable private practice but, from being unable to resist the kind of client who can touch your heart but pay nothing, was continually distracted from that sensible ambition; and Sanford Katz, who, after twelve years at the bar, was the senior of the others. The Law Commune represented the New Left; Mr. Katz's firm, Rabinowitz, Boudin, and Standard, was a powerful and subtly wrought pillar of the Old. Mr. Katz then was, without condescension, divided from the others by a full generation, ten years being more than a generation in radical politics, and constituted the closest facsimile the group had of a Presence, although his was the unobtrusive kind of Presence that expressed itself in acerbity toward the pomposities of judges and district attorneys and even of himself: it was Mr. Katz's style to identify himself as the only lawyer alive who had ever lost a criminal anarchy case in New York.

Mr. Lefcourt had thought that the uneasy trust these clients felt about everything might be strengthened if a Negro lawyer could be added to the team, and eventually Charles McKinney was secured. Mr. McKinney had awhile before been universally recognized as the most promising young black lawyer in the criminal courts and he had risen well beyond the limitations implied by that compliment to a position where there was talk that he was even about to acquire *mafiosi* as clients. He is a tall man of commanding and gentlemanly mien with lustrous hair and a princely smile; and Mr. Lefcourt would think it the only stroke of luck he had so far experienced to have anyone of Mr. McKinney's proportions pause in his ascent and engage himself in this desperate a cause for persons of the kind he had left behind.

Yet the defendants did not at once trust even Mr. McKinney. The luster that identified him as a success to the world outside was the suspect mark of betrayal to them. "When we first saw you, Charlie," Afeni Shakur said much later, "we really wondered about you. We ran lots of changes on your hair." By the time she uttered this confession, Mr. McKinney had established himself as preeminent among their counsel, not because he was black or because he was so shrewdly experienced that all the other lawyers so obviously deferred to him, but because he was so regal. For these defendants were early Americans and thus deeply and subtly appreciative of the obviously well-bred. Their affection had increased for the rest of counsel, with its unconcerned dress and its untidy hair, but they had come to revere Mr. McKinney especially for what was traditional about him—for those questions with their majestic overture: "And did there come a time, sir, when you—"; for the suits invariably black with the faint, perfectly chosen, white stripe; for this whole air of property, this living proof that they too could afford true luxuries; for this achieved embodiment of them in him not as defiance but as authority itself. They were proud of him not because they were black but because, being black and from our oldest families, they were also snobs.

But Mr. McKinney would not arrive until well after a summer when Mr. Lefcourt, having surrendered all hope of lower bails, had to limit himself to protest against the conditions under which his clients were being held. He cast his complaints in the language that is so often received as evidence of how irresponsible the New Left is, even though what Mr. Lefcourt himself might have thought hyperbole, dependent only on his imagination as it was, may well have been rhetoric rather inadequate for the actual malignity of the conditions described.

35

On June 11th, Mr. Lefcourt had informed Justice Murtagh:

"In our papers and oral arguments, we have consistently argued that [Lee] Berry is an epileptic. The district attorney knows this, for he was arrested in the Veterans Hospital suffering from epileptic fits. Now, just yesterday, he woke in a pool of blood suffering from an epileptic attack. He is not provided . . . with the medicine that is required to fight these attacks and he cannot eat anything. And, in those conditions, he is being kept in that hot dungeon next door."

To which plea, Judge Murtagh gave answer:

"All right, let me interrupt you to say that the commitment in this case with respect to—*what is the name of the defendant?*

MR. LEFCOURT: Lee Berry.

JUSTICE MURTAGH: —has been marked for medical attention.

MR. LEFCOURT: Your Honor, medical attention is not——

JUSTICE MURTAGH: I use these words with thought.

MR. LEFCOURT: It seemed to me it would be reasonable to transfer him—for observation at least—to a hospital.

JUSTICE MURTAGH: I am not passing judgment on the matter. I am taking precautionary measures and I so order. Continue.

When it came the turn of Mr. Phillips that day, he offered and saw accomplished by the silence of the court the dismissal of this complaint:

"In relation to the complaints about jail conditions, your Honor, we have submitted a prior affidavit by the deputy commissioner of the Department of Corrections in which he outlines the conditions of each of these defendant's incarcerations and we have already made that a part of this record. It effectively refutes the complaint that Mr. Lefcourt is raising today. Specifically, in relation to the man who claims to be ill, he has received medical treatment, he has received all kinds of things and he has——"

36

"That's a lie," Lee Berry interrupted. "I haven't received nothing."

He was cut off by Justice Murtagh and Mr. Phillips completed the suppression of these grumblings by holding up a diagnosis of Berry's ailments as transmitted by the deputy medical director for Corrections:

"[The inmate] states that he has had epileptic seizures since he has been in the institution, but there have been no witnesses to confirm this statement, nor have the *sequelae* of *grand mal* seizures been observed."

Defense counsel returned July 22nd to complain that Lee Berry had been beaten with a blackjack by a guard during one of his seizures and therefore punished with five days of disciplinary confinement for having failed to get out of bed for the afternoon head count. Commissioner McGrath's rebuttal was a further affidavit from the attending physician:

"Dr. Collins indicates that plaintiff Berry had a small laceration on his left eyebrow, which was treated by applying a Band-Aid. Dr. Collins concluded that the wound did not require sutures and that X rays were not necessary to rule out further injuries. The doctor further concluded that the injury did not appear to be caused by any sharp or blunt instrument. He suspected epileptic seizure because of the findings of postepileptic shock at the time of the examination."

The *sequelae* of postepileptic shock had appeared upon the inmate Berry, at last and most fortuitously, to explain an injury that might otherwise have been most distressingly blamed upon a prison guard. This diagnosis, of course, would not excuse him from forthright punishment with a diet of bread and tea and the withdrawal of medication.

The protests of defense counsel against the treatment of their clients worked their way through the federal courts against the resistance of Commissioner McGrath, devotedly supported by Mayor John V. Lindsay's corporate attorneys. Beyond the adoption of the district attorney's language about his wards as his own, the commissioner had no other argument for his conduct except to cite the uniform degradation of his

37

jails as proof that they were no worse off than ordinary prisoners:

"In respect to the assertion that on occasion plaintiffs have been without a mattress, the department, during the last two years, has been purchasing specially covered mattresses for all its cells. Prior thereto, the incontinence of some of the inmates prevented the use of regular mattresses. However there has been no policy to deprive plaintiffs of a mattress. Almost all of the cells in the Manhattan House of Detention are equipped with mattresses."

Commissioner McGrath would continue morosely to growl over this bone until December when he had to give it up and submit to Federal Judge Tyler's order that the male defendants all be transferred to common quarters at the Queens House of Detention and that their lawyers be granted unlimited visiting privileges; he continued thereafter to howl to Mayor Lindsay; what would happen, he wrote the mayor, if all our inmates should demand the same treatment?

But the summer before had held only defeats for the defense; and, when Mr. Lefcourt and Mr. Katz came on schedule to Justice Murtagh's court on November 17th, their clients were in the main still strangers to them. They came this time with a wispy but provocative new precedent: the weekend before, Federal Judge Marvin Frankel had refused to hold four white radicals, caught in a series of bombings, in the $100,000 bail demanded by their federal prosecutor. Mr. Katz and Mr. Lefcourt would have noticed the difference in treatment and felt the duty of reminding Justice Murtagh of it even if young Lonnie Epps, the only Black Panther defendant on bail, had not stopped by Mr. Lefcourt's office that morning and observed in passing, "Did you see where those white cats got only $25,000 bail? And they DID shit."

So Mr. Lefcourt rose as soon as he could that day to remind Justice Murtagh:

"All of the defendants still remain on the astronomical sum of one hundred thousand dollars bail. And I bring to the attention of this court a decision that was just rendered Saturday in the case of four people . . . charged with much more serious crimes . . . Judge Frankel wrote [and I think you can apply this sentence to this case]: 'It is apparent that, in this instance, as in so many others familiar to us all, the statement of the astronomical numbers is not meant to be literally significant. It is a mildly cynical but wholly undeceptive fiction meaning to everyone "no bail." '

"And that's what this court has imposed on these defendants—no bail for eight months. . . . Now I think it's time, your Honor, that everyone knows what's going on. Four white people had bails originally set in federal court of $500,000 each. . . . Judge Frankel ruled that this was preventive detention, that what you're doing is unconstitutional—and the federal court has told us so."

The comparison passed quietly enough for a while and then Mr. Crain heightened its measure:

"Our defendants [are] staying incarcerated, under bail which Judge Frankel has decided for white people is clearly unconstitutional and clearly a setting 'no bail'—and I would concede that the appellate courts have confirmed this bail for black people—and I would say that this is a pure and simple suggestion that there is a double standard for setting bail in our country. But your Honor, I would further say that——"

And then the defendants, so long only shadows, took sudden form and commenced to shout:

THE DEFENDANT MOORE: This is a farce. You're a racist judge—a racist pig judge.

JUSTICE MURTAGH: What is the name of the defendant who spoke out there?

MR. PHILLIPS: Your Honor, Lumumba Shakur and the gentleman standing next to him.

JUSTICE MURTAGH: This gentleman who is number two, what is his name?

MR. PHILLIPS: Tabor, I believe, Michael Tabor.

And Richard Moore, defendant number two, confused at this sign that Mr. Phillips, otherwise master of their intimacies, could not tell any one of them from any other, could only shout back, "You can include me," at which there was applause and Justice Murtagh cleared the courtroom. Matters then proceeded soberly enough until Mr. Lefcourt applied for permission to record the fact that his clients had been quiet and patient until this day when they had arrived aware that "four white people who were charged with significantly more serious crimes had their bails drastically reduced on worse records."

"It's a denial of constitutional rights for black people that has caused the problem in this courtroom today," he concluded. "I ask the court to disqualify itself from reviewing these bails."

JUSTICE MURTAGH: Application denied.

THE DEFENDANT MOORE: Why don't you plug yourself in?

JUSTICE MURTAGH: You will remain quiet.

THE DEFENDANT MOORE: I be quiet? You can put me in jail.

Then, with a crash, they seemed all to rise up, these undifferentiated blurs become an army with banners; and it was as if they were all shouting at once—the organ swell of Michael Tabor: "Where is the equal justice? The Fourth Amendment says you cannot—"; the mocking street pitch of Richard Moore: "You crazy, you IN-sane. You sitting there so cool and collected because you don't have to be in jail and eat that slop for eight months"; and then, riding over and quieting all, the breaking-out of Lee Berry:

"I plead not guilty because of the fact that I was in the hospital, I was in the hospital for one thing. I called the pigs. For two, I plead guilty to epilepsy. I have that. I'm guilty of that. *I'm guilty of that.*"

40

JUSTICE MURTAGH: Be seated.

LEE BERRY: Can you dig that? What the fuck did I do? What the fuck did we do? I was in the hospital.

JUSTICE MURTAGH: I direct you to be seated.

At last he ordered them back to their pens, and so ended Lee Berry's final utterance in that courtroom. In November he was transferred to Bellevue Hospital, half-conscious with a high fever; on Christmas day he was operated upon for what was incorrectly diagnosed as an inflamed appendix; he developed pneumonia and was operated upon again for thrombosis in January of 1970, and thereafter judged too sick to stand trial.

For the moment, Judge Murtagh had no more to do than coldly inform the shaken lawyers who remained behind that their comparison between the federal courts and himself had been in all ways uncalled for and that they had been using words to incite their clients.

Mr. Katz replied that his only task was to defend these defendants and Mr. Crain reminded the court: "Our own government says we live in a racist society. I didn't think that up on my own, your Honor."

But hold their ground though they tried, they departed it aware of how it had begun to yaw and pitch under their feet, between the cold face in front of them and this new rage at their backs. Mr. Katz wondered to Mr. Lefcourt what would happen to them all if these defendants, having abandoned hope, now abandoned all containment. The course remained to run, by every sign to be lost, and by every prospect with disbarment trials at its end. Mr. Katz sought the relief of an aesthetic consolation: "Who's the one with that deep, rich voice?" he asked. "I think that's Michael Tabor," Mr. Lefcourt answered. All these persons, even this late along the road, had been preserved, by act of their jailers and indeed almost by order of their court, as strangers to the eldest of their counsel and only vague acquaintances to the one who knew them best.

"I finally got in touch with Sekou again in April, 1965. We got together and smoked some reefer. He joined the Organization of Afro-American Unity too, and we both agreed that we will always be activists in the struggle for the liberation of black people."—Lumumba Shakur

A man's spirit can be marked as moving most clearly from the reform to the revolutionary impulse at the moment when he decides that his enemies will no longer write his history. Yet it is not the smallest of those cheats which life works upon the revolutionary that more often than not his history remains the property of his enemies. And so the police own all that is official in the history of the New York branch of the Black Panther Party that began in April of 1968 and that either ended or was changed beyond recognition with its arrest in April of 1969.

Its character was painted by district attorneys; what records it has were compiled by policemen; even the strongest bond its protagonists would share was finally owing to their prosecutors, since we have small reason to believe that these prisoners had ever known one another as well as they would after they had been collected into the pens of the Department of Corrections.

Even what these persons would write in their own cause would survive most frequently as a document in some criminal dossier, enduring for no purpose except its service to the kind of history which records what men say as the description of what they do. Against all this weight, there is only the history whose prime evidence is intuition, a history in ruins, broken yet still obstinately claiming, salvageable if at all only through the surmises that come out of conversation with its lost personages.

Its only formality was in its beginning. In April of 1968, Bobby Seale and Kathleen Cleaver came to New York as legates from the Oakland Black Panther Party. They had little baggage except their fame and the transient letter of their agreement to merge with Stokely Carmichael's Student Non-Violent Coordinating Committee (SNCC), then in the terminal throes of its agonizing progress from trust as integrationist to defiance as black separatist.

SNCC's spirit had fled to Harlem, but it had no noticeable presence there; its flesh was still bound to the downtown Manhattan headquarters it had established while it still evoked the tenderest aspirations of the gentle white left. So it was there and not Harlem that Seale and Mrs. Cleaver set up their standard and it was there that they found Joudon Ford, an eighteen-year-old SNCC activist, and regularly commissioned him as acting captain of defense for the Black Panther Party in the East.

For the next ten months, Joudon Ford would pass through stresses enough to crowd the lifetime of an ordinary politician; and then he would resign his commission while he still had two years to wait before being eligible to vote for even a borough president of Manhattan. At times, during that tenure, a police lieutenant would solemnly attest and a judge would believe that Joudon Ford was commander of an army disciplined to his every command; but he would remember it only as a troop with room in it for Sekou Odinga who thought of robbing banks, Ralph White who worked for the police as a cvil servant, and Shaun Dubonnet who worked for them as a subsidized volunteer.

Joudon Ford had the common sense of that rare refinement which expresses itself in contradictions; before he arrived at the Black Panther Party, he had at the same time, and with equal commitment, been a member of both the Student Non-Violent Coordinating Committee and the Civil Air Patrol.

"The Panther Party seemed to be the most serious black organization," he remembers. "But there was also the military aspect. I had this natural psychological thing for being a soldier."

Now it is certainly normal for Panthers to think of themselves as warriors; but Ford seems to have been unique among them for conceiving of himself as a soldier, a job description which avoids romance and summons instead images of order, caution, and chains of command. The warrior erupts; the soldier plans. The warrior scorns clerks; the soldier assigns them a place in his table of organization no less worthy than the one appointed for riflemen, truck drivers, and mess sergeants. Ford was a regular among volunteers. His campaign, if it can be called such, was only a succession of confusions; somewhere along in them, he relieved himself of command, because that is the way things are done with officers who fail, and because—there being no one in Oakland with the soldierly quality to be unjust to him—he must, in honor, be unjust to himself. A warrior would have blamed his circumstances; but, as a soldier, Captain Ford could accept no such excuse. He had always known his circumstances to be bad and he had never expected them to improve, being romantic only in demanding too much of himself.

And yet he had never had an army, if, when we speak of an army, we mean an institution assembled in order; he had never

44

been a captain if, when we speak of a captain, we range behind him a company of men at the ready to obey. He had only a title to command troopers recruited by a shout in the streets, drawn together not by an oath of enlistment but by a shared response to an attitude, to whom Huey Newton was only a name on a flag and Captain Ford only an acquaintance. He set out, as a soldier would, with the notion that armies begin with house-keeping, that there is first the training and then the campaign. He began with classes in weapons; we have no way of saying what he might have done once this drill was accomplished; men can equip themselves after all for self-defense or assault upon others, and the basic training is rather alike in both cases. Captain Ford would have neither the time nor the force in being for it to be known what he would do if he had. Still, cautious as he was, the results were no different than if he had been reckless. In the end, he experienced every vicissitude— the turning of the coats of the defeated, the prisoners taken by the enemy—which attends the final disasters of military adventurers.

His command base was in Brooklyn and Manhattan's Harlem was for him a province so distant and mysterious that its exploration was left to Ron Pennypacker, an Oakland Panther with some acquaintance among its nationalist tribes. In April of 1968, Pennypacker had managed to enlist and commission Lumumba Shakur as section leader for Harlem and Sekou Odinga as subsection leader for the Bronx.

They were guerillas as Ford was a soldier. If there had ever been a disciplined long-range plan, it would have been designed by Joudon Ford; and, if there had really been a desperate and isolated deed, it would have been conceived by Lumumba and Sekou because, by conviction, they disdained alike the crime for profit and the life within the law. They had known one another first as Shotgun and Beanie at Andrew Jackson High School in Queens; they had met again as the prisoners Nathaniel Burns and Anthony Coston at the Comstock Correctional Facility where they had been sentenced for street fighting; and, for their part in an inmate disturbance there, they had been parceled off together to finish their sentences in Attica.

Back on the street, they were Sekou Odinga and Lumumba Shakur who had followed the ghost of Malcolm X into his relict Organization for Afro-American Unity. Very soon they lost patience with what they thought of as its evasions and timidities; and they went exploring together to turn over and discard every other black nationalist group in their city.

And, while they were searching, there broke upon them a revelation from the farthest shore—a leaflet with the photograph of Bobby Seale, Eldridge Cleaver, and twenty-eight other Black Panthers carrying their guns into the California State Capitol in the spring of 1967. That was a moment of triumphant display undeflected in Bobby Seale's recollection by all the various punishments that followed it:

"So Huey says, 'You know what we're going to do? We're going to the Capitol.'"

The real thing thus rising in the West had become a tangible presence in the fall of 1967 when Huey Newton shot it out with two policemen and one of them died and the hungry imagination of the street could fall upon what few scraps the East Coast radio and newspapers afforded of this embodiment both of victim and avenger in his prison awaiting trial for murder. The Panthers had become the stuff of legend while they were still the unprocessed material of police reports.

And here was the image for which Lumumba and Sekou starved. Someone, far away, had *done* something. Life in Harlem was even more conducive then than it usually is to the exhaustion of any illusions that words can provide. The shade of the Malcolm X who was so largely unheeded when alive would have been amused to observe that the main effect of his death was the excuse for doing nothing it gave those who had been almost strangers to him and now called themselves his survivors.

The feverish torpor of those times is retained in the recollections of Gene Roberts, the policeman, and Afeni Shakur, the wife, who would each bear so unexpected a part in Lumumba

Shakur's destiny. As a third-grade detective for the police department's Bureau of Special Services, Gene Roberts had spied upon Malcolm X and come so to revere him that, two years after the death of the man he had begun by betraying and ended admiring while still betraying, he would be approached by a membership solicitor for one of the nationalist sects that Lumumba and Sekou had inspected and scorned and he would report to his commanders, "I told him I was tired of joining bullshit organizations." The life with Mr. Malcolm had ingrained Gene Roberts with the snobbishness of someone who has known the company of grandeur and, faithful steward of the enemies of that grandeur though he otherwise remained, would never lower himself henceforth to spy upon anyone he could not take seriously.

Afeni Shakur, dropped from the High School of Performing Arts and cast into the theatre of the streets, was introduced to the struggle when she lived transiently with one of Malcolm X's former bodyguards. He called himself Omar and she, with her indelible nativism, called him Cheyenne. "Omar," she remembers, "was hustling roogie and coke and of course he was fly." He would talk to her about Malcolm X and Elijah Muhammad, mixing the hunted and the hunter up in a mind mulled by drugs and despair until this pair—enemies to each other—seemed to her brothers equally to be reverenced and holding a common torch. "I wasn't doing anything else except shooting dope and talking about how great Malcolm was and this drag about the misunderstanding he and Elijah had." She would never again be closer in spirit to the streets around her.

Sekou and Lumumba, since they lived among Harlem's desperate indifferences, had only to look about them to bow down to Oakland's active self-assurance. Those guns on parade evoked those crazy niggers their hearts exulted to see at last; and they could neither recognize how little they had in common nor imagine any future moment when Huey Newton, with hardly more foundation in intimacy than when he had first accepted him as a brother, would decide that Lumumba Shakur was no more than a thug.

Still, they did share with Oakland that need to be taken seriously which is the finest part of—as it can so often be the part most perilous to—submerged persons. And there was no show that could be taken so seriously than the show of the gun, trigger that it was for the fears of the otherwise unnoticing majority, occasion it uniquely gave for those photographs whose wide dispersion alone makes possible the recognition of the anointed by a faithful so buried and fragmented that even to whisper his instructions he needs the loudest public clamor

So the merest appearance of this light from the West was enough for Sekou and Lumumba; they had little chance to suspect a difference between its source and themselves no less important than the similitude of being black and revolutionary. For one thing, geography separated Oakland's mind from Harlem's. Huey Newton and Lumumba Shakur were equally Americans against their own insistence and equally Americans of that old-fashioned stamp that used to make it easier than it is now for their countrymen to tell one another apart by region and even by clan. An American raised in the West is inclined to look at Asia. And Huey P. Newton had looked at Asia and brought back from that scrutiny the thoughts of Mao Tse-tung and the dictates of Kim Il Sung, which even his familiars could not study without being made drowsy in their Oakland office and which Sekou and Lumumba would accept with a loyalty to the source of light that could not always overcome their puzzlement over what such formulas had to do with them.

An American raised in the East will look to Europe, or, if his case be Sekou's and Lumumba's, to Africa; and they had brought back from there exoticisms of nomenclature and occasionally of costume that Huey Newton, being their leader, could dismiss with the same scorn for their inexplicable tastes that they, being only followers, would have had to mask as their mystification over his own taste for Kim Il Sung.

They were, moreover, separate tribes, strangers to one another because they were from different neighborhoods. Oakland's was the older gang and one already ingrown; its brothers, however conscientious their reach toward all the outraged and oppressed, had no felt need for close comrades except themselves. And Oakland was already under seige: and Huey Newton was a prisoner when Lumumba Shakur recognized him as the liberator; and Eldridge Cleaver was in prison too when Sekou and Lumumba were introduced to Captain Ron Pennywell, and appointed to the offices they owed less to their very real, if different, energies and talents than to the condition that they seem to have been two of the only three recruits Pennywell enlisted on this mission. Oakland's emissaries were uncomfortable in New York, tarrying there unwillingly to complain about its cold, its confusion, the rubble its defeats seem to have made of it, and leaving with the unconcealed relief of Protestants leaving Rome. New York, in its turn, would remember these missionaries for the glowering silence that identifies the man not too sure of his authority when he is engaged with strangers he does not understand. It was in this period that Richard Moore, who early experienced its emissaries, began mockingly to refer to Oakland as"Western civilization." In time, New York would decide that Oakland was selfish because Oakland seemed involved only with itself. Yet Oakland had so many good reasons for preoccupation, having been beleaguered well before New York even went into garrison; and its fiercest concentration had turned by necessity to the Newton case, the Cleaver case, and inevitably the Seale case. Four young men had set upon a course that, in two years, brought them the notice of the world and the respect of all the corners of all the Street; and, within ten blocks of Oakland, the police already had enough Panthers in trouble to consume all the resources the party could hope to acquire.

And some of their troubles were in their triumphs. The same *badness* that had speeded the propagation of their legend worked to inhibit the spread of that appeal to the sympathies which make men feel themselves comrades. They seemed so *apart*.

To those Negroes who competed only to be noticed and favored by those property-holding institutions whose permanence they essentially accepted, the Panthers had no greater

49

usefulness in alliance than to serve as mute supernumeraries in a theatre whose license as impresarios was the jealous possession of their betters. "They were," Bobby Seale discovered, "just trying to make guards of us, for some artwork shit sitting around there. They were trying to give us orders. What kind of shit was that?"

And Oakland's posture of command was, if anything, even more estranging to the type to whose imagination it most appealed. Huey Newton's flame was that of the man who had turned, ill-armed, at bay; real commitment to any such image can only come from those with their own proud memories of confrontations with power; and such persons do not make docile followers for a commander cut off from intimate association with them.

They were, these recruits and their captains, men who governed their bearing before the unfamiliar so habitually in terms of test and showdown that it is not easy to imagine those first passages of Captain Pennypacker's with Sekou and Lumumba as conducted otherwise than between parties continually on the balls of their feet, one side's eye set for cowing, the others for refusal to be cowed: behold, the Redeemer cometh, and just who does He think He is?

And yet they did share the heightened consciousness of the struggle between the good and evil in each one's interior that had stirred in Richard Moore in the weeks before his release from prison:

"When I came out, I asked myself why I should ever go back for nothing, like stealing a pocketbook. Why shouldn't I go back for trying to change things, for trying to deal everybody a new deck?"

That divided self had been there at the very source of light. Huey Newton was a symbol, because the response to him could encompass two quite contradictory reasons for admiring his character. On the one hand that he had killed the policeman proved how *bad* he was; on the other that he had not meant to kill the policeman proved how *good* he was. The insistence that he had been unconscious from his wounds and fired back only reflexively, founded as it turned out to be on unexpectedly strong evidence, was necessary not only for his legal defense but for the legend that depended upon Huey Newton's *innocence,* indeed upon that *goodness* which would impel him finally to urge his followers to go to church and which had already shown itself in his vision of a party identified both with the gun and the free school breakfast program, in his concern that Seale not leave weapons in sight around the party office because they were both a danger and a bad example to the children who came there, in the request he relayed to Cleaver that, since Huey's mother watched him on television, it might be better if Eldridge were less scatological in the brilliance of his language.

So delicate a balance between social service and aggression is altogether too rare for Lumumba Shakur to have found it equally weighted in every one of his recruits. They tended, as is normal, to divide between persons who had a firmer bent for blessing or who had a stronger one for cursing. Later Ralph White, the policeman who was intimate with their councils from the beginning, would try to mark the difference by describing a division between those drawn to the party's political and those attracted by its military side. Lumumba Shakur himself seems to have been able to balance those impulses and to have drawn real satisfaction from haggling with and occasionally bullying landlords, school principals, social workers, and like objects of the discontent of his neighbors. The leaflet and the explosive charge seemed to him each useful in its place. But this equilibrium so admired in statesmen and *mafiosi* was an achievement beyond most of the others.

As a man of the deed, Sekou forgave Lumumba his distractions into mere propaganda because Lumumba was his oldest friend; but he was otherwise so scornful of such tendencies that he is said continually to have complained that all talk of politics was only shucking and jiving and that it was time to come down from the hills upon the pigs.

By August of 1968, they were joined by Afeni Shakur, who had wandered in to find Lumumba and Sekou after a process

51

that had begun a year before when she heard Bobby Seale, "this cute little nigger," speaking on 125th Street.

"It was the first time in my life," she would say of this rough pair, "that I had met men who didn't abuse women. It was as simple as that. I used to sit around and they knew that I had what I thought were important problems, with my family and stuff like that. Sekou would help me understand my mother."

Still, if she had stumbled into this unlikely refuge from the experience of being used by men, she retained the habit of deference to them and fought to make herself into the hard model their own commonplace vehemence suggested as their ideal. She had long been trained that no wants count except the man's, and had grown up without knowing how charming she was—as perhaps Sekou and Lumumba had. If she did know, existence would still have taught her that, where she lived, charm was no resource at all, and approval the only hope against desertion, and that love died when the man felt either that he did not measure up to the woman or that the woman did not measure up to him. She felt it her duty then to talk as Sekou and Lumumba did; and, afterward, when she would press the main witness against her to tell the jury one thing she had done, he could remember only what she had said; and the growing conviction that she had not meant most of it would be strengthened by the suspicion that even Sekou had meant less of it than he thought.

Then there was Joan Bird, a nursing student and the daughter of Jamaicans who had scrimped to send her to a Catholic high school as insulation against the plagues of the street. Since her mother worked at night at Mount Sinai Hospital, Joan Bird and her father often had supper alone together. One evening, in August, 1968, their conversation strayed to the Black Panther Party; and her father said that such movements seemed to him just one more example of the sauciness of American Negroes who, being incapable of handling their own affairs, demand the supervision of everyone else's. He remembers that his daughter only nodded her head with no demurrer at this testament to the endurance of West Indian loftiness against every blow from 155th Street and St. Nicholas Avenue.

And yet Joan Bird must have been a member of the Black Panther Party even then; her docility at table seems unexpected from someone engaged in a cause whose pride it is to speak out at whatever damage to one's own convenience. Joan Bird could hardly have been afraid of her father, who is a weary man sinking into mute deference at every interruption from her mother; the wrath of David Bird would weigh as a feather; still his melancholy weighs as a mountain and to quarrel with him was to risk wounding far more than being wounded. There was, then, kindness rather than fear in the deception of her silence. Later, when her parents knew the worst, Joan Bird's letters to them from prison were unfeignedly affectionate and homesick, wistful in reflecting that "it may never be possible for me to be with you again," and all the same unbending in her affirmation that she would die a Panther. It became her mother's particular pride that the attendants at the Women's House of Detention never failed to remark what a lady Joan was. And she did seem a curiosity in the assortment of the others with the muted browns and beiges of her dress, the decorum of her laughter, the cool slimness of her body, the shy voice that said "Power to the People" in the tone she would have used to say "How do you do?" If there was about the others so much that was exotic and even aristocratic—the red band like a plume on Richard Moore's black hat, the loud chorus of voices with which a circle of the elect announces itself in the largest, most crowded assemblies—her demeanor was in every aspect genteel. To see her was to imagine the relief that would flood over some Mississippi merchant, under injunction to provide fair employment opportunities for Negroes, if his first applicant had been Joan Bird.

She had been drawn to the Panthers, her lawyers finally decided, by the very appeals to social service, the promises of free clinics and breakfast programs, that seemed so irrelevant to Sekou. And yet Joan Bird would be the only one of them all who would be caught by the New York police in a circumstance suggestive of a deed of violence actually undertaken.

53

Sekou's harsh and impatient bearing was, of course, rather more typical of Captain Ford's enlistees than Joan Bird's gentle one; and neither seemed appropriate to his temperament. Quite beyond that, there was the difference in kinds of sophistication: the experience of most of his subalterns with the confusions of the street ran deeper than Captain Ford's, and his own with the broader world was wider than theirs. He had preserved some access to the white left from his association with Stokey Carmichael and Rap Brown. He could find lawyers like Kunstler and Lefcourt for persons who, in their prior troubles, had known only the languid and docile attentions of Legal Aid. By June 1968 he had persuaded the Brooklyn campus of Long Island University to lend him a hall for monthly citywide meetings.

But, even though he made it certain that his party's functions would neither be totally obscure nor its legal posture anything but securely contentious, Captain Ford was very soon aware of how small a distance his real mandate ran outside the few blocks of his own Fort Greene, Brooklyn, neighborhood. Harlem was quite beyond his reach, being the province of a stiff-necked sect, whose members seemed to think of their relationship even to Huey P. Newton as alliance rather than allegiance and were so indifferent to Oakland's strictures against cultural nationalism as to cling to their *dashikis* and their Swahili sobriquets.

Around a few of them, there hung intimations of dark and desperate deeds; but he had no instrument to measure the truth or falsity of such stories except what gossip he could hear. Whenever he comes to talk about what he could learn about the Harlem sections, he described the gap between the letter of his commission and its reality; he speaks, not of checking the posts, but of reaching for the grapevine.

His own disposition was for housekeeping, for the distribution of informational bulletins, for classes in Franz Fanon, karate, and the dismemberment of the rifle, for open confrontations of speech with the police, and for internal struggles for order and responsibility. Still what he remembers of his stewardship sounds very much like that round of dealings with the private deficiencies of the enlisted personnel which fills the day of the company commander in garrison:

"A brother would beat up on his wife or was living with two women; and it would cause some static in the street. I had to tell so many of these hooples to remember that they were representatives of the community. Guy be dealing dope and I would tell him to give it up, and he'd answer, 'I can see how it conflicts, but I got to do my thing.'"

What order and discipline could be detected in the subsequent history of Captain Ford's command all belonged to the Bureau of Special Services of the New York City Police Department. Patrolmen Ralph White, Carlos Ashwood, and Leslie Eggleston were breveted from their recruit classes at the police academy for service as undercover agents in the Black Panther Party almost as soon as it was formed. White, buttoned and bereted, was a conspicuous figure at the first meeting assembled by Captain Ford at Long Island University. His easy social graces quickly moved him not just into Lumumba Shakur's intimacy but into treasury of the city's antipoverty program as well. By August, White had got himself appointed director of the Ellsmere Tenants Council, a Bronx grantee of the Office of Economic Opportunity, and could prove his worth by appointing Lumumba Shakur as his deputy and a number as his staff assistants; the tenants council seemed, he would later explain, a most suitable vantage point for keeping an eye upon them.

Detective Eugene Roberts, the veteran of the police cadre, became an almost permanent charge of quarters at the party's Harlem office. His gift was for silent service. Patrolman Ashwood made himself useful in his dour way as manager of the party's literature sales program. But then Special Services was very used to climbing over the outcroppings of the rebellious impulse in a Harlem where the revolutionary seldom traveled without there trailing behind him some attentive confidant he did not know was a police agent. Brooklyn was a less developed society; Patrolman Eggleston had been assigned there to

55

watch over Captain Ford's command post; but he could report so little speech let alone acts suggesting aggression that his superiors commenced to doubt whether any informant this drab could be trustworthy, and resigned themselves through the summer to the sense that, so far as Brooklyn was concerned, the Bureau of Special Services might as well consider itself unstaffed.

Captain Ford, at his end, recognized that he was unstaffed everywhere. Below him there was only confusion and above him there was only Oakland, a God rather like Graham Green's and thus given to dissolving into mist the closer he came to It. Oakland's own troubles had rendered it useless as guide in his own perplexities. Once he telephoned to ask David Hilliard, Huey Newton's chief of staff, how he could keep shady persons out of the party. "When I find out," Hilliard answered, "I'll let you know."

Then there was the unbridgeable chasm of cultures between New York and the flintlike spirit of Black Oakland. In September, Eldridge Cleaver came East as a presidential candidate; and Captain Ford provided Vernon Gassaway, the most street-smart of his intimates, as chief of security for the Cleaver rally in Harlem's Mount Morris Park:

"Vernon showed up in a freakin' blue suit that was just right, because it enabled him to blend right in wth the crowd and watch everyone unnoticed. But Eldridge said he was a fool who didn't even know how to dress with revolutionary dignity. When he got back, national office ordered me to fire Vernon as security chief."

The personage whose deportment best recommended itself to Oakland as a replacement for Gassaway seems to have been Shaun Dubonnet, a stranger who had appeared in September with no noticeable credential except a brooding, portentous appearance weightier than his twenty-nine years and certain rudimentary skills in revolutionary tongues picked up from transient association with Communists, Trotskyites, Black Muslims, and Columbia students. Dubonnet had a gift for first impression; his prior arrest record ran strikingly to those

56

offenses of the confidence sort—impersonating doctors, forging checks—which attain their lòftier heights of plausibility when the swindler can believe his own fabrications. From his birth in 1940 as William Fletcher across his progress through four other aliases before arrival at the terminal elegance of Shaun Dubonnet, he had been in four prisons and fifteen mental institutions, twice as the hearer of hallucinatory voices. Their psychiatrists had united in diagnosing him as "paranoid schizophrenic, chronic." Four of them added the judgment that he was a pathological liar.

That summer, its agents in Harlem could report all manner of conversation that intrigued the Bureau of Special Services, but most of the events that aroused it seemed to center in Brooklyn. On the first of August, 1968, Joudon Ford got into a quarrel with a policeman outside his party headquarters and was charged with striking an officer and calling him a pig. A little after midnight on August 2nd, while Ford was still in custody, a voice with a Spanish accent telephoned the Crown Heights precinct house to report a disturbance on Eastern Parkway. Upon their arrival at the spot, two patrolmen in a police car were ambushed with a shotgun and bloodied by the glass from their shattered windshield. Patrolman James Rigney, one of the targets, had an unexpected response: "It made me understand," he says now, "that the best way of combating these things is to be more friendly with the people."

The department's official response was to commission a special investigatory detail under the command of Lieutenant Angelo Galante of the Seventy-first Precinct Homicide Squad. Galante's special pride was his knowledge of revolutionary guerilla warfare; he had served the Office of Special Services with the partisans in Italy and the Central Intelligence Agency in Korea. As a reservist, he belonged to a special forces group whose primary interest was the conduct of guerilla operations behind enemy lines.

Galante's faculties were languishing in a Central Brooklyn homicide detail when they were called upon by this ambush in his own precinct. A Black Panther button had been found near the site of this shooting; and this small suggestive object was enough to bring forward in Lieutenant Galante's mind all the luggage of his special experience, first with revolutionaries and then with counterrevolutionaries, and to set in motion all those probings of the mind of the enemy unseen, and those diagrams of infrastructures which serve in the absence of any visible structure. The fantasies about revolutionaries to which studies of the speculative nature tempt the scholar were fortified for Lieutenant Galante by the fantasies of the Panthers about themselves. Their literature was a litany of adjurations to an iron unity of will and discipline amounting to a confession for anyone whose mind was too ordered to entertain the suspicion that anything could occur unplanned. Lieutenant Galante could study the rules the Black Panther Party prescribes for its members, come to Regulation 11 ("All [party] personnel will be responsible to the defense unit . . .") and feel confident that, having found the Word, he had defined the Deed, when he explained to his superiors that, according to the illusion thus made fact, "any direct action . . . must be cleared by the Central Committee of the Black Panther Party." To Lieutenant Galante this disorderly troop had ordered itself merely by announcing its procedure; henceforth he could conceive no act of a Panther as independent of Captain Ford's direction.

But the pattern prescribed by the party manual was no part of Joudon Ford's real experience. The Eastern Parkway ambush was, of course, offensive to his canny disposition, since it added injury to insult and could only arouse a shrewd and disciplined police department against troops of his he had every reason to know to be meagerly equipped, disparately motivated and inadequately trained. Still he could not be sure that some of them had not laid this trap for the police. Visions of *attentats* like that were common in the conversations around a headquarters by no means without its complement of serious persons but populated as well by children, street hustlers, and windy braggarts, all talking apocalypse.

"Oh, sure," Joudon Ford remembers, "a lot of it was Afro-American kidding. We were niggers and niggers talk."

58

Lieutenant Galante was not even privy to the fortification such talk might provide for his suspicions. He was a spymaster without a spy. Even so he pursued his investigation of the ambushed police car.

His Panther studies had of course fixed his theoretical convictions; but the physical evidence he had was less adequate to his needs, adding up as it did only to the Panther button, two shotgun shells, still untraceable, and a recording of the accented voice that had called in the alarm which thus induced the dispatch of the patrolmen to their trap. But by September Lieutenant Galante had found what seemed to him his first usable clue. Captain Ford had been arraigned September 4th, 1968, on charges arising out of his August confrontation with a police officer. He and a party of his supporters were set upon and beaten outside the courtroom by 150 spectators, some of whom proclaimed themselves off-duty policemen. The police department announced at once that it would investigate itself; nothing has been heard of this inquiry since, but, during its course, the department did stumble on an object demonstrating that even the hollowest show of conscience can have its serviceable contents. The evidence assembled for the department's self-scrutiny included a tape of a radio broadcast by Jorge Aponte, a lieutenant of Ford's, accusing policemen of having beaten him in the courtroom. The department's investigators cannot be imagined as absorbed in attention to material which amounted in their minds to no more than a protracted defamation of their fraternity. But Aponte's voice waked them at once because it sounded so like the one that had telephoned the Seventy-first Precinct and brought two of its patrolmen to their bleeding. The radio tape was turned over to Lieutenant Galante's detail and carried by it to a voice print specialist in New Jersey. This expert could only report that although the voice on the precinct telephone tape registered a close resemblance to Aponte's on the radio, he would need more samples before feeling safe in swearing that they were the same. On Lieutenant Galante's behalf, the district attorney thereupon asked and was granted the Supreme Court's permission to tap

Jorge Aponte's telephone in pursuit of more extended samples of his voice. This device turned out of little use; Aponte had already commenced to drift from his ties both to party and to home, and the taps produced almost nothing except the complaints of Mrs. Aponte.

That posture of Shaun Dubonnnet's which had seemed so purposeful to Eldridge Cleaver in September had already come to be for Captain Ford only the bearing of a nut with a gun. He assessed Shaun Dubonnet as a nuisance useful, if at all, solely to distract and afflict the other side; and the one assignment found for him was fitted to that estimate. Through the fall of 1968, Brooklyn was convulsed by the quarrel between the small Ocean Hill–Brownsville school district and the United Federation of Teachers. The Ocean Hill board asserted the demand for community (amateur) control of local schools; and the teachers union the tradition of civil service (professional) immunity from any direction except its own. In essence these events were a contest between two schoolmen—Rhody McCoy, Ocean Hill's administrator, and Bernard Donovan, the city's superintendent of schools—the first reaching for ground, the second defending it. Ocean Hill was black and the civil service establishment essentially white; and each of these antagonists, being quite alike in cunning and temperament, knew the rules appointed by such conditions: their argument would be decided not in a debate over educational philosophies but in confusions of other men's epithets confusing the issues and even their captains. Donovan would fight unseen behind those instruments of his authority, the teachers union and the Council of Supervisory Organizations, while McCoy did his dexterous best with a broad, but in no case very satisfactory, range of resources—rather like an irreparably out-of-tune piano—parents, engaged but disfranchised; street militants, engaged but intractable; politicians, black and white, franchised but prone to desert at any whisper of alarm; and distant benignities like the Ford Foundation and the Urban Coalition, quick enough with the cloak of respectability when his cause began but hardly engaged enough to thicken the cloak when the cold

60

came. McCoy masterfully deployed these ill-matched forces, so weak when they were committed, so indifferent where they were strong, turning on the militants when a show of force was needed, shutting them off when they intruded too horridly upon the nightmares of the middle class. He knew that his only power was to convince Donovan that the schools of Ocean Hill could not be open if its community control experiment were suppressed; but he also suspected that Donovan didn't that much care whether Ocean Hill had schools or not, while Rhody McCoy very much did, at least so long as he ran them. His struggle was an unsleeping maintenance of some balance between these two givens; and, when he lost, he could say that he had been beaten by power and not by higher craft.

Captain Ford observed these events from their periphery and early recognized his duty to help McCoy. It is a mark of how politic he was that he seems at once to have understood McCoy's tactics and his own subordinate function in any such alliance.

"Our only use," he says, "was to attract enough attention on to us to take it away from the residents of the community, so they could do whatever it was they had to do without the police on their backs."

As a suitable instrument for this policy of distraction by nuisance, he assigned Shaun Dubonnet to Ocean Hill-Brownsville. Dubonnet's exhibitions there seem to have had little impact on anyone around him except the more contained of his comrades who commenced to suspect that only a police agent could so persistently advocate deeds reckless so far beyond even their casual imaginings in language lurid so far beyond even their accustomed vehemence. In October, Panther Lieutenant Victor Perez decided to test these dubieties and told Dubonnet that the officials of the Ocean Hill–Brownsville School Governing Board had just offered the Panthers $15,000 to kill Albert Shanker, president of the teachers union. Perez said afterward that he had contrived this fable because he assumed that if Dubonnet really were a police agent, he would carry it to the district attorney, who would confirm the party's

61

suspicions by being unable to make a public announcement that he had discovered a plot.

Perez's surmise that Dubonnet had sold himself had been sound but premature. A few days later, he was arrested while driving a stolen taxicab. The arresting officers found a wad of Panther Party documents in the vehicle, an indication that their prisoner was in a fair state of revolutionary grace when this misfortune fell upon him. Dubonnet adjusted himself to this change in circumstance with the alacrity of habit, having but to see the interior of the station house before discovering himself disgusted with violence and ready to cooperate in the Black Panther Party's exposure if the police department would overlook the matter of his car theft. He had moved with perfect instinct to the ground where permanent paranoia can call out to transient paranoia and be assured a welcome. Lieutenant Galante claimed him; and, after a few long talks, he was certified as a witness to the Brooklyn Grand Jury.

His testimony was long and circumstantial: sometime around August 1st, he had been called to a meeting at Captain Ford's apartment where there had been revealed a national office directive to "ice some pigs" and plans laid for the act of compliance. On the morning of August 2nd, Jorge Aponte had summoned the patrolmen to Eastern Parkway, where a Killer Joe Foiville had shot them; Dubonnet's only function had been to meet Foiville after the fact and pick up his weapon for safekeeping.

No grand jury could be blamed for believing a recital whose manner had been refined by long practice at such concoctions and with proper appreciation of the artistic purpose of the ornamentally irrelevant detail, lingering as Dubonnet did over the Drambuie, the marijuana, and the girl that occupied his hours waiting for the rendezvous with Killer Joe, adding mountains to his weight as a serious man by the ponderosity of tone preserved even in the recall of unhallowed pleasures.

But audiences are there to be fooled; the mystery commences when the stage managers are fooled too. Lieutenant Galante needed only the most ordinary fingerprint check to discover Dubonnet's history as a man who would swear to any story appropriate to its hour. District Attorney Aaron Koota's office still held a warrant for Dubonnet that had been open since his escape from a mental hospital in 1967 when it presented him to the grand jury in November, 1968.

And Galante, determined though he might have been to neglect Dubonnet's past, was sustaining repetitive refreshment of his untrustworthiness in the present. Dubonnet had led the police detail to a shotgun which he identified as the assault weapon entrusted to him by Foiville; the splendor of this prize was immediately tarnished when the ballistics laboratory found that it could not have fired the shells found at the scene. Galante, in fairness, had no reason to know that Dubonnet had not even made the acquaintance of the suspects he represented himself as conspiring with before the shooting until a month after it. But there were facts of indisputable record to make Dubonnet's account suspect in essentials: Ford and Aponte had each been in police custody during the hours when Dubonnet had, on his oath, been conferring with one in his home and the other on the street. Since Galante had spent weeks concentrating most intensely on both Ford and Aponte, he could hardly have been ignorant of those skirmishes in their war or of the existence of police records constituting the only rebuttal to Dubonnet's allegations that he could not refuse to believe. Yet Galante did not bother either to question or to tidy up such details in Dubonnet's scenario as were refuted by his department's own records and confidently recommended him to Acting District Attorney Elliott Golden. Any small impulse Golden might possess to inspect this gift was dissipated by his first encounter with the witness: Dubonnet, being a man most economical in the management of his reserves of false coinage, had saved his story of the $15,000 offer to the Black Panthers to assassinate Shanker and presented it to Golden now. In his uncritical delight, Golden opened another investigation, put Dubonnet on a maintenance allowance of $100 a week, and sent a transcript of his grand jury testimony to Appellate Justice George Beldock as single and sufficient support for an order permitting the police department to tap the telephones of Ford, Aponte, and four other Black Panthers identified by the witness.

Long afterward, when Shaun Dubonnet had squeezed away the last drop of their credulity, Golden and Galante united in vaguely affronted puzzlement when anyone asked how they could have trusted him in the first place. Galante did remember having ordered a detective, now deceased, to check on his treasure, and having been informed of Dubonnet's criminal record, but having avoided pursuit of its details, since, he still insisted, "it was not important." Nevertheless there seems to have existed a diffidence toward Dubonnet suggesting that these officers might have known his history better than they wanted to confess now that his conduct under their patronage had confirmed everything it had so clearly prophesied. Assistant District Attorney John Cianci explained that, in drawing the wiretap affidavit, he had not supported it with "the usual allegation where a police officer has an informant, describing him as reliable and having been of use in the past"; instead "we just used the grand jury minutes."

We are left to suppose from this explanation that the district attorney, being too scrupulous to certify Dubonnet as a reliable informant, would go no further than to guarantee him as a witness. The wiretaps were maintained through March of 1969, when they were abandoned for want of useful fruit. Shaun Dubonnet had managed, on his errant course, to be a more lasting instrument of history than Black Panthers more purposeful; the immense bulk of these eavesdroppings, laboriously transcribed, endures to provide us pretty much with all we can entirely trust about the inner life of their party, which, like so much of life, manages to speak to us as both desperate and trivial, at once ridiculous and dignified, a mixture of nonsense and common sense, of fustian overlaying caution, being an invasion, and investiture and looting of privacy, being the capture of those conversations during which bound brothers, thinking themselves free of pretense before the world, pretend before one other. The solicitude of our courts for private

64

liberties requires that no wiretap be continued beyond six weeks without an affidavit attesting to the enormities the district attorney has already learned from it and the worse enormities to come whose discovery it promises. The task of wrestling out the sinister import of conversations that hardly bore it on their face was Galante's, who brought to it a passionate insistence.

His line of argument was to set down a fragment of telephone conversation, often innocent and never worse than ambivalent to the untutored, and then to interpret the meaning made plain to his special experience with revolutionary terrorists.

On December 22nd, 1968, Deputy Minister of Information Fred Richardson told Captain Ford, "I have your shit here and I'm not going to keep it anymore." Lieutenant Galante explained: "Use of word 'shit' is a reference to either weapons or demolition or some form of contraband."

On December 23rd, Paul Milkman of the Students for a Democratic Society called Fred Richardson to tell him that SDS was planning a confrontation at the site of the State Office Building in Harlem and that the Panthers ought to help. Lieutenant Galante explained: "It should be noted that the Black Panthers do not believe in peaceful demonstrations and it is likely that they intend to use violence of some kind when and if a major confrontation takes place." Yet there was no sign that Richardson was in any way aroused by this invitation to battle; if he had hung up and begun telephoning summonses to the troops, Galante would certainly have recorded that response. Later he was asked if he knew of any Panther demonstrations that were not peaceful; he could only think of "some difficulty down at the court building," a most curious citation since all the violence in that demonstration had come from the bystanders.

Mayor Lindsay's office had commenced an investigation of this courtroom assault on Captain Ford and friends; on November 27th, two and a half months along in its gingerly progress, a Lieutenant Edme would telephone Richardson to report the finding of a mayoral assistant "who right now was in a position to help the party." Richardson answered that, of course, "when the revolution comes, he will be shot or maybe before." It was a historical observation no less abstract for being unattractive. To Lieutenant Galante it meant that a "Statement as to the killing of a particular representative . . . of a political office is the standard procedure followed by numerous organizations of the same nature as the Black Panther Party, with which I have had previous contact and practical experience, and that the practice of these organizations is to eliminate elective or appointive officials which could be in a position to hinder or unnecessarily obstruct the achievement of their ultimate goal."

On December 1st, 1968, Stokely Carmichael, then prime minister of the Black Panther Party, called to ask Fred Richardson what the New York Panthers were doing. Richardson answered, "We got a retreat going" to which Carmichael responded, "It's time to do a little freezing for a while." Richardson then stated, "Yeah, up until December 21st and then we plan to come out again." Carmichael responded "Good." Lieutenant Galante proceeded to uncover the alarm concealed in the torpor of this exchange: "[It] shows that [these individuals] have temporarily postponed their overt criminal activities with relationship to the crimes of homicide, assault [etc.] and . . . other crimes of violence but that they indicate they intend to commit such overt acts of violence as abovementioned in the near future."

The Panthers, being the currently fashionable revolutionaries, seem to have suffered some jealousy from formerly fashionable and now unnoticed ones. Bobby Seale stayed at Captain Ford's on the night of December 27th; there he talked on the telephone to May Mallory, half-forgotten heroine of the Monroe, N.C., armed confrontations of the late 1950s. "Things are going slow," Mrs. Mallory said; after this implied reproach for inactivity from the previous decade's Menace to this year's Menace, Bobby responded, "Many, many times we might not hear of the Viet Cong themselves . . . but all of a sudden we look up two months later and read in the papers 118 GIs wiped out by the Viet Cong. This is the way things move many times. . . . Many more things we have set up will be happening across the nation." This vague promise of an active future as an excuse for a passive present had for Galante the most vivid and material portent: "This conversation is an allegory. The use of 'Viet Cong' in their conversation means Black Panthers and 'GIs' mean police. The conversation further shows the object and intent of the Black Panther Party in regard to their plan to kill police."

Aside from such prodigies of inference from talk so desultory, the police department seems to have gained from its wiretaps evidence about only one act of violence and that rather an embarrassment. On December 18th, 1968, Shaun Dubonnet called Galante to report that Ford had ordered him to place a bomb in a patrol car near the Eightieth Precinct. The bomb was thereafter discovered where Dubonnet had said it would be. Galante reported this incident with this caution: "The foregoing is qualified in that our informant was subsequently overheard in a conversation with Fred Richardson, in which conversation the informant told Richardson that he had done something on his own because the party does not trust him. That it is my opinion at this time that it is likely our informant is engaged in acting the part of 'double agent.' "

Assistant District Attorney Cianci remembers that it was about this time that he got around to asking his own probation department about Dubonnet and learned of his repeated diagnosis as a paranoid schizophrenic. Yet Galante informed Justice Beldock of his suspicion that Dubonnet might be a double agent, while Cianci saw no need to burden the court with the fact that his major informant was mentally disturbed. But then, the double agent is a rational creature, a figure normal to espionage, and useful with caution; suspicion of him indeed is a proof of how watchful one's own agent is being; such revelations fortify rather than disturb a judge's confidence. It is quite something else to confess that the witness whose testimony is the main support of all your assertions is an escaped lunatic.

Even all these incidents did not exhaust Dubonnet's powers of illusion. The district attorney went on paying him through January of 1969; and "our informant" went on being cited as expert witness to the lurid reality beneath the dreary surface of this wiretapped conversation or that. Shaun Dubonnet's authority did not subside until he was arrested for jumping bail in the stolen car case in mid-January.

The focus of police alarm and black revolutionary unrest had shifted that summer and fall from Harlem, its traditional scene, to Brooklyn. The Manhattan Panthers seemed to have felt no very lively discontent over their loss of precedence; they studied, intermittently, and recruited, slowly. Police agents had been most consequential among the earliest recruits. Then came high school students and then redeemed street bravoes like Richard Moore recently home from an assault sentence in Green Haven Prison and Michael Tabor, a defector from treatment at a New York State drug rehabilitation center. Joan Bird and Afeni Shakur were among the few women with a commitment that extended beyond hanging out. The latest to arrive were the employed and the formally schooled—Clark Squire, the computer specialist who had been Neil Armstrong's tutor; Curtis Powell, a biochemist at Columbia-Presbyterian Hospital; and Robert Collier. One of the last recruits was William King, honorably discharged marine, subway token change-maker, and author of a mimeographed handbook of urban guerilla warfare. King had arrived in September a stranger to all of his new comrades except Eugene Roberts, the police detective. He burned with a rather chilling flame and at first was so distrusted that only Roberts' recommendation finally won him admittance.

The founding captains of this band seem at the outset to have had little agreement about such notions as they had for its employment. Lumumba Shakur was more and more diverted by his services to the Ellsmere Tenants Council; but those endeavors at peaceful, if raucous, advocacy for the poor had the meagerest appeal to Sekou's temperament; and restlessly his thoughts turned to scenes more stimulating to the blood.

In November, 1968, as Nathaniel Williams, he was arrested in Connecticut, while driving a stolen car in which there were found two shotguns, a tear gas spray, fifteen pairs of handcuffs, and a ski mask. The police charged him with having planned to rob the Stamford National Bank. It was the first effort at direct aggression ever imputed to any leader of the Harlem Panthers.

If Sekou's trip to Connecticut had been that purposeful and he had mentioned it to Lumumba, there is small reason to believe that his old friend would have found it distasteful. The Black Panther Party had more needs than resources; Shaun Dubonnet's testimony about the August police ambush had been enough to get Captain Ford indicted and jailed for attempted murder; and several other Panthers were in prison because they could not find bail on charges that the police asserted were criminal and the party insisted were political. In those days, it would have been most difficult for anyone to conceive of ways to get emergency funds for the movement except by stealing them; the financing of politics is in the easiest of circumstances an enterprise founded on the most elastic ethical notions. As respectable politicians pay their way by being polite to bankers, the Black Panther Party could get their money only by robbing banks. This necessity had occurred to Huey Newton, and early in their collaboration, he and Bobby Seale had planned a bank robbery.

They were barely into the preliminaries when, Eldridge Cleaver reports:

"Huey jumped up and said, 'Later for a bank. What we're talking about is politics. So later for one jive bank. Let's organize the brothers and put this together. . . . And it will be like walking up to the White House and saying, "Stick 'em up, motherfucker. We want what's ours." ' "

The idea, then, had existed at the cradle; and, if Sekou set forth in its pursuit, he would have had Lumumba's hopes if not his full complicity. That month, when Ralph White expressed worry about the paltry condition of the bail fund, he said that Lumumba assured him, "Don't worry; I'll have plenty of bucks soon."

Sekou had been traveling with William Hampton, a hanger-about on the party's edges, when they happened upon a map of Stamford, distributed "With the Compliments of the State National Bank," and conveniently locating all its branches. On November 18th, the Negro driver of an old Chevrolet was stopped at gunpoint at a Stamford traffic light by another Negro who ordered him out of his car and drove away. Sekou and Hampton bothered only to substitute stolen license plates on their prize and then confidently drove it about Stamford for the next two days. On the morning of November 21st, a passing citizen happened to notice them coming down the front steps of a State National Bank branch; Sekou was wearing a green fatigue jacket and Hampton a gray tweed coat, from beneath whose hem there protruded some four inches of what appeared to be the barrel of a shotgun.

Later this witness observed these two strangers riding purposelessly about in an old Chevrolet and alerted a passing police car. The consequent search and interrogation produced three pistols, two shotguns, several handcuffs, and two wool ski masks. Sekou and Hampton were held in $25,000 bail for stealing the car; their intent to rob the bank, assuming it had existed, had not gone far enough to give real grounds for accusation.

This is evidence that can persuade us to Sekou's doings while almost dissuading us from taking his intentions seriously. He steals an easily recognizable car in the same neighborhood where he plans to use it for a larger crime; he drives it about Stamford for two days in whose course he and Hampton so frequently visit the bank which is their presumed target that its manager is easily able to describe them. They finally enter it with Hampton carrying a shotgun and leave it unmolested with a departure that Hampton made most demonstrative by showing more than enough of his weapon to make any beholder aware of its concealment; and, after this tableau sure to arouse the suspicions of every passerby, they linger in Stamford until the police can answer the alarm their own behavior has made inevitable. All this suggests the conduct of someone who, whatever his previous training as an enemy of order, has been so altered, so divided by his conversion that he cannot bring enough fixity of purpose to crime as a votive offering. There was less of the pure terrorist in Sekou than he declared and seems to have realized.

On November 25th, when Sekou was in jail waiting to be arraigned for his displays, Lumumba Shakur and his friend Ronald Hill drove over to Stamford to lend him support. A policeman saw them "acting suspiciously" and stopped and searched their car. Lumumba Shakur had a twelve-gauge shotgun at his feet; he and Hill were arrested for its possession and held in $5,000 bail. In a while, the Stamford police, presumably fortified by the rumors Patrolman White relayed to his superiors in the New York Bureau of Special Services, came to assume that the party had come to liberate the prisoner Sekou forcibly. It was this explanation of the Stamford trip that would carry Mr. Phillips to the hyperbole of reminding any judge who might be slipping toward tolerance of Lumumba Shakur as a bail risk that *here was a man who had been caught in a Connecticut bank with a shotgun concealed under his coat.*

The prisoner, instead, had been taken in an automobile on the street, where if his intentions had been quite so desperate, he had recruited an unusual complement for carrying them out, since two women and three small children were among his seven fellow passengers. In any case, these events, defined by all prosecutors as pursuant to a plan to raise bail funds by robbing a bank, had no more tangible result than to increase by $60,000 the bail obligations of the Panther Party.

Some bond was made for Lumumba at the end of December and he returned to New York, took up his work with the Ellsmere Tenants Council, and resumed a debate within himself where neither side gave as much satisfaction as his restless spirit demanded; the badness of the Panthers was confined to rhetoric, and the goodness could only express itself in wrangles with institutional agents who had almost as little power as they had. Sekou was freed, his bail having been reduced to the proper proportions for a criminal suspect charged with nothing

71

worse than stealing another nigger's used car, and he came home to be another reminder of failure and another voice for those who insisted that some way must be found that makes it possible to tell the Panthers apart from all the other agitations and proclamations that were the Street's normal futilities.

The controlling influences on Lumumba Shakur's life in those days were, all unknown to him, the agents of the police. He had been hired at the Ellsmere Tenants Council by Patrolman Ralph White, who conceived this employment as a convenient way to hold his quarry under surveillance. And, when he sought the dynamite that could provide the one gaudy night that might set the Black Panther Party higher in the public imagination than its rivals, he had no resource except Roland Hayes, an informer for the FBI.

Lumumba Shakur had spent much of his youth in those gang fights he calls "the bad-nigger-kill-bad-nigger-process"; and he still remembers those as nights when weapons were there to waste:

"Some of the gangs were better equipped militarily than some African and Latin American states when they first got so-called independence. . . . In [The] Fort Greene project, the Mau Mau chaplains would rip off the navy yard for guns at will; any kind of gun you could name, bishops and chaplains had them."

Now Lumumba was twenty-five years old and had acquired whatever superior wisdom there might be in the understanding that the gun would better serve for other targets than his opposite self. Yet the weapons supply had narrowed while his horizons were widening; the party had to travel 150 miles to procure just one of those rifles that Lumumba remembered as piled within reach when the passion of a young Negro was only for killing another young Negro. The recollection of growing up is, of course, generally inflated; even so, there are inescapable differences in the urgency of occasions. The preparations for the deed of the Panthers in maturity have a rather aimless air about them as against the simple desperation of Lumumba's adolescence.

72

But then perhaps he who once got ready to shoot a rival warlord had understood that he better had or risk either death or unspeakable disgrace while he who has decided to shoot a policeman need not be all that purposeful, since the command he responds to had been less enforced upon him by the instincts of his flesh than arrived at by the operation of his reason. One can always wait awhile for a policeman. For Lumumba Shakur had merely decided that he ought to have dynamite if anyone was to take him seriously, and that is far below the pitch of sensing that, unless he armed himself tonight, he would likely be dead in the morning. He did not so much actively look for dynamite as casually ask if anyone knew anyone who might have some.

The dynamite came his way by complicated accidents of providence, working through Gordon Cooke, a soldier absent without leave, who had taken cover with Trudy Simpson, a lieutenant in the Black Panther Party's Brooklyn section. In the summer of 1968, Roland Hayes, a chance acquaintance of Cooke's, had mentioned in general conversation that he knew where to get dynamite. Four months later, another acquaintance told Cooke that he needed some explosives for purposes of blackmail and extortion. Cooke thought of Hayes and sought him out; the motives all around seem to have been commercial.

Hayes was familiar with wider precincts than Bedford-Stuyvesant: for two years he had been supplying the Federal Bureau of Investigation with five reports a week as an informer; and, more transiently, he had been a student at Goddard College in Vermont, a neighborhood so rural that commercial suppliers of dynamite would sell it to any white radical bothering to pretend that he needed to blow up a tree stump.

At Goddard, Hayes had studied American History, Reform Movements, What Is Religion?, and Biology Cell Structure. He had also stored dynamite against the day when, he told his friends, he would use it to blow up a police station. One of them, alarmed, told Hayes that if he didn't get rid of his stuff, the dean would be informed. Hayes sold it at a ten percent

73

profit; and the local explosives dealers were thereafter on notice not to sell to "the little colored boy." Even so, Hayes knew that almost anyone who was white could buy dynamite around Goddard on the most transparent showing of peaceful purpose. In December of 1968, he traveled to Goddard, and a white friend did the office for him and he came back with fifty pounds of dynamite and detonators for $57.85.

Hayes' shadowy status as a law enforcement officer would produce the surmise that the Federal Bureau of Investigation provided the explosives with which the Panthers set out to make themselves masters and managed instead to make themselves victims. The record rather suggests that Hayes acted for no purpose more devious than to make a simple score for himself; home again, he looked up Cooke and offered the dynamite to any customer who could use it for $130, twice the price he had paid. Cooke found the original prospect who asked for time to find the cash and then after two weeks reported that the bloom was off his extortion project and that he had no use for explosives.

Once the market vanished, Hayes seems to have thought that if he couldn't make a profit, he could still give satisfaction to the FBI. He suggested that Cooke take custody of the dynamite and hide it in Trudy Simpson's refrigerator except for twenty-five sticks that were given to Fred Richardson, the party's deputy director of information. On January 15th, 1969, the FBI, acting on information whose provenance could only have been Hayes, raided Trudy Simpson's apartment and seized Cooke as a deserter. A Bureau of Special Services detective accompanied the party, went unerringly to the refrigerator, opened it to the dynamite, and arrested Trudy Simpson for possession of explosives. In the interim, Richardson had been keeping the odd twenty-five sticks from Hayes' consignment as a display item in the rear of his bookstore. Late in December, 1968, Juan Martinez, a Brooklyn Panther, had told Lumumba Shakur about them. Since Martinez would turn out to have a zeal so obliging for serving necessitous parties as to extend even to informing to the police, it is conceivable that

74

the Bureau of Special Services knew that Lumumba had found his dynamite just as soon as he did. In any case, the police knew soon enough, because Shakur had no place to cache it except the Ellsmere Tenants Council where, official history asserts, his sense of fun betrayed him into telling Patrolman Ralph White that he had it and where he had hidden it.

With the goods in hand, Lumumba Shakur could assemble his small cadre for the direct assault upon the police that until now had been no more than the smoke of its night talk. These vapors were formed into hard purpose not by any offense of the police but by the announcement that, on January 17th, 1969, a black cultural festival in Harlem's Rockland Palace would present as its orator-in-chief Ron Karenga, commander of a Los Angeles sect that was most savagely contending with Huey Newton for the allegiance of the Street. It is a perversity of politics that partisans content only direly to talk about the enormities of the appointed enemy will rouse to passionate activity when annoyed by the factional one.

Lumumba Shakur would, then, use his dynamite primarily to upstage Ron Karenga and only incidentally as an outrage against the police. He appears to have planned his demonstration of the Panther Party's kidney as the simultaneous bombing of two police stations and a board of education office in Queens. He himself would go to Rockland Palace and be there when his sappers reported; and, when news of the Panther strike circulated through the assembly, it would be universally understood that the Panthers had acted while Ron Karenga was only jiving; and all the glory of the deed would be concentrated in the pride of the doer and the abasement of the mere talker.

Lumumba Shakur's plan was nicely enough constructed by the rudimentary standards of carpentry for any violent act in a city as vulnerable as New York; but it would most miserably miscarry in the execution. Its fault could have been in the failed seriousness that so often accompanies projects designed more for the impression they may make than for whatever effect they might have. Its captain was as careful in his assignments as the scarcity of personnel allowed; it would afterward be testified that he found various uses for William King, Richard Moore, Ali Bey Hassan, Clark Squire, Alex McKiever, Joan Bird, Kuwasi Balagoon, Sekou Odinga, Michael Tabor, and Afeni Shakur, all of whom would endure the worst of his trials with him thereafter; and he excluded from any part in the project that faithful auditor and occasional seconder of Sekou's demands for direct action, Ralph White, the secret policeman. Still, dubious goods though he felt him, Lumumba Shakur may have been unable to resist telling White where he had stocked the dynamite; and the police would afterward credit White with effecting its exchange for a mixture of clay and oatmeal and thus making certain that the assault teams would do very little harm even before they could move to do anything at all.

The chief objective of the Shakur plan, the state would assert, was the Forty-fourth Precinct police station, which sits on a slope in the Bronx directly across the Harlem River from Manhattan. The scenario was for the station house to be bombed and for a sniper to fire across the river at any policemen who might come running out in the confusion.

The arrangements for this crowning outrage strained all Lumumba Shakur's resources, what is simple for the middle class being most intricate for the property-less. Clark Squire, the computer analyst, had a job and access to his employer's credit card; he could provide the mission with an automobile. The finding of a rifle for even one of the two snipers required a borough-wide search until one was turned up on the Lower East Side. Kuwasi and Sekou were chosen for the task because they had the most experience with shooting at policemen, even though it seems to have been an experience confined to talking more about shooting policemen than anyone in their company.

The teams were to attack their assigned objectives at nine in the evening and then return to Rockland Palace and meet Lumumba and Afeni Shakur and taste their triumph over the pretensions of Ron Karenga. At half-past eight, Joan Bird took over Clark Squire's rented car and drove it to pick up Sekou and Kuwasi and carry them to the sniping point on the high ground above the Harlem River Drive, at 170th Street, 560 yards from the Forty-fourth Precinct.

The police would afterward find the rifle unused in the back of the car's trunk. It had four cartridges in it. Sekou thus proposed to take his station on a freezing night at a point where, however clear his line of sight, he would need to fire more than 180 yards with a rifle that had no telescope, that he had apparently never before even seen, and that would be empty after the fourth time he fired it. If he could not sensibly be said to be no menace at all to the objects of his mission, it could still be suspected that some guardian angel who watched over and inhibited his every essay at revolutionary action had once again so hedged him about as almost to insure that whatever he was likely to accomplish would have no greater effect than as a display increasing the respect of his friends without asking too much of them and stirring the fears of his enemies without harming them.

Going to the Harlem River Drive, Joan Bird noticed that the gasoline gauge was low; no matter, Sekou said; there was no time to stop at a filling station; they had a schedule to meet. They arrived at the foot of their sniping point on time but short of gasoline and ammunition.

Sekou was opening the trunk for his rifle when they were surprised by Louis Scorzello and Roland McKenzie, two policemen who happened to have parked their patrol car nearby. Scorzello and McKenzie made brief inquiry; and then Sekou seems to have shot at them with his pistol. McKenzie and Scorzello would afterward describe a gun battle in whose course Kuwasi and Sekou fired ten or twelve times upon them; since the parties were no more than six feet apart, an exchange of these proportions could hardly have left everyone unscathed. The probability is that Sekou fired a cautionary round or so to cover his flight and Kuwasi's, and that afterward the sight of so many superiors mustered in response to his alarm suggested to McKenzie, less from malice toward the Panthers than sensible self-interest, that, after eleven obscure years in uniform, he might usefully abandon scruples about artistic license for this unique occasion when his commanders were there to notice him.

Sekou and Kuwasi gone, the two patrolmen approached the automobile they had immunized with their gunfire and there found Joan Bird, huddled under its dashboard. McKenzie, who had at least been shot at if not quite so incessantly as he attested, might have been pardoned a word of reproach; still he would swear that he had neither spoken to his prisoner nor touched her, once she had been dragged from her refuge. Even so, when she reached Harlem's Thirty-fourth Precinct station, Joan Bird was damaged enough in appearance for Frank Ruggeri, the admitting detective, to remember asking McKenzie, "Did you work her over?" This recollection hardly assisted McKenzie's reputation for unswerving probity; and the prosecution would have been better off with no such shadow upon one of its few witnesses able to testify to having caught a defendant in an act. But then policemen are more parochial in their loyalties than the iron unity of their appearance makes them seem.

In due course, there would be pictures of Joan Bird with a black eye; and, though it might be difficult for the defense to establish that a policeman had blackened it, Detective Ruggeri took care to recall that he had noticed her injuries as soon as she was brought to the station house, which was to say that any excessive force used against her that night was the doing of no one inside his precinct house. Detective Ruggeri, knowing his duty, would sacrifice the patrolman and protect the squad.

Joan Bird began by giving her name as Judith Johnson, Sekou's as Tommy Williams and Kuwasi's as Bill Roberts, and contributing enough other false leads about her companions and their purpose to set the Thirty-fourth Precinct to vain scurryings about the city for several hours. An hour or so after midnight, having professedly abstained from attacking her with severities, her interrogators assert they managed to cozen Joan Bird with kindness. She would have been exhausted by then and consumed with the largest of her worries—what her

78

mother was going to say—when there most delicately intruded upon her Detective Delmar Watson, a fair-spoken and confiding officer who is a department specialist in taking confessions.

Detective Watson remembered that Joan Bird had been sitting by herself and crying a little and that he had gone over and asked her how she was doing. She had replied, "Not so well. I'm in a lot of trouble. I've been telling lies." He had suggested that they talk about it; and she had looked at the thirty other detectives and their supervisors around her and, just that one time, objected and said, "Not here." Then he had taken her to the locker room where they could be alone; and, in a very little while, he was calling her "Joan" and she was calling him "Scotty."

They talked on and off for four hours, at whose end she said she was glad to have gotten all this off her chest. Detective Watson had, of course, reminded her early on that she had a right to keep silent until she could reach a lawyer. She had, he said, answered that she knew more about her rights than he did and that she had taken courses in guerilla warfare at the Black Panther chapter on Seventh Avenue and that she had learned that "the barrel of the gun was power."

"I asked her how this group from Seventh Avenue was going to overthrow the government," Detective Watson remembered, "and Miss Bird got very insulted and told me that this was not the only group of Black Panthers . . . and that they had chapters throughout the country—just about all the cities. She told me that they were trained in guerilla warfare, snipers like the Viet Cong, hit and run. She told about persons being trained in the use of dynamite. She spoke of breaking the back of the law, of explosions in public places, in precincts—that it would cause mass chaos in the United States and that this was how they were going to overthrow the government. . . . She said, 'We even have a lawyer.' She mentioned his name as Kunstler. . . . And I told her that I'd never heard of Kunstler, and she said, 'You've never heard of William Kunstler? He travels all over the country.'"

She had told him about Lumumba and Afeni Shakur,

79

Lumumba's second wife—"people in the party have two wives"—and how Afeni had brought her word that she had been chosen to prove herself and how she had gone forth to commit an act of violence.

The armor she boasted seems to have rendered Joan Bird secure against every terror except the reproach and indignation of her family.

"She told me that she lived with her mother, who worked in a hospital. She told me her family were hardworking people. She told me that her dad was a carpenter, and that she believed that they wouldn't understand and that upset her. She led me to believe that she was very close to her mother. She said, 'I can get a job anywhere, but what about my mother?' "

Detective Watson at last won her proper address from her; and a police party was dispatched to bring her mother to the station house. When Mrs. Bird arrived, Detective Watson went down to see her.

" 'I noticed the last few months something has been wrong with Joan,' " he recalls Mrs. Bird saying, " 'I don't like her friends, and she is saying crazy things around the house and the way she dresses and all. I knew she was going wrong and she was telling me how hard she worked.' "

He left her then to report her arrival to Joan Bird.

"Miss Bird asked me if I thought she should see her mother and she was afraid. I said, I have children at home. And, as a parent, I said, if one of my children were in trouble, I would feel insulted if they didn't want me at their side when they were in trouble and she agreed to this."

"[Mrs. Bird] looked at Joan and began to cry. And then she started to scream at her about you disgraced us, what are you doing to us? 'What's the family going to think?' she said. 'I want to talk to Joan. I want her to tell the truth. I want her to tell you everything.' "

A little while afterward, Joan Bird confessed the last details and Watson asked her how she felt. "I feel better," she answered, "I feel better. I feel I got it off my chest."

Detective Watson's recitation of her statement was persua-

80

sive enough; Joan Bird very probably did talk like this, with one part of her assured of the majesty of the secret army whose soldier she was and upon whose mystery she so confidently—to Detective Watson's mind, even "arrogantly"—expatiated, and with another part more afraid of her mother than of any of her captors.

No policeman could have invented these naïvetes, this invocation of a power that could create two wives for every brother, that could call upon the shield of William Kunstler, that could at will create mass chaos, the source of all those fantasies of what a "bunch of young people on Seventh Avenue" could do which left Detective Watson, in his street wisdom, wondering how anyone could believe what she was telling him and which could only be accepted in their awful portent by the better insulated, hence more susceptible, imaginations of policemen at the level of inspector.

Detective Watson's summary of what Joan Bird had said was, then, plausible. What failed to convince was his insistence upon the ease, almost the comfort, with which she had been induced to say it. He would describe a suspect who was cooperative almost at once, who had confessed to lying in the first minute of their encounter and who had in the first ten given her true name and those of her companions, told him that she was a Black Panther and embarked upon the details of her mission on the Harlem River Drive. That free flow would have put Detective Watson in possession of all she knew by twelve thirty in the morning. The conversation that followed could not, in his reconstruction, have taken more than another half-hour's time, even allowing for tears and painful silences. His entire interrogation, then, should have been concluded by one o'clock.

Yet they were still talking when Joan Bird's mother arrived at three in the morning; and Detective Watson had been the prisoner's only companion until then, having, he says, been granted exclusive access to her by superiors who appreciated his particular talents for interrogations of the gently persuasive sort. Even so, well into the third hour, he was still anxious for Mrs. Bird's assistance in her daughter's total conquest; and it could have been as late as four when Joan Bird, in words appropriate only for the moment of delivery of her final secret, spoke of how relieved she was that she had at last got it all off her chest.

The events of three hours would, then, be left unexplained if Detective Watson's recollections of the dispatch and grace of Joan Bird's conversion were all the truth there was. But then, along with the paternal bearing of his ecclesiastical models, he could hardly have avoided acquiring that discretion, or more properly, that vanity of theirs which, when the secular arm had force, used to inhibit them from looking behind those conditions that made the saving of souls a work more of fear than of hope.

Nearly two years later, Detective Watson and Patrolman McKenzie would come together in court as witnesses against Joan Bird—Scotty Watson, with his soothing demeanor and his sandy red hair balding at its crown as though Nature had blessed his image by tonsuring him; and Roland McKenzie, with his motorcycle puttees, his cruel angry eyes, his way of holding the pointer he used to indicate features on the diagram of the incident as though it were a pool cue: the detective so like the priest, the patrolman so like the conquistador as to fix inescapably the picture of Joan Bird's rescue from darkness; she would have been the Indian girl subdued by the soldiers of Spain and only then released to the ministry of the Church.

The evening had, of course, traveled more tortuous paths than the smooth one remembered by Detective Watson, and can never be traced to more than a probability. By nine thirty, on the evening of January 17th, Patrolmen McKenzie and Scorzello had brought Joan Bird to the Thirty-fourth Precinct, the only conspirator to add getting caught to the lesser misfortunes of the adventure. Most of the rest of her comrades had made their way to report to Lumumba Shakur at the Rockland Palace. There they were closely watched by Carlos Ashwood, to the police an undercover patrolman, to the Panthers their delegate for literature distribution. Ashwood reported to the Bureau of Special Services that Sekou had come in limping and gone at once with Lumumba to the washroom, from which they had emerged laughing, apparently more exhilarated that every Panther seemed to have gotten away unharmed than depressed because the police had too. Ashwood said he heard Clark Squire say that there were going to be a lot of tickets on his car when he got it back. It would be awhile in the general amusement before they noticed that Joan Bird was missing and, with that chastening thought, went off home, only later to discover that only one piece of their dynamite had worked.

Back at the Thirty-fourth Precinct, Joan Bird was still insisting that she was Judith Johnson. The police, while they fended with her, traced Clark Squire through the car rental agency, and brought him in a little after midnight. He had been booked and was waiting to be questioned, cool in his dark glasses and his inscrutable little beard, when Joan Bird, still Judith Johnson to her captors, was led by him. "Hi, Joan," said Squire fraternally; and what scrap remained of her false identity was destroyed by that greeting; shortly thereafter, the police drove her to what would have been the address she had given them and confronted her with the fact of its nonexistence. At that climactic moment of exposure, she admitted her true name and address. She was carried there; two patrolmen went upstairs to awaken her mother; and, as they climbed, the police took Joan Bird back to their precinct.

All these passions must have played themselves out during those hours when, Detective Watson would swear, no policeman except himself was allowed to talk to the prisoner. The likelihood is, then, that he did not take the stage, at least as leading player, until nearly three o'clock, when Mrs. Bird arrived and he was summoned, the daughter being still recalcitrant, to work his delicate craft first upon the mother.

Since she found her child in a place making entirely clear her abandonment to every temptation against which her upbringing had been contrived to protect her, we may accept the fury of Mrs. Bird's entrance that Detective Watson describes and she denies. But she seems to have turned very quickly to tenderness:

"I looked at Joanie and her face was all busted up. 'God in heaven,' I asked her, 'Who did this to you?' And Joanie was too scared to speak. She could only point to Roland McKenzie."

After a while, as her mother still struggled for faith that her daughter, having been in the worst of company, was now in the best of hands, the kindly Detective Watson went away, Mrs. Bird says; and Patrolman McKenzie employed the interval of her confessor's absence to take Joan Bird into a separate and closed room, from which Mrs. Bird heard first the words, "You lying little bitch," and then a thump and then a scream. After McKenzie brought her back, her daughter whispered that he had kicked her.

Somewhere then, between three and seven in the morning, among the soft persuasions of the detective and the hard ones of the patrolman, Joan Bird finally uttered a statement full enough of circumstances that only she could have known to make implausible its dismissal as a police fabrication.

It was a transient conquest. By daylight, she had gathered again the armor of her silence. Lumumba Shakur, with that gallantry that for him so habitually drove away all calculations of safety, came to the precinct to ask about her and Clark Squire and was at once arrested as their coconspirator. By then the police could see little use in confronting him with Joan Bird's confession; they recognized that she had already drawn back from her brief, painfully induced cooperation. Detective Watson had neglected to reduce her confession to a form preserved immutable and irrefutable; her voice on a tape or her signature at the bottom of a transcript. When, twenty hours after her arrest, Joan Bird and her mother were at last taken to criminal court, she seems already to have commenced to recant. There was nothing to do except arraign her for attempted murder and to hope that the penitence fleetingly established at the police station might be restored at the Women's House of Detention.

Alone the child recants; in company, the child affirms. And Joan Bird had been taken back into both her families. When Lumumba Shakur had come, in disregard for himself, to pro-

84

test to the police against her arrest, he had risked his freedom and preserved her allegiance. Her mother had tried for a few days to help the district attorney and rescue the family from trouble. But, before long, Mrs. Bird could only accept the mystery of a child both loving and obdurate, and, in spite of all appearances, return to her assurance of her daughter's innocence. No intimate of Joan Bird's was left to urge her to cooperate with the district attorney. Even without her testimony, of course, substantial elements of a case for conspiracy remained: there was Detective Roberts's memory of the things she had told him; there was Clark Squire's signature on the car rental slip; and there could be, if the exposure of an underground agent were worth the price, the witness of Patrolman White, who would swear that he had seen Lumumba Shakur possessing and dispensing dynamite. But, by then, the police were already too involved in anticipation of greater affairs to worry about this minor one. They did not even bother to arrest Sekou and Kuwasi, even though Ralph White could report their every movement through the secret passages into which they had dived after the police alarm went out for them.

Sekou was inactive underground; Lumumba Shakur was inhibited by a cluster of legal troubles. By now William King had emerged as an enemy with a firmer hold on the imaginations of the police than any of his predecessors. He was a man of system, a soldier taking the place of the night fighters who had managed the party's prior endeavors. By February, 1969, he had made his way to command of the arm of the party that Oakland called its security section, that Lumumba Shakur called its taking-care-of-business squad, and that King called its guerilla team. As his oldest friend, Eugene Roberts very soon established himself as King's most trusted subaltern. A police detective was an intimate of the guerilla team's every secret and an actor cast in its every project. The Bureau of Special Services need only wait to catch them all.

IV

The case of The People against Lumumba Shakur and Others was called at last on February 2nd, 1970. There were minor preliminaries to be got over; Lee Berry and Eddie Joseph were separated from the others for later disposition, Berry because he was too sick to be in court and Joseph because, being only sixteen, he was too young to be judged as a responsible adult criminal and was set loose on bond for later trial as a youthful offender.

The alarm and indignation of some imperial race at bay were all about the trappings of the morning: downstairs, the rows of policemen, the rims of their caps seeming fixed to their chins, so tightly armored were their faces; upstairs the court officers searching every visitor, making each one plant his hands to the wall, distend his buttocks, be felt over by embarrassed fingers, and, having appeared as Defiance, to pass through Humiliation, and to take his seat as Effrontery, reminded by Majesty of how certainly eleven men well armed can subdue a single man in his shirt. But, then, Lumumba Shakur and the others made their entrance; and, among these reverberations of the powerful suddenly there crashed the thunder of the helpless—Lumumba Shakur, a pencil in his hair, his glasses gleaming, his chirrup of "Power to the People," his right fist half-raised and then withdrawn in a gesture that seeemed less to proclaim defiance than to exchange complicities with some vast secret army that would arise whenever he chose to whisper whatever signal had been agreed upon in some smoky grove among cypresses and Spanish moss; Michael Tabor (Cetewayo, "True King of the Zulus"), gaunt, shaven of head, with "POW" painted on the back of his denim jacket like the heraldic device of some captive chieftain whose tribe would come in vengeance; Richard Moore (Dharuba, the jail name he had never bothered to have translated), sad of eye, laughing of mouth, dancing toward the bar as to his own street corner; and behind them the others in a line, a reel to unheard music of persons who owned no more than the air around their own bodies but who owned and commanded that element as fish do water. Afeni Shakur, bailed three days before with funds found for her by the feminists, came up from the audience, and turned—as though beginning the first figure of the reel—and presented her radiant smile, almost her bow, to Mr. Phillips.

They had arrived so undisguisedly to renew the quarrel they had broken open in November that their counsel, who could only be alarmed for its consequences, may have been as earnest to establish some formalities as their judge was when he suggested that each lawyer open by identifying himself and his clients.

Mr. Lefcourt arose to give his name and address and to say:
"I am representing Lumumba Abdul Shakur——"
(The defendants applauded.)
"The defendants will refrain from demonstrations," Judge Murtagh said.
"—Analye Dharuba," Mr. Lefcourt went on.

The defendants applauded again. This time, Justice Murtagh did not comment; and, at that suggestion of colors struck, they subsided; and each lawyer's recitation of his name and his clients' passed uninterrupted.

In the quiet, Mr. Lefcourt moved the formal severance of Lee Berry from the trial—"He has been ill for several months. He has lost fifty pounds. He is unable to walk." And here, sensing an intrusion of the incendiary, Justice Murtagh interrupted to say that he understood that the district attorney had already consented.

Mr. Lefcourt proceeded to a defense motion requesting the judge to withdraw from the case.

"Your Honor," Mr. Phillips cried out, "this motion has previously been made to the appellate division and has been denied."

Justice Murtagh replied that whether or not such was the case, he would still hear Mr. Lefcourt out. Mr. Phillips remained on his feet, paltering between his duty not to be impudent himself and his rebellion against authority's toleration of the impudence of others. Richard Moore told him to sit down. The court cautioned the defendants not to speak out.

"We will speak out whenever we want to," Richard Moore answered, "unless you want to do the two hundred and fifty years for us."

What the judge had allowed as a lapse, the defendant had affirmed as a course of conduct. And Justice Murtagh stared down from his nation upon the separate nation of Richard Moore, that alien entity so unmanageable because it at once comprehended you and was itself so uncomprehensible. The court's language was one of those antiqued reproductions whose effect depends on acceptance without examination. It was in style and cadence very like those expositions of the terms of the loan that the law requires the lender to print on the back of the finance contract and that meet the lender's convenience rather better than they protect the borrower, being most useful as a kind of auxiliary character test, since the

88

customer who reads and asks questions about them shows himself that most untrustworthy of debtors, the one who distrusts the creditor.

For the court's were formulas whose force depends on the resignation of the offender who is their object, upon his abandonment of struggle and recognition that he is at the mercy of his prosecutor, his judge, and, often, even his lawyer. Most of the dignity of courts depends upon the defendant's consent to his own humiliation. This strange wild tribe was, then, most alien because it insisted upon being so unabashedly natural and upon bringing with itself, unmuted, all the cacophony of the very Street where its imputed crimes would have had their inception and the display of whose posture was almost a boast of guilt, being so flagrant a scorn of convention.

Richard Moore's utterance could not be translated because its meaning was so clear; and Justice Murtagh could only puzzle over a speech foreign to his every experience—the flat statement of a relevant reproof to the court by a man on trial before it.

For want of an interpreter, Justice Murtagh gave no reply. Mr. Lefcourt was free then to proceed to review all their prior disputes, which, he confessed, had left the defendants and their lawyers with no remaining faith in the fairness of the judge before whom he had the embarrassment of saying such things. He wondered, with the chivalry that was the most surprising of his virtues, how Justice Murtagh hoped to be detached in his judgment of parties who had made their feelings as explicit as these had. When Mr. Lefcourt concluded, Mr. Phillips asked leave to rebut him; and Justice Murtagh told him that there was no real need to, and went on to say:

"The defendants are assured that they will have a fair trial. The motion is denied."

RICHARD MOORE: How can it be fair if Hogan picked you?

JUSTICE MURTAGH: You are represented by counsel.

89

RICHARD MOORE: But I still got a voice and it's going to be heard in this courtroom whether you like it or not.

And thus he proclaimed his sovereignty. For the next two weeks, he would be Lord of Misrule in this courtroom, reducing every other actor to his chorus. He had been ordinarily foolish before these first few days, his one almost perfect fit to his situation; he would be extraordinarily foolish afterward; but, when he came to that place that he and all who saw him must ever afterward remember as his summit, he raised himself and became divinely foolish.

He owed the sudden fleeting focus of himself to the district attorney. The life that drifted when he was free had been made ordered and purposeful in prison. He was, for this little while, entrapped in the only community that had ever offered itself to him as strengthening rather than debilitating, in an anchorite order whose founder was that Mr. Phillips who had so passionately sustained those bails that forced its members into the cloister of the Queens House of Detention. And, in jail, the revolutionary commitment of the self that had so long been only the drowsy boast of his doorstoops had become an undistracted exercise.

His fellow prisoners, who would hardly have chosen him to lead any other enterprise, turned to him in this one, as though both memory and instinct instructed them that the more misspent the life, the quicker the head in trouble and the richer the vocabulary of insult to the common oppressor. A thousand nights on so many corners, Richard Moore must have done The Dozens, the game that is to the man who hangs out what golf is to the lobbyist. There he had made himself an adept at its intricate interchange of challenge and response, where the insult is offered and its object risks no shame except failure to return an insult of ruddier hue and higher fancy. For The Dozens is a counterpuncher's game whose rules prescribe that the player stick to the point.

It would be hard to conceive any employment except The Dozens where Richard Moore had ever felt required either to pay attention or be relevant in response; but he brought The Dozens with him as his only training in such disciplines:

JUSTICE MURTAGH (to Defense Counsel Bloom): All right, just try to be orderly in the making of objections and don't make speeches.

RICHARD MOORE: And you be orderly in denying them.

MR. KATZ: This is a political party and defendants who are politically involved are before this court——

JUSTICE MURTAGH: We are trying a criminal case.

RICHARD MOORE: No, you are trying a political case under a criminal guise for the elite ruling class of this Babylon.

JUSTICE MURTAGH: From the defendants I expect to hear this, but I do not from counsel.

MR. KATZ: Well, I have tried to be as temperate as possible.

JUSTICE MURTAGH: You are not being lawyer-like.

RICHARD MOORE: You are not being justice-like. I have never heard the word justice uttered in this courtroom.

He was, for this wild occasion, the leader who quite ob-scured the rest, leaping suddenly into the light and leaving them still in the shadows where they had always been. And yet, as time went on, one came to notice these others as exercis-ing an instinctive control upon him, so that in those moments when his mother wit failed and he lost his relevance and commenced only to rail, their voices would surround his, railing too, covering his temporary lapse from the point with their own pointlessness. They let him stand alone when he was precise, and salvaged him when he floundered by floundering more wildly than he, as though to make sure that his would be the leading voice only when he was pertinent and they would group him into the chorus whenever he stumbled into mere invective, as in:

(Mr. Phillips arises to make a point.)

RICHARD MOORE: Why don't you give us our time in an envelope? You know you're a faggot.

LUMUMBA SHAKUR: It's on your birth certificate.

RICHARD MOORE: Old Phillips' Magnesia.

LUMUMBA SHAKUR: He's full of shit.

Their insistence on being heard at last was an entrance upon empty space, for here at the beginning Justice Murtagh was listening to disputes of little consequence to their real trial. He was sitting to measure their treatment by the police against the Supreme Court's prescriptions for propriety in arrests, searches, and the seizure of evidence. The most numerous subjects of defense challenge were the weapons the police parties had brought back with their prisoners. Mr. Phillips had not obtained search warrants, chiefly, he asserted, because the peril was too imminent to afford him the time. The defense contended instead that Mr. Phillips had known that a search warrant would have had to specify the items to be seized and that he preferred the potluck of any useful surprises the police might come upon in the course of the arrests.

Mr. Phillips very much wanted the weapons in evidence, and had even drafted a fresh indictment adding them as counts to the conspiracy and charging all the defendants with their possession. Some of the seized items, like Collier's pipes and gunpowder, were important elements in his case; but the guns themselves would be useful largely for display to the jury, even though persons remotely familiar with his party's dicta would hardly be more astonished to learn that a Panther had a gun in his home than they would to be told that a nun had an image of the Madonna in her cell.

Still the Supreme Court had generally, if not invariably, held that the Fourth Amendment constrains policemen without a search warrant from gathering any evidence not within reach of the defendant at the time he is arrested or in plain sight in the room where he is taken. Without search warrants, there was a cloud then on all these trophies of the district attorney's;

and its removal was the business of the police witnesses, whose recollections were richly tailored to suit the Supreme Court's taste:

Detective Coffey opened with the image of Michael Tabor standing near the doorway until the police party entered and then turning and running to his bedroom, which deviation from the rules of common sense and party rule for conduct in such confrontations had provided his captors with a tour of the premises that brought them into the clear view of a P-38 pistol lying on one bed and the stock of a shotgun protruding from under a coat on another.

Detective James McDonnell remembered that Robert Collier had himself gone into his bathroom and returned to hand over his can of gunpowder. Things had so conveniently arranged themselves that no police witness could recall any case where he had had to soil the Constitution by rummaging through any defendant's bureau drawer; and, on the only occasion where such fortunate circumstances did not prevail, the suspect Collier had repaired the deficiency by going off and bringing back the evidence himself.

Justice Murtagh's did not seem to be a temperament that would have impelled him to lively concern for the property and person of the criminal defendant unless the Supreme Court had guided him toward it. Still his respect for all proprieties made him dutiful toward its dictates; and the recitation of so many happy chances must have been a relief to him, since their establishment eliminated any need to consider the lack of search warrants as relevant to the case; and he heard these witnesses with that absence of dubiety produced by so many years of hearing and believing the arresting officer when he recalls that, when approached, the suspect gambler had taken the numbers slips from his pocket, thrown them to the floor, and thus saved his taker from the hellfire appointed by the Supreme Court for any law officer who lays his hands upon a defendant and searches him.

By habit then, Justice Murtagh absorbed the police version of these events with the faith that assures accommodation

93

between a judge's deference to the higher courts and his sympathy for the problems of prosecutors; and he cut off, as beside the point, all Mr. Crain's early efforts to inquire behind the district attorney's failure to get a search warrant.

After this ruling, Lumumba Shakur clutched at Mr. Lefcourt and told him, "If you don't get up and say something about that, me and Dharuba are gonna just rip up this courtroom." Mr. Lefcourt came to his feet, suffering the bad to avoid the worse, to beg the court's pardon for intervening while Mr. Crain was at work and to explain that his clients had been so disturbed at this turn that they had wished him to ask the court to reconsider.

"Your motion has been denied," Justice Murtagh replied. "Your clients have an exception. I ask you in the future not to interrupt——

RICHARD MOORE: We will interrupt because you·deny us our constitutional rights.

JUSTICE MURTAGH: You will have the opportunity to express yourself on the record.

RICHARD MOORE: You can tell him to proceed and I will keep yapping. You deny us our constitutional rights according to the Fourth Amendment of the racist Constitution of this country and you know you are denying us those rights.

(Noise from the audience.)

MR. CRAIN: Your Honor——

RICHARD MOORE: You must be insane. And let it go on the record that all the defendants say that, Richard Moore, first off.

DEFENDANT LEE ROPER: And defendant Shaba Om.

DEFENDANT ALEX McKEIVER: And Katara.

DEFENDANT JOHN CASSON: Ali Bey Hassan.

DEFENDANT ROBERT COLLIER: Collier.

DEFENDANT CURTIS POWELL: Powell.

LUMUMBA SHAKUR: Abdul Shakur, too.

THE COURT: Will you kindly record those names?

MR. CRAIN: Your Honor——

94

THE COURT: Would you address yourself to the question?

MR. CRAIN: If the court pleases——

THE COURT: I have made my ruling and I ask you to continue your questioning.

MR. CRAIN: Your Honor——

THE COURT: My patience has an end——

RICHARD MOORE: Your patience! We been laying here for ten months and you're talking about your *patience?*

He seemed from these retorts to have listened to the voice of judge and prosecuting witness alone, oblivious to the tumult of other voices he had raised, as unswerving as a gyroscope in a storm. Here, among the few extended days of fierce concentration he had ever known, when he had created the atmosphere of a carnival, he yet managed, now mocking, now magisterial, to maintain his posture as a serious man.

Once, early in his remonstrances, Justice Murtagh asked which counsel represented this defendant and he himself answered.

RICHARD MOORE: My name is Richard Moore.

JUSTICE MURTAGH: The record will so reflect.

RICHARD MOORE: Reflect what? Racism? It's already reflected there. If I had one hundred thousand dollars, I wouldn't even bail myself out. You serve to educate black people better than anybody in the world. . . . All we ask for is justice. That's all we ask for. Four hundred and fifty motherfucken years we ask for justice.

At one point in these disturbances, Justice Murtagh detected a smile on Mr. Crain's lips, rebuked him, and extracted an apology.

RICHARD MOORE: You better hope he smiles, because that's the only hope left for this racist country, is people to understand what's happening up there. Not you, you dried-up cracker in female robes. . . . You don't understand why nig-

95

gers don't love whitey. You don't understand anything, but *you* administer justice. You are an instrument of oppression; and you know and I know it. And he smiles and he excused himself for smiling; but I am going to keep on smiling, even when you give me one hundred and fifty years, because the people are going to keep on getting arms.

He was cheered and laughed with by an audience that was in the main white; yet, more and more, one felt the difference between him and so many of his admirers, the serious as well as the trivial ones. Every now and again, on the louder occasions, Justice Murtagh would fix upon someone in the audience to cite for contemptuous behavior. The trivial ones would apologize and be loftily and ornately dismissed to sin no more. Their embarrassed departures carried away with them their recognition of having advanced too far toward reality and being now in full retreat and leaving Richard Moore behind as that vicarious martyr the street Negro is for the middle class of every identity. He was separated from them by the fact of his doom. The serious ones read to the court spiky statements of defiance and definition and were stonily ordered to jail for contempt. He was separated from them by the fact of his divided self.

For Richard Moore was one of those tragic men who is insufficiently satisfactory to merely serious ones. Time made it more and more difficult to think of him as someone with a party or, for that matter, with a community. He had been infused for this brief hour with the fraternity of the prison. Comradeship was not so much something he had himself embraced as something that had been enforced upon him by Mr. Phillips. He was, and his curious honor would not long let him deny that he was, simply that Street Negro who judges and mockingly dismisses all promises of salvation and escape. He let himself be called Dharuba; yet African names and costumes and all other flights to the source offended a nativism stubborn enough to constitute a resistance to his whole century. Signified as Dharuba, surrounded by Baba Odinga and

96

Shaba Om, he went on proclaiming his intact identity with the pavements that he had as a boy claimed as his own:

"They've turned their backs on their own culture," he would complain of his brother Africs. "I stay with my culture. Ain't nobody can break a hat like a nigger."

Jail had formed him as jail had transiently uplifted him. He had spent five years at Attica prison for a street fight, the maximum term of his sentence, because he rejected every temptation to acquire good time or to adjust himself to the parole board. There was in his retorts the echo of a thousand rehabilitation sessions, their overtures scorned, their language fixed in his memory:

ASSISTANT DISTRICT ATTORNEY WEINSTEIN: I renew our application that this bandolier or bullet holder be marked in evidence as People's 12.

RICHARD MOORE: I don't understand the colloquial terms that are whirling around this courtroom. What does he mean by the People?

And yet, beneath this voice that slammed the door upon every pretension of the institutions that had brought him here, there was contained and unconcealed in Richard Moore a wholly unexpected trust in the America of archaic illusion. A memory of Lumumba Shakur's suggests how common such credence is among prisoners:

When he was in the fourth year of a five-year sentence for second-degree assault, Shakur read the criminal code and discovered that the maximum term for sins like his was two and a half years. He filed for immediate release; and a circuit judge came to Attica to hear his appeal.

"The judge said that my writ raised some very valid constitutional questions," Shakur remembers. "And then, he said that if he granted my writ thousands of inmates would be released within weeks on the same grounds, so the court will deny this writ of habeas corpus."

It is just this mixture of innocence and shrewdness that

drives the jailhouse lawyer; he assumes at the same time that the words of the primal covenant mean exactly what they say and that those who administer them mean everything else but what they say; and he wears out his life proclaiming what the covenant promised against what the institution does. And, out of such conflicts, there comes that contradiction, that quarrel with oneself as well as one's enemies, that is embodied in Richard Moore crying out, "You deny us our constitutional rights according to the Fourth Amendment of the racist Constitution of this country."

For the revolutionary, being an outsider, may go on believing that the society is better than he says it is and not even recognize the degree to which it is worse than he knows. As symbol, for example, the assistant district attorney was the appointed object of all the taunts of the defendants; and yet, since they did not know as much as he did about his case, they were far from imagining the cruelty that Mr. Phillips brought to the wars against them. When defense counsel urged that Lee Berry be bailed to a better hospital than a prison ward and that Alex McKeiver deserved severance as a youthful offender, Mr. Phillips successfully rebutted the first plea with intimations of Berry's dangerous and untrustworthy nature and the second with the declaration that McKeiver had been too key a figure in these crimes to deserve the kindness the law might accord some peripheral adolescent. Few of these defendants, being less privy to their own affairs than the district attorney was, could have known as he did that Lee Berry's name was essentially unmentioned in all the evidence he had gathered and that his own witnesses would testify that Alex McKeiver, that vital force in all the schemes imputed, had asked to be relieved of all responsibilities to the Black Panther Party hardly a week before being arrested on the very day appointed for its ultimate outrage. So Mr. Phillips had no more scruple about concealing what little he knew that might have reflected favorably upon one defendant or another than his imagination had a bridle when it came to describing the infamies of them all. Still when they looked at Mr. Phillips, they were enraged only at

98

the type and they were much less apt to recognize a special malignity in this man than they would have been to notice an unexpected kindness in another official with a better personal nature.

The defendants took it for granted that judge and prosecutor were their common, indistinguishable enemy; and that assumption was hardly alterable by the regularity of agreement between Justice Murtagh's rulings and Mr. Phillips' arguments. And yet, within the type, there were real variations of disposition; and if a large part of the district attorney looked upon them with malice, as large a part of the judge looked upon them with essential indifference.

The question of their guilt must have been closed for Justice Murtagh when, as guardian of all their affairs, he had read the minutes of the grand jury that had indicted them. The law would prefer, of course, that the trial judge not have his detachment deflected by advance knowledge of the evidence against the defendant; still it concedes that the bail judge cannot properly assess the size of the bail unless he knows the weight of the case. Justice Murtagh had done his duty as a bail judge and read the grand jury minutes before ascending to these spheres where the trial judge is presumed to float ignorant of them. He had the knowledge without the remorse of improperly possessing it. And he seems on at least one occasion to have dispensed it with the munificence a *grand seigneur* might show with his own property.

In the fall, a young lawyer had come to his chambers representing a client temporarily involved in the indictment and departed remembering that Justice Murtagh had hoped that counsel would not have to struggle all the way through this trial because "they have enough on these people to hang them." That expression seemed to his visitor to have been employed less from any special passion of the justice's against these defendants than from his concern that a young man he liked might have to spend months in association with clients who would continually embarrass him by being contumacious and finally depress him by being convicted. That sort of com-

99

ment from an embodiment of judicial detachment would, of course, have scandalized Richard Moore in his innocence as someone freshly come upon the fundamental writ. But to Justice Murtagh it seemed only grace and kindness to sympathize with a young friend facing entanglement in a hopeless enterprise; he had, without alteration in his consciousness of rectitude, long ago subsumed most of his innocence about the writ in his experience of its gloss, those writings-over, those accommodations by evading and overlooking its apparent dictates that are so much a part of its history and may so intimately have attended its conception that Richard Moore himself, when he invoked "your racist Constitution" as ground for his declaration of right, may not only have revealed his own interior quarrel but lighted up the ambivalence of a document at once sacred and spotted all over.

Having disposed of the guilt of these defendants, Justice Murtagh's concern quite sensibly moved from the substance of the case against them to its formalities. What would be done was assured. The remaining uncertainty was in the way it would be done. It was natural that he should cleave to Mr. Phillips, because, along with a common opinion about the parties before them, they had a common interest in getting over the process with dignity and some dispatch, the reputation and the budget of the Supreme Court of the State of New York being the only matters that either regarded as remaining at issue. Their judge and their prosecutor, then, accepted the case against these defendants; and even their lawyers approached agreement with that view at least to the extent of most uncomfortable surmise. The shared assumption of guilt, of course, brought a response from defense counsel directly opposite to the court's. As it was the business of Justice Murtagh and Mr. Phillips to expedite the end, it was the business of Mr. Lefcourt and his associates to defer it, to exhaust the most implausible remedies for it and to wander down any path, however unpromising, that might lead out of it.

Such desperate exercises of their sense of duty very soon made them enemies of Justice Murtagh's sense of order, so objectionable that he could not restrain himself from observing that for Mr. Lefcourt to say that the defense had not "sought with every device to delay these proceedings is to lie."

The clamors of the defendants deepened his distaste for their lawyers, in part because he could hardly conceive these defendants as persons capable either of this much rage unless incited or of comments even this pertinent unless coached by their betters in training and education. Later on, after Afeni Shakur and Michael Tabor had undertaken to represent themselves, he would commend their brevity and precision in cross-examination; still these compliments were never offered except in a tone that made clear that he noticed their virtues only to underline the vices of their lawyers.

The affront of what he felt as the bad manners of Messrs. Lefcourt, Bloom, Crain, and Katz seemed quite to have displaced from his passions what he was sure were the bad deeds of their clients. He had attained, in this displacement of his anger, a quite genuine judicial detachment about these defendants. For Justice Murtagh's true animus was directed at persons who he thought ought to know better; and that is the one form of intolerance from the severity of whose standards the pariah is comparatively safe.

He would, to be sure, accept Mr. Phillips' description of the character of these defendants whenever Mr. Phillips felt the need to remind him of it. When Mr. Crain persisted in asking for the addresses of the police witnesses so that their reputations for truth could be tested by questioning their neighbors, Mr. Phillips flatly refused such information with the explanation that "Mr. Crain does not appear to have adequate regard for the safety of the law enforcement officers of this community."

Justice Murtagh agreed with the assistant district attorney for reasons, he told Mr. Crain at the bench, "I do not think it would serve the interest of your clients or your personal interests if I express publicly."

He was fortified in the harsh assumptions this language implied when his own home was bombed two weeks later. The

101

Weatherman faction of the Students for a Democratic Society later claimed credit for that act and thus provided its own useful reminder of how much of the burden upon these defendants by the white community might be imposed by the rebels who admired as well as the officials who feared and hated the Black Panther Party.

Just before the attack on Justice Murtagh's home, the defense had formally applied for the addresses of the police witnesses, and he had denied their motion. Now, with his personal experience to certify his suspicions, he demanded that defense counsel withdraw its request for anyone's address, and thus almost confess that events had proved that it ought never have been made. Mr. Lefcourt's immediate compliance was so entire a revelation of how helpless he felt among so many strangers who shared his cause but were beyond his control that any observer less certain than Justice Murtagh that counsel were accomplices in every courtroom disturbance might have commenced to recognize that Mr. Lefcourt was in a circumstance where his clients and, what could be worse, friends of theirs unknown to him would do what they felt they had to do without needing his inspiration or asking his advice. That thought could have passed to feeling some measure of respect for someone who would need better reasons for deserting persons in trouble than a reminder from the bench that counsel rather more eminent than he had found it proper for a lawyer to withdraw from a case where his client disregarded his guidance. But there was no alteration in Justice Murtagh's demeanor to suggest his softening by speculations of such complexity. He did not unbend until Mr. McKinney, the appointed exception to his general displeasure with defense counsel, asked leave to speak. Mr. McKinney said that the defendants had chosen him to express their sincere sympathy with their judge in his ordeal and their condemnation of all such acts of aggressive terror. Justice Murtagh expressed his appreciation, formally for the sympathy of the defendants, and heartfully for that eloquence of Mr. McKinney's which seemed

102

to him one more evidence of its bearer's invariable reflection of the best traditions of the bar.

But, hardly an hour after this comity, the defendants were back to full mocking cry against Mr. Phillips. He clambered up to say that such conduct was proof of how little Mr. McKinney's fine sentiments had to do with "the intent or attitude of any of his clients." Justice Murtagh agreed; and, when Mr. McKinney most spiritedly replied that men can give vent to the harshest opinions about their judge and still find it most objectionable to bomb his home, the coldness of the court's eye and the compression of its mouth were a statement of its ruling that such distinctions were nonsense, that the word is equivalent to the act, and that bad manners lead so implacably to bad deeds as to constitute the most persuasive evidence of them.

That was the assessment of most respectable persons, who looked at the judge going home at night to brood over his sufferings and at his tormentors driven back to their jail presumably to exult in the freedom they were abusing, and who had no trouble recognizing who was the victim and who his oppressors. The tumults that afflicted Justice Murtagh were indeed deplorable. Still, on those occasions when he could be seen presiding under circumstances more appropriate to the dignity of courts, the contrast was insufficiently more appetizing. On Mondays the justice would suspend the Panther proceedings awhile to keep house on the rest of his calendar and run through a dispirited parade of persons whose criminal cases were suited for summary action, either for disposal or postponement.

The courtroom was quiet and its atmosphere languid enough to make more noticeable the dusky meanness of its appointments; there grieved unrepaired on one wall a hole—the shape of a large map of Norway—left behind by falling plaster and prompted the reflection that if our agencies of justice cannot promise the criminal defendant a jury from his class, they at least provide him a setting very like his home.

On one such calendar morning, Justice Murtagh looked upon

a convicted Negro, his defeats much easier than his age to read on his face, and plainly a stranger to the woman lawyer from Legal Aid beside him. The convict, his judge, and his counsel must have all been meeting for the first time at the moment of sentence. The transactions were an indistinguishable murmur; the assistant district attorney said a few words, defense counsel fewer still, and the prisoner none at all. Justice Murtagh sentenced him to a year. He did not appear quite certain that he had heard what had happened; a year seemed worse than he had resigned himself to. The Legal Aid lawyer explained, not really annoyed but under clear pressure for time, that this was as good as they could have gotten. Then he was taken away; and Justice Murtagh had to turn from the comfort of defendants who were humble, lawyers who were accepting, and routines that could be gotten over with neither expenditure of grace nor trial of patience to contend once again with their disconcerting opposites before him.

He had his sporting side or, at the very least, parts of himself more accustomed to accommodation than Mr. Phillips could be imagined as having. He was, of course, prepared to give Mr. Phillips any point needed to prove the substantial elements of the case. But he would not concede him his trivia. The defense's protracted attack upon the seized evidence would be disposed of, then, by a judgment at once affirming the probity of the police search and denying Mr. Phillips the most numerous, although least significant, portion of its fruits. The police had brought home bundles of revolutionary literature, Lonnie Epps' bomb timer, Lumumba Shakur's primer cord, Collier's pipes and gunpowder and ten guns. Possession of unregistered guns was the least of the charges against these defendants; still it can be a felony; and Mr. Phillips had made the unlawful ownership of these weapons a count against all parties. Of the offenses imputed, gun possession was the one whose proof was so overwhelming that the most fractious juror could hardly dismiss it. But Justice Murtagh made it clear quite early that his disposition was to preserve the explosives and the writings for Mr. Phillips as adornments to his tale but to discard the

104

gun charges because to him they trivialized the graver issues and could only confuse the jury. If he would hang, say, Richard Moore, it would be as a sheep and not as a lamb.

There was, moreover, less firmness of mold in him than his stern bearing attested. He was engaged, to be sure, with persons so powerless as to be for the moment beyond any power of his: "What you gon' do," Richard Moore mocked him, "put me in jail if I don't shut up?" Still he did have that *gravitas* that suggests resource; even so, one grew daily more conscious of a kind of immobility, as though the justice were some sentient parish church across whose facade urchins had written an obscenity and that could only sit, hooted, humiliated, and helpless. And, as he watched and threatened and could do nothing, except to remind them that he might be their sentencing judge in the end, the defendants extorted from him the time to give themselves characters and features and become strangers no longer, until observers who had felt insulted by their course on the first day were laughing with them after the third session or so. Every day there increased the disturbances of an audience dominated by the young who were involved with the defendants although not quite seriously enough to recognize that the man under arrest who responds with contumely to his jailers has, after all, chosen his penalty, while his supporters, when they add their bit, more often than not increase his risk rather than theirs.

Three times members of the audience gave way to expressions so vehement that Justice Murtagh called them forward to be punished for summary contempt. Two of them, Maryann Weissman and Alan Katz, were adult white radicals of stiff enough principles to carry their defiance to his face; he gave them thirty days in the correction facilities. The third was a young woman from one of the news magazines, caught by Justice Murtagh markedly applauding one of Richard Moore's sallies; she appeared for punishment the next day with counsel from her institution's law firm, who both wrapped her in his mantle and stood by as she crawled according to his instructions.

105

"The court," Justice Murtagh informed her, "has tremendous respect and admiration for the profession that you represent. I think it is unfortunate that you have cast discredit upon these loyal people. In measure out of compassion for you in what was perhaps a human error and partially out of respect for that great profession, the court will not press its intention to adjudge you in contempt."

And she departed, wearing that smile of the martyr which is most infuriating as it is most frequent upon the lips of those with no inclination to be martyrs, leaving very little dignity to the attendant journalists. She had first and rather mildly embarrassed them with her demonstration and then last and most painfully humiliated them by providing the occasion for the court's compliment to "these loyal people," which was, in fact, the most precise and too-often-merited denigration in his power.

All these scenes and his Forcible-Feeble contentions with them suggested something else in Justice Murtagh just as alien to Mr. Phillips: he was cursed with the need to be liked that seems born in the Irish along with the knack for its achievement; but he had retained the need while losing the ease of manner that is the whole knack throughout his apprenticeship to the Puritans. It could be felt how he must suffer from having kept the desire and mislaid the instrument of its satisfaction. He could never achieve the peace of that Covenant whose elect are untroubled by ignorance of the ways of getting themselves liked, because they do not overmuch care whether they are liked or not. Somewhere, behind that Presbyterian garrison, there was an Irishman, as lonely as a chapel might feel in a prison. For, after all, if ever there was a spoiled priest, it was John Calvin. And, living with Justice Murtagh, as one came to, it was impossible not to think of LaFontaine explaining his sympathy for the banker Fouquet, fallen because he was caught in peculation: yes, misfortune *is* a kind of innocence.

But, as an added misfortune, his need to be liked had survived only to be distorted into the form that needs most the good opinion of persons well above or well below or equal to his social station. Defense counsel's reminders of the bias that no human judge could avoid in this atmosphere offered him the soundest excuse to withdraw. Yet he sat and endured these torments until the mind could conceive no explanation except that he felt a duty first to the superior judges who had charged him with command of their outer works and then a duty to himself as someone assailed by persons claiming to be his victims when he, as author of so many remonstrances for whores and junkies, felt his unique claim to be the shield of all victims. For, most of all, he needed approval from above and reverential trust from below. That one can very seldom have both at the same time was a condition of fact that had so escaped him that the "Motion denied," without explanation, which he returned to every protest in the papers defense counsel sent up to him seemed a designedly curt expression of his disdain for young men of the middle class who had not chosen his way of rising and were, worse, so callous as not to care whether he liked them or not. But then there is no one crueler than the oversensitive; and the patience, however ungracious, with which he bore these days may have contained the consolation of coldly counting the punishments Mr. Lefcourt was daily piling on his account, punishments that would have to wait until his clients came to verdict but that could be avoided only if Mr. Lefcourt got his clients acquitted, for Justice Murtagh was a sportsman and sportsmen do not punish winners.

Still the heart curiously insisted on going out to him, having, as it very well should, a weakness drawn to any human substance that is being called a pig. It eventually becomes a defect in victims that their language is either lower than we would appoint or higher than we could imagine, and that, in either case, there comes a time when we cease to identify. The style of Richard Moore, pointed though it was and evocation of complaints too infrequently heard, was approaching that bottom of the pail that can be so shallow for the techniques of nightclub insult. Just at that juncture when laughter was commencing to

embarrass and the need for something else of the spirit beginning to press, Michael Tabor came before the court to describe
his arrest by Detective Joseph Coffey.

Michael Tabor assumed the witness chair wearing dunga-
rees, a Huey P. Newton sweatshirt, and an expression that
appeared to the unknowing stranger to reflect less the sorrows
of the earth than the annoyance of the day. He seemed smaller
than required by the first extensive opportunity for formal
utterance afforded any of them for the last ten months; but
then, taken one by one, these were not persons whose entrance
proclaimed a Presence; we do not notice the trombonist until
we hear the trombone.

Mr. Crain asked him if he recalled the morning of April the
second last.

"Yes, I do," Michael Tabor answered.

All that was noticeable in his reply was the timbre of his
voice. It was the voice of the organ in the cathedral, a voice
that made the ceiling above him seem like a vault over which
angels and archangels leaned to catch the word of God arising.
As Mr. Crain plodded toward the next stop on his schedule of
questioning, those three syllables of Michael Tabor's sounded
on, leading their choirs, extending their fugues in the silence of
the inner ear. The outer ear could not at first hear the words for
listening only to the music that calls children home and grown
men to judgment.

Michael Tabor was remembering how he and "my wife"
Rosalind Bennett had come home and he had taken off his shirt
and thrown it across the copies of Eldridge Cleaver and Mao
Tse-tung on the couch and they had stretched across the bed,
picking up a copy of *The Black Panther,* and, while he read
that sacred study, he and his wife began to talk.

"We were," he explained, "discussing our coming child—she
was pregnant at the time—and we were also discussing ways
and means by which the party could serve the needs of the
people, specifically the free breakfast program."

The elevation of tone ought to have been ridiculous. And yet
it was all else but. The same divinity who had given him the

108

instrument of this voice had added the most perfect instinct for its employment; he invariably chose the stately as against the common word; and where ordinary persons would say, "Help the People," Michael Tabor would always say, "Serve the needs of the People."

His narrative had reached the point of Joseph Coffey's assault upon the chasteness of the haven just described: "I was standing there with my hands directly in front of me with my fingers spread apart. . . . There was a shotgun; I saw bullet-proof vests, white faces, handguns. There was no question in my mind; it was definitely the police. . . . They were screaming, 'Don't move, black bastard. Don't move, we got you.' And other such terms. . . . They grabbed me and threw me against the wall of the kitchen, handcuffed me, and put me face down on the floor, and placed a shotgun at my head. And they kept repeating, 'We got you, black bastard. You like to shoot police,' something like that."

MR. CRAIN: Did you run into the bedroom?
MICHAEL TABOR: No, I didn't.
MR. CRAIN: Did you ever have your back facing the policemen with the shotguns and other guns?
MICHAEL TABOR: *Definitely* not.

There was laughter from the defense tables at his emphasis on that modifier; and it defined the inadequacy of such themes to an instrument like his. Mr. Crain was hardly the most adroit conductor for motifs that swell the emotions; he had called the witness to challenge Detective Coffey's account of the chase to the bedroom that justified the provenance of the weapons in dispute; and he carried Michael Tabor through that exercise with a compulsion to detail that seemed merely fussy to the judge whose conviction it aimed to unsettle. Well before being exhausted, the subject seemed beneath the voice, the cadence, and the bearing and no more able to involve its auditors than is the organ at a baseball game.

But then Michael Tabor was yielded up to Assistant District

109

Attorney Phillips, who approached him with the coldness, contempt, and assurance of the rectitude that is armed with the witness's criminal record. And all this absolute certainty delivered the assistant district attorney up to his prisoner; for, if Michael Tabor had found by himself the precise tone, archaic without ever being primitive, for the spaciously old-fashioned instrument of his voice, he would owe to Mr. Phillips the one theme worthy of it, a nineteenth-century man's exposition of his salvation by grace.

Mr. Phillips opened by asking Michael Tabor how many times he had been convicted of a crime.

MICHAEL TABOR: At that time, I was addicted to narcotics, you see, and I was in the process of securing funds to take care of my habit. I had become addicted, as a result, really, of the conditions that underlay my existence.

MR. PHILLIPS: During the period of that addiction, is it fair to say that you would lie to get narcotics?

MICHAEL TABOR: It would be fair to say that, during the period of my addiction, I might have done anything to get narcotics owing to the fact that I was a slave to hair-o-wine.

MR. PHILLIPS: In other words, you would lie, cheat, steal, and kill for narcotics; isn't that correct?

His tone had risen to a pitch of contempt and distaste that the police witnesses, for all the solicitude of judge and prosecutor for their feelings, had never had to suffer from defense counsel, who, however intense their distaste, could not possess the authority of hate that belongs to the man who is sure he has its object at his mercy. Mr. Crain protested the district attorney's tone, facial expression, and general demeanor; he was overruled by Justice Murtagh; and Mr. Phillips could screw up his face and press his hunt, unprotected by any restraint on the full play of its vulgarity.

MR. PHILLIPS: What wouldn't you do for narcotics?
MICHAEL TABOR: I would not kill for it.

110

MR. PHILLIPS: Other than that, you would do everything else I said, isn't that correct?

MICHAEL TABOR: I had lied, I had stolen, I had cheated to get narcotics.

MR. PHILLIPS: And you would lie in this courtroom.

MICHAEL TABOR: I have no reason to lie in this courtroom; I am not addicted to narcotics.

MR. PHILLIPS: When did you become truthful, Mr. Tabor?

MR. CRAIN: Objection, your Honor.

JUSTICE MURTAGH: Objection overruled. And I will admonish the audience.

MR. PHILLIPS: When did you become truthful, Mr. Tabor?

MICHAEL TABOR: After I liberated my body and soul from the plague of hair-o-wine.

MR. PHILLIPS: And is it fair to say that from nineteen sixty-six or nineteen sixty-seven, when you stopped with this heroin, that from then on you led a model existence?

MICHAEL TABOR: It depends upon what *you* define as a model existence.

The game went on that way, the district attorney lunging, the witness gravely, even sardonically pulling him back to earth, until the defense suggested a recess.

"Your Honor," Mr. Phillips said, "the difficulty with granting that application is that it gives the defendant an opportunity to be coached."

Nothing he had heard from the witness had altered the caricature he had brought with him; to him there still could be no source except coaching for a performance of this high a style from an actor so contemptible. The criminal prosecutor's weakness is that his experience teaches him so little of life: Joseph Phillips must have processed a thousand felons, most of them Negroes and all of them too commonsensical ever to talk back to him; and he had never had a chance to know that the Street, for a thoughtful inhabitant, is our one best school for counterpunches. When Justice Murtagh heard the ground of Mr. Phillips' objection, the sight of the reality that he had just watched was obliterated by the district attorney's reminder of the caricature; and, once again, he returned to his image of Michael Tabor as no more than the puppet of Mr. Crain, someone he regarded as inept in all things except, of course, the manipulation of the criminal poor; and he recognized the peril of allowing this mesmerist a further chance for his dark arts, reversed himself, and ordered the hearing to go on.

So Mr. Phillips was free to hector on, his questions rising in their passion as Tabor's answers descended into their indifference; and it would be the next afternoon before the district attorney ceased to hammer this cold iron and gave the witness back to Mr. Crain who asked him if he had any further reflections upon his death in heroin and his rebirth in service.

Michael Tabor leaned back, half-closed his eyes and began:

"Roughly around the age of thirteen, I began using hair-o-wine. It was conceived as something slick and something sly. Then, for a while, I did not feel my nauseous and disgusting reality. It had the effect of like helping my nose not to smell the urine-soaked tenement hallways, like I didn't feel the uncollected garbage that littered the street under my feet.

"I didn't hear the deafening sound of the police sirens as they tore through the black jungle. Under the influence of heroin, things were, like, what you wanted them to be, everything was beautiful. But I was plunging myself deeper and deeper into what you might call a pit of degradation.

"In order to attain this euphoric sensation, it became necessary to shoot more dope. So I began stealing, you see. Roughly around the age of seventeen, I became convinced that if I did not alter my course, if I did not stop shooting heroin that I would eventually die.

"I think the turning point came by way of a piece of literature entitled *The Autobiography of Malcolm X*. It uplifted me."

The organ had found its key; there had fallen over the courtroom the silence that accompanies the presentation of the

112

Mystery of the darkness broken by light, of the fallen raised by the intercession of the Word. Without mark of irony upon their faces, judge and prosecutor listened to a man on trial for arson and attempted murder telling how his soul had been saved.

And in that silence Michael Tabor's testament swelled on and on until it ended:

"Hair-o-wine addicts and alcoholics are all woven from the same fabric. It is just that their disease manifests itself in different forms. And I became convinced that the only way these various psychological diseases could be overcome was by effecting a radical overall change in the system. And it was at that point that I joined the party."

And the spell broke for Judge Murtagh; he roused himself and, by what was now habit, signaled the restoration of business with a rebuke to Mr. Crain:

"Counsel, don't you think that we had better get back to the issue before the court?"

So Mr. Crain returned to a line of questioning less conducive to incantatory response and finally wound his way to a concluding question that asked the witness what he had meant when he told the district attorney that all his arrests had been frame-ups.

"When I say that ultimately I was framed," Michael Tabor answered, "I am saying that the conditions, under which not only myself, but black people per se in America are forced to live, drive them to such a state of desperation that they are forced to extend beyond what society defines as the bounds of law."

At that, Mr. Phillips smirked, again in command of, if he had ever been really unseated from, what he had been. The once-born were back to trying the twice-born. Still, Michael Tabor went on reverberating; he had altered the face of the event. To the curse upon the present, he had added the promise of the future: Richard Moore had fiercely, derisively pointed up what was, and Michael Tabor had glowingly imagined what might be. Each had so made himself a personage that, as funds enough appeared to bail two of the male defendants, Moore

113

and Tabor were selected as the ones whose release and public display would best serve the case. In their emergence would be their common ruin; and Richard Moore's would be the deeper, because no one had more felt the difference between them than he did at the moment of Michael Tabor's crest.

Then the Street had bowed down to the clouds. In that time to come, when, free on bail and thus more vulnerable than in the pens, they began to drift away from the others and back to their old isolation, Richard Moore would follow Michael Tabor downward as his faithful squire, being that very familiar victim, the man with only the gift for definition in the thrall of the man who offers the gift of prophecy.

For a few days after Tabor's witness, the defendants generally suspended their interventions, as though having heard themselves expressed in the lofty tones of the saved had given them a dignity above expressing themselves in the earthy terms of the humiliated and the endangered. Police witnesses came and went, comparatively unbaited; but then the chorus began to stir again. On February 25th, the rage of its members at the present displaced whatever remained of the balm of Michael Tabor's assurance of the future, and they surged up together in the courtroom, a common fist thrust upward, a common shout of "Power to the People" into Justice Murtagh's face.

And then they turned about to raise that summons to an audience that did not respond, the judge's three contempt citations having been enough to subjugate it. Then, reminded of how little it can take to fragment the people and knowing themselves without hope of rescue or resource except their own despair and self-esteem, they set themselves again to upbraiding their captors:

LUMUMBA SHAKUR: I think you should put on the record that this is going to be a daily procedure.

ROBERT COLLIER: I think that you can also put down that it's part of the Declaration of Independence.

RICHARD MOORE: Right.

LUMUMBA SHAKUR: Anytime we say "All Power to the

People" we're just expressing our definition of government for the people, by the people, and of the people.

The detective who had arrested Ali Bey Hassan was the day's witness and, as their gibes against him mounted, Justice Murtagh returned to telling the defendants to be silent.

Walter Johnson told him to shut up and Curtis Powell announced, "We ain't gonna be silent, pig." And Mr. Phillips seized the chance that never escaped him to note for the record his observation that counsel had watched these excesses with no show of admonishment; and, while Mr. Katz was directing his disclaimers of complicity at a stone wall, Robert Collier attempted to establish the innocence of the lawyers with less success in their cause than he achieved in making clear the self-hardened obduracy of their clients:

"Let the court understand that we have told our counsel that, whenever we see injustice being perpetrated in this court and being defamed in this court, we shall speak out, whether they like it or not, and there's no use for them even to try to admonish us on it."

That would be their final concerted rebuff to their humiliation. Justice Murtagh at last invoked the remedy for his. He ordered the defendants removed from the courtroom, picked up a sheet of paper, and read aloud his declaration that these hearings stood now in indefinite recess. He was ready, he said, to consider resuming them only after each defendant had sworn his "unequivocal assurance [of] complete respect to the court during the continuance of these hearings and during the course of the trial to follow, and an assurance that the defendants are now prepared to participate in a trial conducted under the American system of criminal justice."

"The court," he concluded, "is responsible for maintaining proper respect for the administration of criminal justice and preventing any reflection on the image of American justice. THAT RESPONSIBILITY WILL BE DISCHARGED."

Justice Murtagh had indicated an expectation of compliance within forty-eight hours. That time passed with no break in the

115

silence from the Queens House of Detention until, on March 2nd, there was handed up to him a reply drafted by the defendants in the form of a remonstrance. It ran across a long history of injuries done to its signers and to generations of Negroes before them; and it refused on their behalf any pledge to respect the court until their claim of right under the Constitution had been honored:

"You have talked about our counsel inciting us. Nothing could be farther from the truth. The injustices we have been accorded over the past year incite us, the injustices in these hearings incite us, racism incites us, fascism incites us, in short, when we reflect back over history, its continuation until today, you and your courts incite us."

"We must," they concluded, "begin anew with a mutual understanding."

It had become, then, a quarrel between the pride and illusions of one side and the pride and illusions of the other. The justice was demanding humility from persons to whom the meaning of life had become rebellion against a tradition of humility; the defendants were demanding an equal station— what else does "mutual understanding" mean?—from an instrument of a court system that appoints the relationship of judge to accused as, at best, guardian to ward or as, at less than best, master to servant. The defendants argued the historic maltreatment of the Negro in these states under the illusion that the suffering of past victims can ever be useful for sympathy with present ones. The justice could only have read that history as without relevance to the business of the present under the illusion that *he* would never have upheld the slave codes, all of us being, as Burke said, enlightened judges of the transactions of past ages. The defendants were crying out their grievances in a judge's ear deafened by his grievances against them.

The defense, meanwhile, under its own conscientious illusion that when nothing useful suggests itself, one ought anyway to do something, had moved sideways into the Supreme Court of Queens County on March 9th to ask Justice John J. Leahy to

116

vacate his brother Murtagh's order of cessation. They were represented in this maneuver by Professors Herbert Reid of Howard University and Leroy Clark of New York University. Professors Reid and Clark argued that Justice Murtagh's language was "totally vague" and that, in requiring the defendants to swear to their good behavior in the future, he was asking them to incriminate themselves by implying a confession that they had behaved badly up until now.

Justice Leahy was both flattered by and flattering toward the eminence of these ambassadors from the academy and must have been surprised to hear that their sensitivity had so survived their rise in the world that their only comment on the atmosphere of his courtroom was the bruised recollection that, since it afforded so few chairs, their clients had had to sit on its floor.

Mr. Phillips came to tell Justice Leahy that the persons squatting behind him were "vicious criminals . . . terrorists rather than criminals for profit," and thus from that worst class of ruffians, the overprincipled sort. "Justice had been trammeled" by them, he declared. He could, he concluded, think of no better argument for Justice Murtagh's formula than was represented by the pieces of evidence sitting behind and beneath him, now housebroken and "starting to act like human beings."

About the time Justice Leahy was sitting down to the record that set forth the offenses against Justice Murtagh, it seems to have occurred to the Department of Correction that, even though the federal courts had removed the defendants from the range of satisfactory reprisal, Lee Berry did remain as surrogate for the punishment they all deserved. On March 11th, Berry was transferred from Bellevue Hospital to the Riker's Island prison infirmary, where his medication was suspended. No notice of his removal was given to his wife, his lawyers, or Dr. John W. V. Cordice, the surgeon who had volunteered to serve them as consultant. Berry had been back in jail a week before a court order allowed Dr. Cordice to visit him, "find his condition deteriorating because of the discon-

117

tinuance of therapy," and get him returned to the hospital. Ten days later, Justice Leahy found for Justice Murtagh, whose treatment he declared to have shocked "the very conscience of the court."

Still there stretched the gulf of pride between the suspension of the event and a renewal possible only if one of the two parties made the crossing; and, curiously enough, it was Justice Murtagh, his pride strengthened by the adherence of Justice Leahy, who found within his temper the means of accommodation. Bail money had been raised for Richard Moore, most of it from Abbie Hoffman, whose nature it is to conceal how generous he is with his own property while exaggerating how rapacious he is for that of others. Mr. Phillips argued that approval of Moore's bail application would be unmerited charity to the worst of these offenders. Even so, Justice Murtagh granted it with unexpected alacrity, perhaps because, as a better listener than Mr. Phillips, he had recognized Richard Moore's advantage over him so long as the threat of contempt citation could be met by that taunting "What you gon' do, put me in jail?" and had surmised that his would be the advantage over Richard Moore once he had freed him from custody and acquired the power to remand him at any breach of the decorum of the courtroom. Justice Murtagh may then have been the first to recognize that, in jail, Richard Moore was armed and, in the Street, naked and vulnerable.

Justice Murtagh had surprised the defense by granting Moore's bail even while the applicant affirmed that its acceptance was in no way to be taken as "compliance with any preconditions." ("It is my belief that I have an absolute constitutional right to a trial without preconditions thereto.") The court surprised the defense further on March 24th by explaining that he would require from its clients no more than the statement that they were now ready to stand trial with neither confession of prior misconduct nor promise of future propriety. He had waived his hard conditions; and counsel hastened to comply with his softer new ones, even while pressing him to admit that the pride of the defendants had outworn his own

118

until he left the courtroom with Mr. Lefcourt still afoot insisting that his clients had in no way conceded a promise to
behave.

Yet behave they did, through April, May, June, and most of
July, while their lawyers exhausted every device of attack upon
the mass of Mr. Phillips' evidence.

Mr. Lefcourt's only conspicuous discovery had a larger ar-
cheological interest than historical effect. A year or so before,
while serving as counsel to Captain Ford then under an assault
indictment, he had demanded that the district attorney of
Brooklyn produce the results of any wiretaps performed upon
his client. To Mr. Lefcourt's surprise, the Brooklyn district
attorney's office candidly yielded up a sheaf of the transcripts
that Police Lieutenant Galante had assembled from his eavesdroppings on Ford and a number of other Brooklyn Black
Panthers after an appellate division judge had permitted him to
wiretap them on the evidence of their criminal pursuits provided him by the grand jury testimony of the informant Shaun
Dubonnet.

The police department which had wiretapped Ford and
subsidized Shaun Dubonnet was, Mr. Lefcourt argued, the
same institution that had developed the instant case against
Lumumba Shakur et al. He felt entitled then to pursue the
Brooklyn wiretaps until he could be assured that the case
against these clients had in no way been developed through
Lieutenant Galante listening or Shaun Dubonnet swearing. Mr.
Phillips attested that nothing in his case relied upon information supplied by either Dubonnet or the Brooklyn wiretaps.
Nonetheless, Justice Murtagh handsomely, if unpromisingly,
allowed the defense to proceed down this line.

What followed would serve rather better to illuminate the
system in general than it did to help the defense along the
track of its particular case.

Shaun Dubonnet had been certified by the New York City
Police Department as a witness to criminal conspiracies worth
taking seriously enough to justify a court to the extreme of
authorizing a tap on the telephones of the parties he accused.

Yet Shaun Dubonnet had been adjudged a paranoid schizophrenic by presumably proper authorities well before he entered Lieutenant Galante's service, had been caught even by Lieutenant Galante in at least one lie, had rendered himself finally untrustworthy as an auxiliary policeman only when he jumped bail on a robbery charge, and was now lodged in Central Islip State again as a paranoid schizophrenic.

Such a history might seem to suggest an unsettling degree of credulity among policemen to any observer less used than Justice Murtagh to gazing into abysses and seeing only neatly ordered acres under cultivation. Mr. Lefcourt would point out to him that a police department and a district attorney had joined to deceive a brother judge into approving a wiretap on no more evidence than the oath of an adjudicated psychopath; and Justice Murtagh would observe from a height no curiosity could bring to earth:

"The court must take judicial notice that police informants are seldom reputable people."

Late in the hearings, Mr. Lefcourt's persistence brought before the court Elliott Golden, the former acting district attorney of Brooklyn who had certified Shaun Dubonnet as a witness first to a grand jury and then to the appellate division of a state court system.

Elliott Golden did not merely concede but quite unashamedly asserted that neither he nor, so far as he knew, any other law officer had made any effort to check Dubonnet's background. The question of why a district attorney had so trusted a witness against whom he held a warrant for escape from a mental institution having been disposed of as the nullity court and prosecution thought it, Mr. Lefcourt moved along to ask Mr. Golden how he could ever have believed that Rhody McCoy, superintendent of the Ocean Hill–Brownsville school system, had entertained the suggestion that Albert Shanker, president of the city's teachers union, be assassinated.

"Well," Mr. Golden replied, "I believe [Dubonnet] told me he asked twenty-five thousand dollars; the offer had been fifteen thousand dollars. He was the only one they were ad-

120

dressing as I recall. . . . He was the only one who was being propositioned."

Suddenly it could be understood that one illusion provided by Shaun Dubonnet had survived all experience intact. The former district attorney of Brooklyn still believed that Rhody McCoy had sat by and listened to a proposal to murder an opponent; the image, on no other evidence, remained as fixed in his mind as at the moment when it was first offered him by a witness he now knew to have been an escaped mental patient.

Late in his performance, Justice Murtagh felt impelled to remind defense counsel that, in Golden, they were hectoring a distinguished lawyer. This compliment was interjected just after the distinguished witness explained that, as district attorney, he had presented to a grand jury a witness who had been in fifteen mental hospitals, certified his testimony to an appellate judge, got curious about his credentials only six weeks later, and, after finding out the worst, gone on paying him for the next month.

Shaun Dubonnet came last of all, wearing a madras jacket, the aura of confident truculence, and the freshly plausible, eventually unbelievable tale of the fantasist. He had, he explained, decided to infiltrate the police department. ("Twice before I had infiltrated the police department.") He had used Elliott Golden's stipend "really for the party."

On cross-examination, Phillips asked him if he had told the police of his background.

"If they don't know my background, that's ignorance on their part," their informant replied. "If they're stupid enough to get out there and give a hundred dollars a week to somebody they don't know they are dealing with, shit."

"Anybody who is gullible enough to believe you is stupid," Phillips pursued. "Is that correct?"

"That's correct," Shaun Dubonnet answered.

Joseph Phillips was laughing. Judge Murtagh reproved him. "Excuse me, sir," he said; he looked down, his great body, working manfully, not quite successfully, to repress its giggles. The pretrial hearings had ended with this glimpse of the fantasies and bigotries of the preindictment investigation. Court and prosecutor looked upon Shaun Dubonnet; neither shame nor anger intruded upon either's countenance; the court was incurious; the Prosecutor was laughing. They were ready for trial.

The defense's motions for suppression of the seized evidence were entered and the court disposed of them as summarily as their presentation had been protracted. Justice Murtagh announced that he hoped to preside over the selection of a jury for the trial itself starting the day after Labor Day. He was reasonably content with the manners of the defendants but still offended with those of their attorneys; and he bade these latter miscreants farewell for August by beseeching them to reflect upon their conduct.

August was not a month offering much scope for attention to the New York Panthers. In Oakland, Huey Newton was released from prison to await the retrial of his reversed conviction for manslaughter, and New Haven began the series of murder trials that would end with Bobby Seale's; among such clangors, the raising of $50,000 bail for Michael Tabor and his bonding out passed off unnoticed.

He and Afeni Shakur could be found two days later at Harlem Hospital, whose seventh floor had been seized by two hundred drug addicts demanding treatment. The hospital's director had welcomed this army of occupation and the publicity it promised. He would, he proclaimed, stand with these trespassers against any police effort to dislodge them. He could offer them his solidarity, his sheets, his mattresses, and his dressing gowns; but Harlem Hospital, though it sits at the center of the distribution of drugs, has few facilities for sustained treatment of their effects. The invaders, occasionally interrupted for routine medical procedures marginally related to their illness, sat around or looked out of windows or slept or read or endlessly played cards, insurgents who settled back with only a change of scene into that life whose function it is to sit and wait. They were only a Display and Harlem Hospital just another stop for an itinerant Trade Show of Social Protest in a city whose managers, being equally tolerant of those who complain of the problem and resigned to the problem itself, yield up their public buildings to persons anxious to exhibit moral reproach as they rent space in their Coliseum to manufacturers displaying their products. In Harlem Hospital, the Panthers and the Black Poets were auxiliary attractions provided by the sponsors, just as Ted Williams might be at the Hunting and Fishing Show.

The public relations director of Harlem Drug Fighters brought Afeni Shakur to one of the card tables. "Here she is," he grandly intoned, "the first Black Woman ever held in one hundred thousand dollars bail in New York City."

Her welcome was fraternal, an unspoken And-What-Did-You-Learn-at-School-Today, Little-Sister?

"They are fixing to give us seventy-five years," Afeni Shakur smiled. "But I am a revolutionary and I know that if I go, there will be someone to come after me."

Just an echo of the tone of recitation remained to suggest how young she still was for the load she carried. The talk, and her awkwardness with it, passed very soon into cheerful chat about the month's wars in various cities—random events to the rest of us but to these imaginations somehow significant of some great plan of their own subgovernment, a power both native and sovereign, with a claim on the prayers, if not the sacrifices, of everyone present. "It's coming," one of the card players said. "When I get out of here, I'm going to get my .357 magnum." Afeni Shakur sensed her duty to bring them back from these idle fancies. "Look," she said, "I don't know much about drugs. But we have this brother Cet who used to be an addict and he's down the hall talking about how to get yourself straight. You ought to come down." And, smiling, she departed.

124

"A beautiful person," one of the card players observed. Still none rose to follow; the game fell back to the routine of so many other afternoons, having only been interrupted and not changed by one of those Performances that occasionally relieve a Street by providing it with the diversion of a Theatre. Afeni Shakur's way had been one not to follow but simply to admire.

For the Street's response to the Panthers is more to the poetry of their motion than to the prose of their message. The Panthers have made the human body itself an instrument of declamation; and they are an embodiment of that effrontery which the street treasures in the celebration of such disparate masters of the Black Style as Marcus Garvey, Adam Powell, and Malcolm X. An audience of surprised, half-laughing Negroes is present and duly noted in every description of Huey P. Newton's passages with the police; there would be no legend if there were not witnesses to that miracle of getting away with it for a little while whose achievement the Black Style embodies. But it is an achievement safer to watch than to imitate; the Street is an Audience that long ago abandoned as perilous any claim to be the Play.

Down the hall, as promised by Afeni Shakur, there was Michael Tabor, lecturing with unexpected abstention from theatrical device on the drug problem. Part of his command on the attention of his audience belonged to him as an old acquaintance. The drug culture is a very small club; and the air of quiet knowingness that had likely been his style even before his redemption must have been a familiar comfort to his auditors. But, then too, his addiction is the addict's main identity and only claim on our curiosity; and it has for him the quality any narcissistic subject has of never growing tiresome, of never needing to be heightened with dramatic effects.

"A hundred years from now," Michael Tabor began, "there will be a museum where they will show a Negro and there will be a sign saying 'This was the Negro who used to be and is now extinct like the dodo and the egret.'" He did not seem to have designed that remark to shock, since he delivered it in the tone of definition, and it seemed, indeed, quite matter-of-fact on a

125

scene where his auditors even sat in the immobile repose one associates with exhibits. He passed in review all the cures which had left them just what they were and ended with methadone:

"The state comes to you and offers this habit in trade for the habit you have now. You take it, and when you've been coming to him a little while, the man will say to you, 'Look we've got a problem. We're running short. But, if you'll tell me what they're saying out in the street, keep open an eye for me on who's talking about revolution, I'll give you some. But, until you perform this little function for us, we can't deal with you.'

"You know what you are now: the dealer says you got to have ten dollars and you're gonna get that ten dollars no matter who you got to rip off. And you'll do this too if you have to; you will have just traded habits and now you are a slave to the state."

We have got, he explained, to have our own institutions, our own programs, our own cures. And there he stopped, having only defined and held back from exhorting. There were neither questions nor traces of doubt on the faces around him. What might seem paranoid to the rest of us was taken for granted here; when Michael Tabor talked of a state that was malignant whenever it was not merely indifferent, he might as well have been telling them that they had lungs and breathed. Logic would have expected him to go on to say that he had found a way that would not only describe the world but change it; yet he avoided any suggestion that they join him, and betrayed indeed none of that snobbery we are so used to when the saved address the fallen. Whatever had changed in Michael Tabor, he retained that politesse according to which the Street grants to every man the possession of whatever special personal business he must take care of.

It was curious, a visitor said, how this audience seemed already to assume as fact a description of America which the rest of us have at most only commenced to suspect. For the first time that afternoon, there was a trace of hauteur in the voice of Michael Tabor.

"Of course," he answered. "I have always said that if you want to have America described for you, you need only ask any Negro."

Since June, Richard Moore had been organizing in Brownsville, an easterly extension of Brooklyn's Bedford-Stuyvesant. There are gradations in blighted regions beyond detection by the tourist but immediately and agonizingly apparent to the native who carries a point of reference from the one to the other.

"I looked right out this window," Donald Cox said one hot afternoon on Lenox Avenue in Harlem, "and I saw a man chase another one down the street with a butcher knife. I never saw anything like that. I've never seen anyone live like these people have to. I can't deal with this city. What am I going to do when it starts getting cold?"

Donald Cox had lived all his life around the San Francisco Bay before he began going about as field marshal of the Black Panther Party. He remembered Oakland as a tough and proud community; he was confronted by Harlem as a mess of broken pieces, far beyond any power of his to offer hope and order. And, as Oakland is shocked by Harlem, Harlem is shocked by Brownsville. "I've never seen people live like this," Richard Moore said.

He was maneuvering through the potholes and the dust raised where the macadam had broken. A dog crossed his path, stopped and faced the car as if it had never seen but would not run before such a beast.

"God damn it," said Richard Moore. "Get out of the way. The streets belong to the people, not the dogs," and with his sudden, always surprising gentleness, turned his wheel and took the long way around.

The walls and the signboards of Brownsville long ago ceased to interest anyone with anything to sell for money; the tattered remainders of a time when commerce had a function there have been covered now with portraits of Huey Newton, of Bobby Seale and those cartoons of babies with rifles that Panther artist Emory Booker has since disavowed. The eye

127

touches no object that has lately been painted except the fire truck which habitually and purposelessly patrols these streets. Brownsville is burning down; more storefronts on Sutter Avenue are fire-gutted than not, as though the hand of some giant child with an acetylene torch, wayward but persistent, had decided to signify the blackness of Brownsville with the blackness of these ruins. There is nothing to explain the fires of Brownsville unless it be some unacknowledged compact between the street and its policemen, who have agreed only on the feeling that Brownsville ought to come down; exuberance mingles equally with horror in discussions of the process.

"The night they *liberated* Key Foods," remembers Tinnie Ibarrando, an ally of the Panther Party, "the cops just watched it burn down until they were sure it couldn't be saved and then they called the fire truck."

And yet there is something almost rural about Brownsville, as though when the ruin of the city is terminal it lapses into desert—the children without shoes, the dogs, the flies, the ponds of water around the clogged sewers, the dry dust where the streets have worn out, the sacked hulks of the cars. Its people seem younger, less used to the city, than the people of Harlem; and Richard Moore in his red silk undershirt, his panama hat, his walk—one part the proprietor, one part the poacher—seems alien somehow, a little too large for the scene, come down, say, from Chicago, where it has been best for him to leave for a while, to see his grandmother in Clarksdale.

Here as everywhere, the question of what to do with Richard Moore seems to be one of those uncertain issues—except for the little boys who knew that he is an adventure and someone to run after ("Day-roo-bah, Day-roo-bah, can I ride in yo' car?") or for the young girls who recognize him as an occasion for defining themselves as ladies, for lowering their eyes, for smiling as if they were thinking about someone else, and for drawing slightly back from the liberating mockery of his approach.

The sense of his being inappropriate seemed to have touched even him. The rest of us may not demand that the tragic hero

128

be a serious man; but he knows he ought to. Tinnie Ibarrando, the neighborhood's resident angel of discord, has brought him to 511 Hinsdale Avenue in response to a report that the landlord means to evict its residents. Dharuba stalks, a prince of the forest, captures a tenant carrying a baby in the hall, becomes suddenly only an intruder. She identifies herself as Barbara Strickland, seems painfully, if unafraidedly, unsure that he is not after her purse.

"We come to stop the rats biting your little baby," he explains.

"I ain't seen any rats," Barbara Strickland corrects him. "It's the roaches."

He had come, Richard Moore went on, to stop the landlord from evicting her.

"He doesn't have the power to take my money and then put me in the street," Barbara Strickland answered.

"I've seen them put old ladies in the street," Richard Moore said. "They don't care nothing about us. From now on you're gonna keep the rent and spend the money on repairs. That is what we have done in Harlem. There's beautiful apartments up there where the rent is only forty-four dollars a month."

The face of Mrs. Strickland maintained its resistance to such fantasies. An old man came through the hall, paused at the party, fixed upon its only member with a necktie, asked, "Are you the landlord?" got the embarrassed denial, and wandered away carrying who-knows-what-long-stored-imprecations. There was beginning to descend the atmosphere of a failed oral exam, as though Mrs. Strickland embodied the poor as a board of examiners that had asked a question whose proper answer was "roaches" and Richard Moore was the candidate who had answered "rats." He had not yet been marked "Failed," yet a visitor felt that Mrs. Strickland knew the exact measure of her inflictions and that Richard Moore didn't quite and that anyone who exaggerated them ran the risk of seeming as much a stranger as someone who denied their existence. Tinnie Ibarrando went up and down the stairs with her notebook; in this place where everything else seemed alien and horrible, she had restored that comfort of the familiar, the reform lady with her

129

pad and pencil, the collector of grievances. Mrs. Strickland's trust was commencing to form; Richard Moore said there would be a meeting of tenants; Mrs. Strickland said he had best slip any announcement under each tenant's door, since the superintendent, who never bothered about much else, would certainly rouse to rip down any call upon the tenants to revolt that was posted in his hall. What had divided them until now, it began to be apparent, had been that Richard Moore's experience was limited to the ordinary slum; he had been talking about decay, which is at least a sign of life. But now this house could be felt as past the point where bacteria could long breathe there. It seemed curiously clean as a picked bone, having no paint to flake; the dirt on the marble facings by the stairs was so old that any hand rubbing it came off with no more stain than a candle would leave; none of its graffiti bore a date later than 1947, and the names they memorialized all came from Eastern Europe; no crust this waxen would take the pencil of a child of a successor culture. There was no glass in the windows by the stairs and not a fragment in their smooth frames to suggest that they had recently known a pane or kept a winter in these halls warm enough to draw a rat in from the cold. There would be a meeting Thursday to organize the liberation, Dharuba said; she would, Mrs. Strickland agreed, array the tenants. Somehow, for a little while, he had lifted her suspicion of strangers in red silk undershirts and other hazards of adventure in life. And now, Dharuba said, let us go to see that avaricious dog.

The landlord, Bernard Levine, has his office in a storefront whose interior is separated by a wall of paperboard, glass, and above that, chickenwire running almost to its tin ceiling.

His washroom is favored by policemen and sanitation workers in moments of need on their rounds; but his is not a premise otherwise proclaiming its station as Brownsville's last vestige of civilization. Tinnie Ibarrando and Richard Moore had to wait their turn while one of his tenants confronted Levine with a bill for repairing his door. The complainant was a black businessman who had rented a store. The grate by its entrance had

130

been broken and, while he was waiting for Levine to fix it, thieves had finished it off and made away with his stock. He had had to close for a month to get a loan to replenish it; and, while he waited, water from the ceiling had ruined his floor. "Look," said Bernard Levine, "the woman upstairs let the bathtub overflow. She does it every week. What can I do?"

The storekeeper had hired a contractor to make the repairs and now he was presenting the bill to Bernard Levine. "That's not how we do business," Levine said. "I didn't rent you a floor. I rented you four walls and a ceiling."

"Man," said Richard Moore, "do you *hear* that avaricious dog?" Bernard Levine merely looked up and surveyed the hat and the undershirt and, without comment, returned to his explanations.

At length, he said, "All right, I'll give you fifty dollars for it. You've had trouble. You been trying."

He plainly meant to be kind. The complainant carried the bulk of his loss away with him, and Tinnie Ibarrando and Richard Moore fell upon Bernard Levine, stated the grievance of 511 Hinsdale Avenue, and he denied it.

"You better talk to us, Burr-NARD," said Richard Moore, making the name an embodiment of all epithet. "There's only one way to talk to people, and that's with decency," Bernard Levine replied.

"Do you consider yourself a human being?" Tinnie Ibarrando asked.

"I consider myself a landlord," Bernard Levine answered. "Are you interested in helping these people or not? Then see that they pay their rent and something can be done."

"The People have no intention of paying you rent while you treat them like this," said Richard Moore. "Make the repairs and you'll get your rent."

"That's not reasonable," Bernard Levine answered. "That's not the way we work. You don't know much about real estate and I don't advise you to take it up. You'll not get anywhere with me coming in here and talking like that. I been through this before. You treat me decent and I'll treat you decent."

131

And then, as if from very old practice, he fixed his face in a mask of inattention and began moving, his back turned, among his desks as though there were no one in his presence. Richard Moore stood outside his partition and invoked the power and the curses of the People upon him. Bernard Levine's back went on looking as though it neither heard these words nor was even aware of these persons until, at length, there was nothing to do but leave with a final "You'll hear from us Burr-NARD; this is not the end, Burr-NARD."

Outside, Richard Moore seemed to feel that the failure, inevitable in all first passages in a combat so uneven, was somehow a sign of inadequacy in himself. "Talking to these pigs is not my game," he apologized. "My game is talking to the People. Did you notice that office? Him, with all his money, and he keeps it so bare that if we took it out with a fire bomb, it wouldn't cost him nothing." Even in anger, he retained that unexpected compulsion of his to be responsible; his first thought was to frame an argument against some violent reprisal; it was hard not to imagine that there would soon come some evening when he would need it when talking to the People.

He came back to the Panther headquarters and railed and pretended to threaten until he was distracted by a boy who needed a bandage on his cut knee, upon which office Richard Moore concentrated as if he were in surgery, first washing the wound, and then sanitizing it, all the while joking with the sufferer; and, by the time he had come softly and tenderly to put on the bandage, his shame and anger had gone away.

Still, a week later, on the return to Brownsville, Richard Moore had gone—transferred to the Bronx—and there was no sign that he had ever been there. His replacement in command was introduced as Oscar, a worried young man with a tam-o-shanter, woven in the red, green, and black colors of the New Africa. Oscar needed to inspect the morning formation, instruct the charge of quarters, and help open the Liberation School, and then he would have time to go with Tinnie Ibarrando to engage Bernard Levine again.

132

As only a fellow traveler, Tinnie Ibarrando had to wait on the street outside while these drills were gotten through. She explained that last week's quarrel had gone better than had been thought in the aftermath of self-criticism. She had called Bernard Levine again, and he had agreed to begin repairs on the Hinsdale Avenue house and had even offered to discuss their progress with her and with Oscar. She had, besides, a new complaint to bring him; she gestured toward a building on the northwest corner of Herzl and Sutter Avenue: "That house hasn't had water for a week."

She needed, she went on, to get all these things redressed before the end of August, because she had to spend September in family court trying to get her children back.

"Some child in school told the nurse that I had beaten my little girl with a dog chain. That was enough for them to come the next day and take four of my children away. My boy, who's eleven, was away from the house and they never come back for him. They took me to jail. I told them to examine the child; if I'd beaten her, there'd sure be marks, wouldn't there? After they did that, they decided to drop the child abuse charge and hold me just for child neglect."

She continued—a plump woman with a kind, innocent, rather childlike smile—an uncomplaining recital of the routine events that had happened since: how two of the girls, nine and seven, had been first put in a home where they had been tied up with lamp cords; how she had managed a transfer to another home from which they had run away and been missing for three days, because, as the man from the children's bureau had explained to her, there were really too few attendants to watch the children; and how since the noise about child abuse had grown so loud as to frighten judges from disposing of such cases, her hearing had been put off again and again until it was set now for September 15th.

"Now they're accusing me of having a gun. I told them I wouldn't have a gun in the house. They might have got that from the children. Before he went to Chicago, my husband used to come by mad every now and then and hold a gun to my

133

head. The children used to see that and you know children can get mixed up. They knew one of us had a gun; they could have forgotten whether it was me or my husband."

Then Oscar came out and the walk to Bernard Levine's began. On the way they talked about Hayward, an intermittent Black Panther, sort of, who had been shot dead over the weekend.

"Are they going to give Hayward a revolutionary funeral?" Tinnie Ibarrando asked. "Two of the girls was over at my house and they said there was going to be a revolutionary funeral and they were going to wear their uniforms."

"We don't relate much to that uniform shit any more," Oscar answered. There was an impression that Hayward was a subject of some reserve.

Tinnie Ibarrando had heard that he had died in the company of members of GWAPO ("power" in Spanish), a Brownsville organization inspired by but in no very easy fraternal relations with the Black Panther Party.

"Oscar, Hayward done wrong," she went on. "He walked into a dry cleaning store with a gun. Only he put the gun in his shirt and put the shirt in his pants. So he couldn't get it out; all he did was point to it. And the woman in there came up shooting. GWAPO's not doing its clothing drive right. They're supposed to go in and ask for the clothes the way you brothers do; but they just went into the dry cleaning store with a gun. Now they're all out of town because the pigs are looking for them. That's just not right."

Oscar agreed that it certainly wasn't. The impression developed that Hayward would be buried with sorrow but no conspicuous honors and with due respect for his mother's wish that there be no revolutionary funeral.

Bernard Levine received them wary but resigned. He set himself with a fair amount of patience to contending with the ignorance of reformers as to what the law defines as the required repair. Between explanations, he made small talk with the third member of the party, an identifiable outlander. "There's people who care," he said. "The bank is always asking

134

me how we can help these people live better." Yes, there was much here to write about; he had a friend who had written *Milk and Honey*—"you remember, the musical"—and that Bernard had often told him that he need only come to Brownsville and find enough to write about for the rest of his life. For the first time, there could be conceived for Bernard Levine another life, not of course the luxury conjured in Richard Moore's metaphor but still comfortable enough, with a son who will go to college and come back calling his father a slumlord and a writer-acquaintance who can indulge subjects sweet enough to be called *Milk and Honey*. Among such interruptions, the negotiations over Hinsdale wandered between vague promises and concrete refusals on his side and not-quite-hardened suspicions on theirs until Tinnie Ibarrando agreed to wait a little longer for the righting of that wrong and turned to the house on Sutter Avenue which had been out of water for a week.

Bernard Levine put both hands up in the motion signaling halt. "I didn't own that building," he said. "I was only the administrator of the receivership there. And I gave it up as of last Friday. It's not my responsibility anymore."

Someone had stolen the auxiliary pipes last month, and he had replaced them. But now someone had stolen the main pipes and that was too much. He had just given up.

"Who has it now?" Tinnie Ibarrando asked. "Who do we see?"

"The city," Bernard Levine replied. The word summoned depths unfathomable, into which the Sutter Avenue building had sunk without a trace. He attempted to help: "I have a court order relieving me of the receivership. It is from the Supreme Court of the State of New York. You could write the clerk."

He handed over a legal-sized document. Tinnie Ibarrando read the first page and turned to the second. There she found five names, the first words to break what had been the seal of a foreign language, the first suggestion of real persons who might be dealt with. Bernard Levine saw her begin to copy those

135

names and fairly leaped through the door of his partition to grasp the paper's edge and try to wrest it from her. "Give me that," he said fiercely and as fiercely she struggled, in a strength of rage almost his equal. Bernard Levine could suddenly be understood. Tinnie Ibarrando had stumbled upon the names of the lawyers for the East New York Savings Bank, which had been left with the mortgages of so many Brownsville landlords, vanished from the sight and memory of their creditors as well as of their tenants. Bernard Levine is only an agent, depended upon by the bank as a shield; now he was possessed by the horrid vision of some descent upon the bank by these people in full cry, of the abuse he had learned not merely to absorb but almost not to hear any longer, and of the blame bound to fall upon him for negligence in causing such embarrassment to his principals. Not insult to himself but the prospect of insult to the East New York Savings Bank roused him to fight with a desperation that scratched Tinnie Ibarrando's arm. They twisted and struggled until Oscar, symbol of the party which is blamed for the intrusion of violence into the Street, felt impelled to intervene. "Give it to him, Tinnie"; she let go and Bernard Levine almost fell back into his cage with the tatters of the prize: "That's what happens when I try to help you people. You take an advantage like that. Just get out of here. I'm not going to deal with you any longer."

"Give me that paper, Burr-NARD," Tinnie Ibarrando rasped at his back. He did not look around. After a while, there was nothing for her to do but leave. But turning, she picked up an ashtray and flung it at his cage. Bernard Levine's back registered nothing whatsoever. At the door she passed an empty pint of Thunderbird and snatched and hurled that too with an impact which threw its fragments straight back upon Oscar. Bernard Levine was dialing the precinct, a number evidently known by heart. "Please send a car right away to 383 East 93rd Street," he was saying as the door closed and Tinnie Ibarrando and her companions were gone.

"Did you see what that man did to me?" She held out her arm, a patch of her soft skin already beginning to turn blue. "In

136

ten years my husband never put a finger on me. I'm gonna go back and call him outside." Her companions had not spoken until now. "Tinnie," one of them said at last, "have you forgotten your case with your children?" It seemed a long while since that accusation about the dog chain had been only a slander to be dismissed out of hand. But Oscar said nothing, and walked the whole way back in silence, contemplating perhaps all the rage around him, a condition ungovernable and almost unemployable except in wayward outbreaks like Tinnie's. The worry that was the most memorable aspect of his expression appeared to have passed beyond concern and to approach despair.

In the Bronx, Richard Moore sat on a stoop outside the Panther Party office on Boston Road. His visitor expressed sorrow at his leaving Brownsville; as a soldier, Richard Moore replied, he went where the command dispatched him. Inside there was an efficiency, almost a grayness, not before felt in a Panther office. One was aware of paper being produced and even of that faint oppression associated with bureaus of administration. The reasons for Richard Moore's transfer had not apparently included a function; he fussed with the tape machine, almost impatiently passing over cassettes of Seale's speeches and Newton's and even one of his own, as if he were seeking only some chance tape from the music of the life he had abandoned to become a revolutionary. "Take us to lunch," he said; but then no one except his visitor seemed to have the time to accompany him, and he departed carrying orders for sandwiches and coffee. In the lunchroom he seized upon the jukebox, staring so fixedly upon it that he seemed about to plunge his head into the speaker in the intensity of his need to remember how the music used to feel. He returned from this immersion to drink his coffee and to flirt with the waitress, who lowered her lashes with no more commitment than his. The passage was clearly form without purpose; Dharuba recruits for the revolution, out of old habit, as Richard Moore used to pick up girls in the days he moved these streets—with the walk which is still one part dance and one part prowl. On the way back, he saw a girl eating an ice cream cone behind the dry

137

cleaner's counter and called out, "I'm gonna come in there and get that cone." She smiled but did not invite. "Bunch of anti-social-ist niggers around here," Richard Moore reflected. Back in the office, he stood about, then suddenly said, "Let's go out. I'm going to show you an automatic bust."

He sat back on the doorstoop, carefully took out and carefully lit a fragile cylinder of green flake wrapped in paper. The tragic hero, with nothing to do now except to wait for Justice Murtagh, was smoking a reefer, all that Energy drowsing on the Street.

VI

"Life is a gift from the few to the many," insisted the dying Modigliani, "from the few who know and have to the many who do not know and do not have." The Tuesday after Labor Day in New York is always a reminder that illusion sustains the artist until the grave. Of all mornings, this one crushes most with the shock of reengagement between those who have escaped and those who have endured the city in August and thus between those who have and are occasionally blessed with not knowing and those who do not have and are permanently cursed with knowing. Justice Murtagh and the district attorney, having rested, for however brief a while with those who have, appeared to have forgotten or not yet to have been reminded by the city's pestilential air of what they had known when they departed.

There were even intimations of refreshment, of beginning anew; the hole in the courtroom wall that had been the shape and seemed the size of Norway had been covered over with plaster and paint. The judge and the prosecutor seemed to have benefited from a summer's repairs. Justice Murtagh had grown through the winter and spring to look more and more like the proprietor of some respected public house suddenly overborne by the tumult of its customers. But now he re-appeared like some antique marvelously restored, back on his throne as father at one of those long-gone Sunday dinners where the old ways still enforce upon the children the duty of quiet at table.

And Joseph Phillips had made himself into such a child of such a family. The old ring of angry declamation was gone from his voice; he had muted himself in preparation for an audience of different tastes, it being an unexpected curiosity of our system of law that public prosecutors must understand that judges will accept a harangue that a jury of mere citizens might find offensive. With the loud colors of assertion put aside for the sober hue of truth, Mr. Phillips seemed much more formidable than he ever had. Even his baby fat seemed to bespeak the plodding schoolboy; the broad blue-serged back need only stand up to proclaim that application is better than brilliance. And what could brilliance do, if brilliance there were in the disparate assembly of lawyers across from him? Mr. Phillips would recite a lesson of which he alone possessed the syllabus; he could speak from drill and memory while brilliance could only improvise. He might not assuredly be said to have the truth, but he alone had the secret. Counsel for the defense could only await the bad while fearing the worst.

Oddly enough, counsel on all sides would begin with the same misconception: Mr. Phillips thought he was prosecuting the armed revolution and his opponents thought they were defending it. Mr. Phillips thought these the worst and Mr. Lefcourt, the best of revolutionaries. The judgment as to the fact, although not the morality, of what these prisoners had intended was so much the same on both sides of the courtroom that the defense could hardly have a theory differing enough from the prosecution's to permit it any course except just to

140

wait for Mr. Phillips to tell it how far matters had really gone. Every now and then, Justice Murtagh had observed, with a mockery whose contempt reached depths more fundamental than the defendants' defiance toward him ever could, that these lawyers were prepared to resort to just about anything to delay a trial and that seemed a sound, if not quite sporting, judgment of their difficulty.

Judge Murtagh and Mr. Phillips were as one man in bulk, authority, and possession of the secret, bishops of a communion that seemed more and more to judge and exclude counsel for the defendants as well as the defendants themselves. Without imagining quarrels between these lawyers, it was impossible not to be conscious of their differences in tradition and temperament:

Mr. McKinney, with his sideburns, his dark suits, his lustrous hair, his being used to courts where judges and even district attorneys occasionally ought to be treated like Lords. Mr. Katz, with the disarray of his hair and a language no less outrageous for its formality. (Once, in the pretrial hearings, he had urged upon Justice Murtagh, as so often before, the propriety of disqualifying himself "as biased toward these defendants." "I beg your Honor to recuse yourself," Mr. Katz had said. "I don't quite get your English," Justice Murtagh had replied. "Recuse yourself," Mr. Katz had said. "That is, remove your body.")

Mr. Katz then could offset the offense of contumely with the defense of high elegance at its forms; and Mr. McKinney had the advantage both of his air of having been so long at the bar and of his blackness, the last pressing a particular claim upon a judge and prosecutor vividly aware that the trial was an occasion that demanded acute distinctions among blacks. Mr. Katz and Mr. McKinney were, then, professionals to be trusted to maintain some of the proper detachment from their clients. Among their juniors, Mrs. Lefcourt was a lady and so gentle a one as to seem almost embarrassed to raise her voice. Mr. Lefcourt was clearly something else. He was possessed, it appeared, of that identification with the defendants which

141

violates every tradition. And yet Mr. Lefcourt was somehow likable, for all of being so engaged with his clients as to have the repute almost of being a coconspirator. Governors can lose all claim to reverence and yet retain their fascination for the unruly governed; and the matter of Justice Murtagh's likes and dislikes came up at the defense table more often than might have been expected in that outpost of alienation. His colleagues had decided that the judge had come rather to like Jerry Lefcourt. There was increasing affection in the "don't-be-a-damned-fool" the judge had come to employ in disposing of Mr. Lefcourt's more imaginative flights of constitutional fancy during the informalities in his chambers. It must still be left to Mr. McKinney's courtly bearing to press upon the judge curious amenities like the ones he granted his enemies even at the pitch of their hostility—a recess for Huey P. Newton's birthday and every Friday off in deference to the Moslem beliefs of the defendants William King and Lumumba and Afeni Shakur. Mr. Lefcourt could not cloak his clients in Mr. McKinney's sable majesty; yet, even so, he had worked his way into tolerance of the sort that might belong to some nephew who comes to dinner on one of those Sundays, his demeanor cheeky, his outside associations suspicious, and who is yet endured because his argument is so free of anything sullen. Mr. Lefcourt was someone Justice Murtagh could imagine growing up. But Mr. Bloom and Mr. Crain were persons Mr. Lefcourt had brought along, friends quite unsatisfactory enough to suggest the raffish ways he spent other days besides Sunday. Mr. Bloom, overborne by the weight of the occasion, handling his duties like an unfamiliar fork, always the last to finish his plate, the young stranger at a seat quite above his social experience, who ought to have had the decency to blush and thus confess himself as someone awkward to be forgiven, yet who had the effrontery not to blush and was thus someone to be bullied. As for Mr. Crain, he was simply impossible; where Mr. Lefcourt could not fail to be attractive even while doing his best to act otherwise, Mr. Crain seemed to have made being unattractive a whole goal of life. The purest, the most likable

142

thing about him, was his commitment to not being liked. He had heroically expelled every appeal to the susceptibilities of the beholder; he had a beard which aimed, not successfully enough, at being a dagger, an eye that seemed to light up only when it could accuse. His voice sounded as though constructed for no function except to recite a bill of particulars; his questions always began by stating the premise that man is in chains and that the witness put him there. His sentences went like freight cars, clack "beast," clack "oppressor." He had even made his own some of Justice Murtagh's ceremonial expressions; things were to Mr. Crain "manifest" or "crystal clear" as they were to the justice, who, assuming as he did the worst about Mr. Crain, probably added some scheme of contempt by parody to the long catalogue of his sins, being unable to understand that Mr. Crain's was the zeal which makes oneself judge with no need for election as it presents oneself as commander of an avenging army with no troop at its back.

Still it fell to Mr. Lefcourt to perform the outrage appointed to remind those who had been on vacation in August how different they were from those who had remained at home or in the cell. His final plea to Justice Murtagh to disqualify himself before the jurors were examined—"we lack the mutual respect which is necessary for such a trial"—began safely within bounds. It was a recital of their prior differences, and it assumed so little hope that it became possible to imagine that Mr. Lefcourt had no purpose beyond improving the record as much as he could for any bar association panel which the court might summon for vengeance upon him and Mr. Bloom and Mr. Crain.

Then suddenly, a quite proper embarrassment entering his tone, Mr. Lefcourt departed the rails of comity.

"There is one final thing," he said, "which has not been brought before your Honor at any time. There was an information filed in Kings County several years ago charging your Honor with failing to report police corruption as an investigations commissioner."

"You are a member of the bar," Justice Murtagh answered,

143

"and I am very pointedly reminding you of your responsibility as a member of the bar."

Mr. Lefcourt persisted. "In Murtagh v. Leibowitz (303 N.Y. 313), there was a report extremely critical of your Honor: 'Strangely and unaccountably . . .'"

It had been impossible until now to think of this Olmec head as needing sympathy. But now it cried out, "Why is this being gone into?" not to a Mr. Lefcourt far beyond the range of any call of his but only to the gods above. Why, it seemed to say, can nothing be forgotten?

Mr. Lefcourt went on reading the report of this long-disbanded grand jury:

"Strangely and unaccountably, all of these memoranda, more than a hundred in number, appear to have vanished in thin air. Neither the *defendant* Murtagh nor any member of his staff appears to have been able to explain the mystery of the missing documents."

"And now," he went on, "the same district attorney has now selected your Honor to be the trial judge in this court. I say this, your Honor, because it does raise questions."

And, having done his worst, Mr. Lefcourt drew back toward propriety, his tone apologetic, as though the contemplation of his deed had reminded him that both he and Justice Murtagh had now and again to obey commands not theirs and that the justice at least might find an excuse to free himself:

"No one will be prejudiced if we have a new judge. . . . The court should deliberate on what I have said. I plead——"

Mr. Phillips was already on his feet, impatient to support Justice Murtagh's dignity with his own indignation. But the justice motioned him down, the victim briefly recognized having already been displaced by the magistrate, and restored to a voice and a syntax that made his sentences sound as impersonal as though he were ruling on appeal from the squalors of some court both far away and far below him:

"The court regrets that a responsible member of the bar has seen fit to make a motion replete with facts which in many instances were misstatements, obviously to achieve ends other

144

than the granting of the relief requested. It is not in the proper tradition of the bar. The court will take under advisement the proper remedy. The application is wholly without merit. The court again assures the defendants that they will have a full and fair trial under the American system of justice."

The mocking laugh of the defendants was like a response to a litany. Mr. Lefcourt had been the instrument of the cruelty of the helpless, and they remained as without mercy as they were without power. More than twenty years before, John Murtagh had been city commissioner of investigation. His most critical duty had been to study charges of police corruption. The subsequent revelation of what appeared to be the purchase of the entire police command by a Brooklyn bookie had been so little the product of his efforts that the sitting mayor's enemies in the Brooklyn district attorney's office had carried Commissioner Murtagh before their grand jury and indicted him for misfeasance. He had been guilty only of innocence; he was then, as now, incapable of believing that a policeman could lie. He had been routinely made the victim of and had exceptionally recovered from that abiding conviction of the public mind and those law officers who cater to it that there are no mistakes but only conspiracies and that an investigator who has been only ingenuous is instead corrupt. The indictment had, of course, been dismissed untried. Justice Murtagh, never really having been soiled, had every reason to think himself washed by anointment as a magistrate and rewashed by elevation to the Supreme Court of New York County. His transient misfortune was so ancient that the Panthers, being young, could never have known of it if the *Times*, with that balance which is so often a source of injustice, had not included it in an otherwise admiring profile of the justice. The Panthers had read it in their jail and made gleeful sport of it in their pretrial intrusions upon his dignity.

Victims have too little community with victims: these defendants believed in the soundness of John Murtagh's indictment as Justice Murtagh believed in the soundness of theirs. For, here were two parties, each with the best reason to know

145

the ways in which the passions and prejudices of district attorneys can guide grand juries; yet neither could entertain the notion that what had been done to one might also have been done to the other.

Mr. Lefcourt, impelled as he had been to a part he could hardly have chosen for himself, had served to remind us of the reckless force and fearsome privacy of any quarrel once it asserts itself as permanent. That shadow having been cast, Mr. Phillips formally affirmed that the people were ready and Mr. Lefcourt resignedly conceded that the defense was ready. Then Justice Murtagh dispatched a court officer to call the first jury panel. For eight months intermittently, this courtroom had been populated by the same persons—even the faces in the audience had become familiar—and it had grown impossible to imagine the intrusion of strangers. Yet these had come at last, entering the courthouse past the thin lines of pickets mustered by the Panther Defense Committee and through the thick clusters of police summoned to contain them, the response as usual greater than the challenge. The timid among the prospective jurors might be confirmed in their fantasies of peril, the self-confident might be amused at the fantasies of the state; but neither sort of juror could be conscious that the true risk of this passage was to his spirit and not his flesh. The room had already hardened. What could the jurors make of it and what would it do to them? The real danger of such an atmosphere was to the juror's assurance of his own detachment and to whatever remnant might survive of the commonsense assumption that private man can establish facts and render judgments. For to sit for any length of time with these defendants was to feel the whole commitment of their lives as a defiance of the facts. If they—or for that matter even their prosecutors—had understood reality, most of them very probably would not have been here at all. It seemed doubtful that, even under impulses of the purest candor, these particular prisoners would have been able to recite the facts: as penitent, any one of them would likely have exaggerated his crimes just as he inflated his deeds when he was an enthusiast. The task would be to accept

146

or reject them as people, a business not often enough to be gotten over just by the weighing of facts.

Only afterward, when the trial panel had been gambled upon—"selected" is too orderly a word for the leaps in the dark of the process—could it be recognized what sort of jury this one had all along been bound to be. The Idea of the Revolution would be the circumstance controlling its selection. The pickets suggesting the shadow of the Idea and the guards around these prisoners attesting the official judgment of Its menace would be enough to frighten away those merely afraid of It. Their own inability to conceal their anger would disqualify those already indignant at It. The residue of the chosen, if it represented any fixed notion, had to be dominated by persons whose strongest opinion was pride in their own capacity to look upon and judge It unafraid. So there would be two trials, one of the Idea of the Revolution in the dock, the other of the Liberal Mind in the jury box, the one with its bodies, the other with its image of itself in jeopardy, the liberal being able no more often than the revolutionary to conceive that the part he is being driven toward is not the one he would have imagined for himself.

Mr. Phillips appeared no less assured about the outcome of this intangible trial than he was about the actual one. His manner when jury selection began suggested the man who fears nothing while his opponents fear everything. The office of the district attorney of New York County had lately come to distrust certain sorts of jurors in cases threatening heavy penalties for Negro defendants. One criminal lawyer had reported the recent surprise of seeing the prosecutor strike *every* Negro from a panel he had thought about to be sworn intact. Yet Mr. Phillips seemed indeed anxious to acquire Negro jurors and serenely indifferent to sniffing after such vague emanations from any prospective white ones as could imply that they might regard society as a criminal worse than its enemies. His affairs seemed to him in that perfect order which allows the traveler to set forth with no need for sense of smell. He was the personification of unlimited cash balance; he seemed as if to

147

say that he would take the first twelve, a customer so rich that he could buy the whole lot, being free even of any limitation of means that would make necessary even the slightest distinctions of taste.

Chance might have invented the first jury prospect to strengthen Mr. Phillips' confidence and the despair of the defense—a sixty-year-old Irishman beleaguered on West 94th Street, his very body a garrison further soured by the three years since his layoff as a department store clerk, able to offset one's suspicion that he hated his new black neighbors only with one's conjecture that he had hated his former white ones almost as much. The defense lawyers fell upon him with a prejudice confirmed by his unashamed responses; he proudly implied even worse things than they had begun inferring.

MR. LEFCOURT: Do you have any black and Puerto Rican friends?

THE JUROR-CANDIDATE: I don't associate with them. I don't associate with nobody.

MR. BLOOM: Can you remember in sixty years ever having made a derogatory racial remark against black people?

THE JUROR-CANDIDATE: I probably did. I probably made derogatory remarks about everybody, including the blacks and whites too. [And, looking markedly at Mr. Lefcourt:] The young are a wild bunch, I'll tell you that.

MR. KATZ: Do you think black people are more violent than white people?

THE JUROR-CANDIDATE: To an extent they are, yes.

Such replies drove defense counsel to the sidebar to ask that the candidate be disqualified for cause as "implicitly biased against black people." "As he expressed himself," Justice Murtagh answered, "the prospective juror reflected no racial bias whatever." So they had at him again, finally getting him disqualified for saying that he would take an FBI agent's word before anyone else's on earth.

The first candidate's temper under examination had seemed

to confirm the worst fears of defense counsel as to the prospect
before them; and yet they would not again look upon anyone
so stubbornly determined upon combat as this first enemy they
faced.

For, as Mr. Phillips moved with routine assurance to ask
William R. Grose II, the next juror prospect, whether he could
ever justify forcible assault upon the government, he got the
calm reply that a bomb, under conditions of proper sanitation,
might indeed serve "to call attention to a legitimate problem."
Surprised, Mr. Phillips challenged Grose for cause and was
further surprised when Justice Murtagh denied his challenge,
being as reluctant to dismiss a juror who rather fancied the
heretical as he had been to dismiss one committedly at war
with it. The day before, Mr. Lefcourt's affronting motion had
instructed the judge in what the trial was going to be like; and
his strongest bias had thereupon become to get it over with. He
would make each side use up its peremptory challenges as
rapidly as he could. Mr. Phillips must turn with skillful patience to the laying of snares; he managed at last to induce Mr.
Grose to. say that he could not be sure of being able to accept
the law as laid down by the judge unless the crime alleged had
actually brought physical harm to someone. Mr. Phillips had
achieved his dismissal for cause; yet his tone in this moment of
success was less triumphant than it would have been if it had
not been shadowed by the temporary, and perhaps, foreboding
absence of his accustomed comfort of speaking to jurors imper-
vious to thoughts of treason and walled against the disreputable.

Still, Mr. Grose's dismissal was a reminder that the juror can
only find the facts and must leave it for the court to define
whether the facts constitute a crime or not. The juror must take
the judge's instructions as to the law; and who could say what
torments that proposition might inflict on the Liberal Mind
somewhere down the road? The citizen, if Grose represented
any number of such, might be bobbing loose from his ancient
moorings; yet the judge was still chained to the rock of the
criminal code, resisting any pull of special exceptions. At some

point unseeable in the murk, a citizen would have to choose either to let himself be tied again or risk the dash against this rock. Mr. Grose had uniquely sensed the crash at the end of the voyage; most examples of the Liberal Mind to follow him would answer with a confidence in themselves as instruments of justice untroubled by intimations of danger ahead.

Still, his unexpected passage with Mr. Grose had reminded Mr. Phillips that no one's capital these days is without limit. He could not, of course, be alarmed; but he was open to entertainment of the reflection that there are risks in life. If only as a libation, he uncovered a small corner of mistrust: he would peremptorily challenge any Negro juror under thirty. Areas of mistrust constituted the only real estate in the defense's possession that was larger than Mr. Phillips'; its lawyers began diffident about almost every other category of candidates: the run of Negroes over forty; all taxi drivers—even the one candid enough to tell Michael Tabor, "I go along with the system; you overthrow this one and I'll go along with yours"; all white civil servants; such white intellectuals as indicated a want of respect for the white left; Irish motormen; Jewish storekeepers; in sum most traditional Manhattan jurors.

Defense counsel's only course, given this mind-set, was to harry and occasionally even to hector, to be reckless about perils of giving offense, and to worry to the bone every suspicion that this Negro might have accepted or that white enjoyed the injustices of what exists.

As the days went on, a number of juror-candidates asked to be excused because they had developed so much dislike for the lawyers for the defense. And this mordant method, conceding it the point of necessity, had in it little room for courtesy and not quite enough for humanity.

For example, there was the figure of Roy L. Blough, emeritus professor of economics at Columbia, former member of President Truman's Council of Economic Advisers, inactive member of the reform Riverside Democratic Club, active deacon of the Riverside Church, and vessel filled, as he said, with

150

"a lot of sympathy for young people, especially young black people, because of their peculiar position."

Dr. Blough, as will happen with professors emeriti, had deplored the Columbia University rebellion, while reserving a paternal tolerance for its black cobelligerents, if only because "they told Mark Rudd he couldn't use them for his revolution." With nostrils thereupon flaring with the scent of the dirty secret, Mr. Crain rose to ask him if he were related to Roger Blough, "former president of the United States Steel Corporation."

The juror-candidate answered that Roger Blough was his fourth cousin. "I know him quite well," he added and his tone suggested how often, if mischance were to lengthen their association, he would feel the need to correct Mr. Crain. "He was not president of U. S. Steel but chairman of the board."

Correction for Mr. Crain was only a spur for confrontation: "Do you believe," he asked, "that you could be fair to these defendants throughout a trial when they will continue to express total disagreement with and hatred of your close friend and *fourth* cousin, with people such as yourself, members of what has come to be known as the Establishment, which is predominantly white?"

"The question," Justice Murtagh intervened, "is so confused that it is not capable of an intelligent reply."

Defense council could only struggle through a fairly decent interval and then exercise a peremptory challenge.

In such scenes, there was something rather like that insistent disregard for human dignity to which the early Mr. Phillips used to give free play when uninhibited by the presence of jurors. One commenced to feel how cruel—how almost violent—the art of advocacy can be, no matter which its side. Most times, of course, the defense is restrained by being aware that it is to some degree at the prosecution's mercy. But defense counsel in this case, having measured the quality of Mr. Phillips' mercy, passed beyond such precautions, fell back on the raw and savage *nature* of the adversary process, and dared on

151

occasion to attack the very insides of a juror-candidate almost as though he were no more than a suborned witness in a divorce proceeding. We were being treated to that rarest of spectacles in a courtroom, the exercise of the despotism of the oppressed.

The juror-candidate Charles C. was a Negro, born in Bessemer, Alabama, a wartime supply sergeant in a port battalion, divorced, no children, working as a clerk in the state insurance department and in the post office at night. He was the portrait of the striver with no goal, since he had no child to work for and was altogether too gentle for private ambition. He held the witness chair as though it were a broom. At fifty-four, his small mustache and slick hair were a reminder of Charlie Chase, the otherwise forgotten film comedian; any effort this appearance represented must have come less from any recollected vanity than from some deep impulse toward that obsolescence which is the subtlest way of announcing oneself as threat to no one. Charles C. subscribed to *Cue* magazine and belonged to a civil service club, which is called the Careerists.

Had it bothered him, Mr. Katz wondered, when he served in a segregated army unit. No, he replied. Did it bother him now? No, he replied, apparently puzzled about the point. Mr. Katz felt himself slipping toward the uncomfortable spectacle of the white lawyer who knows the posture a Negro ought to have, lecturing the Negro who doesn't. He seemed to draw back in embarrassment and left such business to Michael Tabor or Afeni Shakur. Charles C. was everything in their community the Panthers hold in scorn; if he had spoken on the street and they had noticed him, they would have dismissed him with a "Quiet, old man." But here, with strangers watching, the family bond asserted itself; and Afeni Shakur put her final questions so gently that she might have been dressing a wound:

MRS. SHAKUR: What did you think of the death of Martin Luther King?
THE JUROR-CANDIDATE: I think it was unfortunate that had to happen.

152

MRS. SHAKUR: Do you think black people have a right to be angry?
THE JUROR-CANDIDATE: In what sense?
MRS. SHAKUR: Just . . . *ann*-gry?
THE JUROR-CANDIDATE: No.

Very gently she released him and Mr. Lefcourt filed the peremptory challenge.

Of all the juror-candidates, the most opaque, the least susceptible to test by light or probe, was James Fox, the Negro composer. He was born in British Guiana and classically trained. He said that most of his income is earned from lectures at colleges on African dance rhythms: "African music—its cross-thematic complexity—was something that I had never known before." The explanation had a tone more of necessity than of choice, as though Mr. Fox had not so much rejected Western culture as been pinched out of it.

Mr. Phillips, because he wanted him so badly, limited his candor about how long the trial might last. Mr. Fox hoped it would not be too long; he would be going to Europe in November for the premiere of his African music drama. "It is," he explained, "the chance of a lifetime." James I. Fox is fifty-seven years old. He looked at Justice Murtagh, the door of escape open before him. Then he closed it. "If I have to, I have to," he said. For reasons beyond analysis James Fox had taken upon himself the duty to serve.

And thereafter he wrapped the riddle of himself in clouds of explication. He was asked how he felt about revolution:

"Well, we eliminate one particular method, but I think everybody has a revolutionary aspect of feeling within them. I think you'll find lots of musicians revolutionary. Beethoven was a revolutionary. Revolution is in everything. We have revolution going on all about us, today, in writing, in music. . . . You evolve in a revolution or rebellion. The methods of doing I may not approve of; I may do mine by music, another by writing. The theory starts first."

The Black Panther Party?

"Whatever I did read, it was not revolutionary. . . . Much more of a progressive concept of things."

Michael Tabor asked him about the Black Panther breakfast program:

"A humanistic attitude. Of course. You are feeding. *Why are you doing it then?*"

Michael Tabor asked if he was familiar with Marcus Garvey, the West Indian black nationalist:

"Very much, sir. In my early youth I would say I was, and I had a feeling that he had something going for him."

Somewhere, in the infinite distance between Mr. Fox and every question, there were hints, unreadable, and glimpses of light, fugitive, but for no one the right to confidence of being able to define. Mr. Fox would give and at once he would take away. We never quite know what it is to be mocked until we listen to the expositions of a serious man. Mr. Phillips announced that Mr. Fox was satisfactory to the People. That was understandable, Mr. Phillips being a plain man untroubled by mysteries and a public servant conscientious about service to a complicated constituency. He may well have noticed, for example, that *The New York Times*, whose function is the soothing of the dubious, would be grateful for the sentence in its account of the inevitable result: "James I. Fox, the jury's foreman and a black, announced the verdict as guilty on all counts of conspiracy to . . ."

Their heads together, defense counsel argued. Michael Tabor could be observed intensely pressing what answer he had retrieved from the riddle. After a long while, Mr. Lefcourt stood up and said: "The juror is acceptable to the defendants."

"Defendants look upon the juror, juror look upon the defendants," the clerk intoned; and the look of James Fox was as inscrutable as it had been all along. What had Michael Tabor noticed about him that had eluded everyone else? "He is very smart," Michael Tabor explained. So then, the illuminati know no more than the rest of us; the difference is that they cannot resist mysteries.

154

It would be nearly a week before Mr. Fox was joined in the loneliness of the jury box by William J. Beiser, a teacher of history at the New Lincoln School. Mr. Beiser had a way of turning his head as if he longed to put it somewhere in the wings and leave nothing above his neck on stage. Mr. Phillips noted the address in Greenwich Village, judged the deficiency of resonance in the voice, defined the type as the rough boys will the gentle ones, and prepared the ceremony of dismissal with an almost malicious masculinity.

Mr. Beiser's mother was still alive in his birthplace of Algona, Iowa. His hobby was collecting stamps. He was forty-three; he had served as an army clerk in the late forties, had made the mistake of joining the reserves, and had been punished for it by recall to Korea. "Like Ted Williams?" Mr. Phillips asked. Candidate Beiser's reply was inaudible; could it be that he was unfamiliar with Ted Williams? The heterodoxy of such ignorance must have clinched Mr. Phillips' suspicion that he had isolated a pattern of deviance from masculine norms. One could infer something quite brutal from the next question: "Do you have any relatives in New York?" Only his wife and two small children, the candidate replied.

"I see," Mr. Phillips said, having, quite to the contrary, imagined every sort of domesticity except this one; and, from embarrassment at having been unseated in his assumptions of the worst, he was momentarily shaken in his certitude about himself as analyst by plain sight, was left with only enough vigor to put the formal question as to whether he could rely upon Mr. Beiser fairly and impartially to weigh the evidence, got the answer that formula makes inevitable, and turned Mr. Beiser over to defense counsel as acceptable.

The defense accepted him too after a surprisingly brief examination that elicited little to explain why he should be an exception to its fixed mistrust. Mr. Beiser's replies indeed served mainly to support an impression of passivity: he did not read the Black Panther newspaper, because "I just wouldn't read a partisan paper of any side."

155

"I'm not that interested in any contemporary political tendency. Like most students of history, I'm more interested in the past than in the present."

He had read Franz Fanon and found nothing dangerous in his writings or in what little he knew about those of Bobby Seale and Eldridge Cleaver. Earlier on, he had told Mr. Phillips that, if held to this jury, he would likely have to sacrifice his graduate fellowship at New York University. "But that's the breaks, I guess."

So he too passed over his chance to be excused. William Beiser might then be one of those persons to whom misfortunes so regularly happen as eventually to be taken for granted, a man who accepts whatever pit he is cast into. Still the habit of bad luck seems to have left him without resentment, which could explain why the defense accepted him—resentment, anger at life, the need to blame someone else all being qualities it had more to fear than seek in jurors. Mr. Beiser was condemned to˙ be acceptable, because he seemed so plainly an uncomplaining victim, as Mr. Fox had been acceptable because he was so obscurely an enigma.

But juror number three was an active mystery, a stocky young man named Stephen Chaberski, a graduate assistant in political science at Columbia, his field, international relations. One felt in him a fixity of opinion, although in what direction, it did not seem safe to guess. He could as likely be guerilla or CIA agent; one guessed he would go where activity took him. He seems to have satisfied Mr. Phillips by replying that, as a general proposition, he did not think anyone would be justified in committing a criminal act even if he did it for a socially valuable purpose. Still he could leave no one entirely sure of what he would say to the idea of a criminal act if it were done just for fun; there was about the beard, appearing one day and gone the next, and the sharp eyes behind their square glasses, something of the desperado. One came to think he gratified Mr. Lefcourt because he was so much like Mr. Lefcourt. Mr. Chaberski, like Mr. Lefcourt, charmed rather as cats do; still Mr. Lefcourt was that rarest of cats, the one with the social

156

conscience; it was hard to conceive that there could be two such in this one cage.

Jurors four, five, and six were accepted with unexpected alacrity, the package essentially of one day's examination. They were all editors, on the mechanical side of that profession: Edwin Kennebeck, juror number four, at Viking; Frederick Hills, juror number five, on college textbooks at McGraw-Hill; Nils Rasmussen, on film documentaries at ABC-television. They seemed the same man really, each monosyllabic in his replies, each with the glasses and the pale cast of faint depression, the faces from which either dread or gaiety are alike erased of the riders on the Eastside subway around nine in the morning.

What light played upon them seemed iron and Nordic. Their difference from judge and prosecutor was not just in the hair that came down to the collar of each but much more in an absence of readiness to accept America as a success. They seemed like men of cheerless endurance, familiars of long winters—Mr. Kennebeck in Colorado, Mr. Rasmussen in Denmark—no more to be imagined as cruel than as sentimental. They were of that obscure army who serve those persons who need to be noticed, the tidiers-up of writers, the fitters of the frames for television commentators, the adjusters of textbooks to the Alabama and the California markets, repairmen as available to J. Edgar Hoover as to Eldridge Cleaver. It was not easy to think of any one of them as having lately been asked a question on any matter except of the most severely practical sort. And this one was so unfetteredly impractical. Still there was their sadness, that remnant of the unfulfilled impulse that had stirred them at home and brought them to New York. As Mr. Phillips was of such as swell, they seemed of such as withdraw. Even so, one felt the consequence of their apparent newness to these issues: Mr. Fox had read Garvey when young; Mr. Beiser, for all his resistance to the topical, did have Black Panthers in his classes; Mr. Chaberski had about him something of the street gamin; yet these three were somehow apart from associations even as tangential as those. Their being so alien to the subject at hand made them the more important. The relationship between black defendants and white jurors may be the only example of protracted integrated living this society has developed. And, if so, the experience was likely to make its sharpest impress on the unmarked consciousness of the jurors who came there most as strangers. The mystery would work itself through Mr. Kennebeck, Mr. Hills, and Mr. Rasmussen if only because the expression which intimated that their lives had been less important than they must once have hoped had also to suggest they would take this turn in it as one very important to them indeed.

The row behind them was filled after six weeks, on no entirely recognizable principle and with persons much more of the familiar mix:

All but one of the last six jurors were civil servants. Juror number seven was Hiriam Irizarry, the Puerto Rican superintendent of a housing authority building. Juror number eight, the only woman, was Mrs. Eleter B. Yanes, a senior clerk in the state insurance fund, who lives in the project Mr. Irizarry services. Juror number nine was Benjamin G. Giles, a retired black longshoreman. Juror number ten was Charles Bowser, a supervisor of welfare case workers; Michael Tabor asked him whether he had ever been the victim of white racism and he answered, of course, he had been born in Washington.

Juror number eleven was James Butters, a shop teacher at Stuyvesant High School, who had joined the marines after high school and had been a surfer at Laguna Beach. He was a young man given to protracted inspections of the ceiling, as bored and restive with this inactivity as were the defendants. Mr. Butters remembered long talks with the Panthers in his shop class and buying their papers, without, to be sure, reading them. Here was the young man who hangs out, a type like some of the defendants and familiar to all of them.

Juror number twelve was Joseph Gary who works in the post office and has one son in Vietnam and another who is a high school dropout. Mr. Gary seemed that Negro of the defense's most profound diffidence: he had never noticed discrimination

158

in the army and its only perpetrator in the post office had been summarily demoted. His swift passage through the process seemed to imply exhaustion in the defense; yet, once he was seated, its team roused to wrangle another two weeks over the alternates.

Five of the jurors were black; none had been born in New York. The eddyings which had tossed all twelve survivors ashore left little assurance about what the two sides may have had in mind. The defense had challenged Negro jurors who seemed no more offhand than Mr. Gary about the discontents of their people; it had rejected others who had been no less securely masked than Mr. Fox or seemed as footloose and fuzzily focused as Mr. Butters did. Yet it let these pass. The standard of selection was so hard to detect that there seemed no explanation except that of temperaments the pitch of whose suspicion was, except for Mr. Crain's, subject to rise and fall through cycles of fatigue and refreshment. Mr. Phillips was no easier to explain; he had taken no notice when Mr. Bowser made clear his militant detestation of the welfare system he served; he had been untroubled by those suggestions in Mr. Giles and Mr. Butters of that stubbornness which, if it is against you, will unreasonably plant its bottom and hold out alone against the majority; he had even overlooked Mr. Chaberski's undisguised if unspoken certainty that he was smarter than any prosecutor.

But Mr. Phillips was suffering perhaps from the deficiency that Henry James noticed in the late Venetian painters—"that painfully frequent phenomenon in mental history, the demoralizing influence of lavish opportunity." He was too sure of his case to give consideration to attitudes that might pass upon it a judgment at variance with his own. And then, too, he cared about appearances; the bench was embarrassed about how slowly this jury selection was going; and Mr. Phillips, in all things the only proper boy in the class, did not want to appear to dally.

Even so, when Mr. Phillips viewed the results of the process in bulk, vague feelings of disquiet seemed to rise in him. This

159

was not a jury quite obviously enough bound to share his certainties even when scanned by someone as confident that his certainties are universal as Mr. Phillips. He closed indeed disputing over the alternates with, if anything, as much distrust as the defense.

The defense attorneys had done all the things their more conventional brethren decry as alienating to the neutral. They had quarreled with the judge while the panel was watching. They had so foresworn delicacy that sensitive juror-candidates could, with some justice, feel themselves as having been baited. Yet, having done so many of the wrong things, they had achieved a result that decorum could hardly have accomplished, a jury that had at least those virtues of opacity that were the most they could hope for.

Justice Murtagh felt peevish when it was over. The process had lasted six weeks; he could only apologize to the jurors for "any embarrassment, humiliation, or tension" they might have experienced from the deplorable deportment of attorneys for the defense. Clearly, he thought that his kindness had somehow led him astray. Still, even those defendants who assumed that he was determined to see them hang could not fairly think that what annoyed him was any assessment of the instability, the unpredictability of the jury that had resulted; the affront had all been in the untidiness of the process. To Justice Murtagh, the defense's only trick had been to give his brother judges reason to suspect his efficiency as a traffic manager.

But the defense's real trick had been far more substantial; it had accomplished a jury which had somehow changed the frame of reference. That was a change hardly noticeable to a judge still too affronted by the indignity of the process to pay much attention to its product or to a prosecutor so proud of his secret that he could not believe in the existence of any frame of reference that would not swell and fill as soon as he unfolded it. If uncertainty had entered the room and sat itself down, Justice Murtagh was too busy with the bruises of the past and Mr. Phillips with the certainties of the future to have observed its intrusion.

160

VII

On Monday, October 19th, Mr. Phillips began by offering the jury a daylong exposition of what he proposed to prove.

He began with all the deeds of violence that these defendants were alleged to have consummated—an explosion at a Harlem police station in November 1968 and then four bombings at once on January 17, 1969, one at a board of education headquarters in Queens and three at police precinct houses, two in Harlem and one in the Bronx.

The Black Panther Party, he went on, was not on trial for these crimes. Even so, as members of the party, the defendants had been taught to believe that "they were at war with the police department."

"The Panthers are a paramilitary organization . . . and have a tremendous emphasis on weaponry, that is, acquiring guns, using them, training people in the use of them, and so forth." Justice Murtagh thereupon reminded Mr. Phillips to stick religiously to the matters at trial.

161

He went back to his recital of the allegations adding up to proof of conspiracy:

On August 16th, 1968, Lumumba Shakur and Ralph White, an undercover policeman, had taken a trip to Balitmore together. In its course, Lumumba Shakur had suggested to White that they "look for a stray pig [and] kill him."

Two weeks later, Shakur and Sekou Odinga had announced, at a meeting at the Panther office in Harlem, that the party would form a TCB (Taking Care of Business) squad. "The TCB squad were to put bombs in police stations, set police cars on fire, to disarm police and get their weapons . . ."

On September 5th, "Sekou met with defendants McKiever, Dharuba, and a man I mentioned by the name of Kuwasi and he told them that the group must start taking action against the pigs."

Two weeks later, Lumumba Shakur told Detective White that it was mandatory and required that all Panthers see the film *The Battle of Algiers*. "You will see here the film *The Battle of Algiers*. . . . The way a revolutionary is tested in *The Battle of Algiers* is, he's given an act of violence to commit against the police. . . . The bombing of stores is depicted in the film."

Sometime in October, there was brought into their study courses William King's "Urban Guerilla Warfare," which "depicts all types of revolutionary activity . . . describes how you establish a sniper position . . . how you make Molotov cocktails, and how you use them against the police."

On October 13th, Kuwasi told Detective White that he "wanted to kill a pig that very day" and wondered if White would care to join him.

The next day White and Kuwasi taught Joan Bird and Michael Tabor how to make a time bomb.

On November 4th, Lumumba Shakur returned from California to tell White that he had found some dynamite. White asked him what he proposed to do with it. "I say this with apology to Miss Yanes and alternate juror number one, that . . . we'll be using some rather colorful language. . . . All

Lumumba would tell him was, 'I have my shit together.' Seven days later, the Twenty-fifth Precinct was bombed."

The next day Sekou was heard to say, "We've got to get more brothers . . . we have to hit more of these places."

On November 15th, Lumumba Shakur told Detective White that "he had shot a pig already."

On December 4th, Michael Tabor asked Detective White where he might get some blasting caps. White said, "I'll look into it."

On December 30th, with her husband in prison, Afeni Shakur assumed command of the West Harlem section of the Panther Party. She said that "it was not going to be involved with just talk; that they were going to actually get out and blow up police stations."

- On New Year's Eve, 1968, the defendant Ali Bey Hassan led a twelve-man team on a mission to cut the wires on twenty-four police alarm boxes.

Earlier, in this spirit, Robert Collier had instructed a gathering at Long Island University in how "to make up wrong communications to the police, to screw up their communications, to mislead them and set up false letterheads and things of that nature."

As 1969 began, Detective Roberts, on instructions of William King and Michael Tabor, conducted a reconnaissance of a subway station near city hall and returned to report that a bomb would do little damage there.

On January 6th, Afeni Shakur presided over another meeting, this time at Clark Squire's apartment. In its course, she said that the next time a Panther is arrested, the party would kidnap a policeman and hold him for ransom "to the equivalent of bail."

Detective Roberts objected that when they released such a captive, he could identify his kidnappers. And Afeni said, "You misunderstand me. After we get the Panther released, we ice the pig."

"Then Afeni asked everybody in the crowd if they had any dynamite or if they could get any dynamite. . . . And she said, 'In the future when something happens to a pig station, not just a wall will be exploded or destroyed but the whole fucken place would be destroyed . . .' She then asked the section members, 'Do you have any weapons? . . . If you have to off a pig, you have to get a piece.' "

On January 14th, Lumumba Shakur warned Detective White not to be firing his pistol inside the Ellsmere Tenants Council, because there was dynamite behind its refrigerator. White immediately reported this fortuitous revelation to his superiors in the police department. "What occurred is one of the most daring, imaginative, and exciting bits in dramatic feats of undercover work ever accomplished in this particular state."

White was directed to remove the dynamite and take it to the headquarters of the police department's bomb squad. There, a bomb squad detective removed the dynamite sticks from their wrappers and substituted for them a mixture of clay and oatmeal dusted with fluorescent powder for tracing purposes.

White took this counterfeit back and returned it to its hiding place. Mr. Phillips indicated the front row of the spectators' seats and asked Detective White to rise and present himself to the jury. On January 16th, Lumumba Shakur had distributed packets of explosives he did not know were simulated to William King and Thomas Berry. At nine in the evening of January 17th, there was a minor explosion at the Forty-fourth Police Precinct; and across the river, two New York City policemen had come upon a car parked on the Harlem River Drive and there had ensued a gun battle with two of its occupants, who had been caught while setting up a sniper position against the Forty-fourth.

Later that night, Alex McKiever told Detective Carl Ashwood that, after days of surveying the Forty-fourth Precinct and finding it lightly guarded, he had been surprised at the flourish of police force there to meet his party when it came to do the deed.

There had also been an effective explosion at the Queens

Board of Education building; and two days later the police found an explosive packet that had failed to detonate in the yard of their Twenty-fourth Precinct in Harlem. In all three cases, the bomb squad found traces of its fluorescent powder in the debris.

All these miscarriages started the suspicions of the Harlem section and Detective White was among those commissioned to uncover the police infiltrators presumed responsible for the general failure of the enterprise. Doubts finally settled on Roland Hayes, purveyor of the dynamite to Lumumba Shakur. Tabor said, "I think we'll have to kill him. We're going to get a confession from him and then we're going to off him . . ." Robert Collier, to his credit, said they couldn't kill him, because the FBI would come down on them immediately.

The next three months would see the ascension of William King and the crash of them all. On February 3rd, 1969, King enlisted Eugene Roberts into the party's security section. "From there on in, Detective Roberts is privy to the internal workings of the entire conspiracy. . . . [He] is accepted by the rest and he is in on the actual planning of further bombings of department stores, police stations, railroad stations, railroad tracks, and subways."

On February 25th, at King's direction, Roberts and Walter Johnson had surveyed Macy's, Korvette's, and Abercrombie & Fitch, whose gun counter had stirred their imaginations profoundly. King had judged that Abercrombie & Fitch "would be the jackpot" and "they talked about putting a dynamite charge on the first floor of the building to cause confusion and chaos." On March 17th, "the defendants reconned the Bronx Botanical Gardens" and "I think it was the defendant Roper who suggested" that they practice on its greenhouse with Molotov cocktails. On March 18th, King had taken his squad on a survey of the Bronx railroad yards. After their return, King announced to his troops that a schedule of priorities had been established by Lumumba Shakur:

". . . first, police stations and railroads. . . . The second

165

priority was the department stores. The third priority was the botanical gardens."

King had set Dr. Curtis Powell and Robert Collier to working on the necessary chemicals. On March 27th, King had instructed Afeni Shakur to find two reliable, trusted sisters to help the brothers on their mission. There had been discussions of how bombs could be made out of aerosol cans. The defendants had spent the next four days searching for weapons; at the beginning of Easter week they had obtained an M-14 rifle from Baltimore. On April 2nd, four days before Easter, a raiding party of 125 policemen had been assembled and the defendants seized.

He ended with the arrests and the weapons that were the most abundant stock in his arsenal of evidence. The recital had taken him a day throughout which his tread had been majestic but unexpectedly pedestrian.

His structure somehow looked heavier than it weighed. What had departed was the urgency, almost the desperation, of District Attorney Hogan's first proclamation of the peril that he had averted. Mr. Phillips' fervor seemed suddenly just a little too much larger than the passion of any of the parties he had arraigned before the bar. He could put words in evidence; he could even put deeds; but even his own version of them could not quite start the hairs; the deeds seemed to limp too far behind the words, being mischievous, to be sure, but somehow short of the level of portent he worked to impute to either. Mr. Lefcourt, having begun alarmed, was commencing only to be puzzled. He had come there assuming the worst in his clients which, in his innocence, had seemed to him a best beyond any powers of his; he had thought them purposeful, implacable, and ready for any enormity. Now Mr. Phillips had adopted Mr. Lefcourt's description of them; and, the longer the district attorney talked, the better reason Mr. Lefcourt felt for abandoning it. The more Mr. Phillips said how immense these matters were, the more Mr. Lefcourt had to be thinking, "And is it all no more than this?" His respect and affection for his clients endured; all he had lost was his certainty of their

166

revolutionary portent. He had started to abandon the illusion that they were guilty and admirably so; and, for the first time, he had been surprised by the hope that they might be innocent.

VIII

Their imprisonment had brought Lumumba Shakur and the others into a brotherhood far closer than they had ever known when they were at liberty. They could credit that bond, more than to any other outsider, to the Mr. Phillips who wished them nothing but ill. The bailing of Michael Tabor and Richard Moore would turn out to be a separation from Lumumba Shakur and the Others; and they could blame that loss, more than on any other outsider, upon those outsiders who had supplied the bail from wishing them nothing but good.

Michael Tabor would be ruined while his legend increased and Richard Moore would be ruined while his withered almost at once.

The prophet of rebellion asserts his presence through spending the treasury of his anger. Richard Moore came from prison to address a rally in Greenwich Village and almost at once it was understood that his resources were inadequate.

His addiction was to comic excess, the one hyperbole an

audience of the sort that is sympathetic to it cannot forgive a man in his situation:

"There the judge was, looking down at us, his robes flying like a vulture's wings. I said to Lumumba, 'To the floor.' And Lumumba said, 'I don't think he's packing, Blood.' 'Make no mistake, my good brother,' I said. 'At this moment history will be made. They goan shoot us in the courtroom.' "

There was already penetrating into the laughter of the pure that uneasiness which too soon turns to disapproval. Richard Moore did what he could to work his way through rigidities more proper, and then he slipped again:

"I'm not as dogmatic as I talk. I don't mean you should march into the office of the A. T. and T. with dynamite strapped on you and yell 'Free the Panther Twenty-one' and BOOM! I could relate to that, it's true. But somebody that righteous shouldn't go that way."

For his blood could not throw off its hereditary taint of antic fancy. In these moments, he was an incorrigible renewal of his father, the recidivist Collins Moore, who, out of prison and already slipping toward jail again, came by court to watch him one day in September, and at once made it plain that the careless gaiety of his father's company was the only temporary comfort that Richard Moore could ever entirely enjoy.

"I was supposed to be paroled a year ago," Collins Moore said. "I figure I was home and then the board asked me, 'Do you know a Richard Moore?' I said, 'How could I not know him? He's my son!' They said, 'Don't you know he's been trying to blow up the government? We can't let you out with a connection like that.' What you been doing, Richard? So I had to stay up there another year, and the job I was fixed up with was gone when I got out. I went up to welfare and the woman said, 'What's the matter with you? You're not supposed to come out of jail without no job.' I said, 'Lady, I was *ready*. The jail wasn't.' They wouldn't even let me in the drug program, and I've been an addict for thirty years. Then I gave all those offices my grandmother's old house in Brooklyn as my address, and I went out there and it's gone. My parole officer's going to

169

think I was messing with him, sending him to a vacant lot. You'd have thought *somebody* would have written me a postcard and told me."

Here was a man held in prison a year longer than he would otherwise have been if he had not had a son charged with criminal conspiracies, who comes out to find that the only refuge in his memory has disappeared without trace or explanation, and who gazes upon a course appointed for him that is sure to take him back to jail in six months. There were in this account a dozen malignities and misfortunes that were reasons for rage; yet their victim could not recite them nor his son hear them without laughing. Cokey Moore, even to his nickname, was a relic of that good-time-Harlem now forty years sunk in permanent depression; and its memory had power to hold him as it did to call Richard Moore, diffusing his anger with the comic spirit. These were men who could almost enjoy every injustice for the chance it gave them for the last word.

On Labor Day of 1970, the Black Panther Party assembled in Philadelphia for the convention that proposed to write a new constitution for the people of the United States. By then, Richard Moore had been reduced to being only a bystander in the black hat with a red band of a guard of honor. But Michael Tabor commanded the stage for three hours of cold, insistent declamation that "the only good pig is a dead pig":

"Self-defense means that if a pig moves on you today and he's got a gun and you ain't got a gun, you ain't in no position to deal with him at high noon. But come sundown, come sundown [the chilling laughter of approval], and the streets are dark and deserted, and you go up on the roof [laughter] and you take your action out [laughter] and you put your index upon that trigger [laughter] and you see him and you pull that trigger, that's self-defense [laughter], that's self-defense." (And then a long wild cry of delight and the speaker shouting over it, "Power to the People.")

This litany of vehemence stirred its auditors beyond anything Huey Newton would say that evening. The imagined Huey Newton was a familiar; the real one a mysterious

170

stranger. For persons who had never before seen either, Michael Tabor suited the fantasy about Huey far more richly than the actual Huey Newton who was so puzzling a mixture of the physical cultist with the gentle mother's son. But, if the Supreme Commander was bound by a duty to the self forbidding any posture this humorlessly uncontained, he must also have felt a duty to those unknown parties, his followers, that made him grateful for a surrogate who could so freely utter thoughts and conjure images he would be troubled at giving way to. Michael Tabor had always possessed qualities of bearing that compelled the admiration of persons quite unlike him: long afterward, Justice Murtagh would attest his respect; and Ralph White, Mr. Phillips' chief police witness, would say that there slept in Michael Tabor a power like Malcolm X's. Even then, for the sake of the image he conveyed, Huey Newton suspended the insular customs of Oakland and anointed Michael Tabor as the first member of the national committee of the Black Panther Party ever drawn from the foreign space beyond California. For Michael Tabor had an intensity that overrode precedents; by mere presence, now and then unabashedly malign, he enforced the illusion that the insulted had come to vengeance.

He did not, to be sure, rise to these paroxysms so much as burst into them from a state of withdrawal passive in everything except its anger and suggesting a man who scowls while he sleeps. The fits of the orator were awakenings from the torpor of the spectator, not at all unlike, perhaps, those convulsions of energy which, when he was an addict, had roused him to climb and run and so swiftly and purposefully to steal the means he needed for nodding and drowsing.

Still he was a sovereign with no dominion. There was no stage that fit him. American liberalism has never been comfortable unless provided with some pariah to its left for good men to repudiate and thus allow liberalism its claim to a place somewhere in that center between declared extremes. The Panthers had become as essential to liberals as objects of scorn and evidence of sound discrimination as the Communists had

171

been when Senator Joe McCarthy's mace still had its weight. There were no forums open to them by now except tiny ones of the already churched or too large ones where one of their speakers could be grouped with so many others less brazen and given so fleeting a part that he could be passed through almost unnoticed as a token of duty done in the general struggle against injustice. The Panthers were an embarrassment, less for what they might say than for what had been said about them. There was a Committee to Defend the Panthers; but it was staffed and supported largely by the young and the unpropertied. The few persons of substance whose sympathies for the troubles, if not the styles, of the defendants had led them to support their legal fund had been most cruelly jeered into silence well before Michael Tabor emerged from confinement.

He and Richard Moore had been selected for bail because their different talents seemed to suit them as agitators for the funds that could bail the others. They would later be blamed for not even having tried; still, if they had, the air around them would have been altogether unpromising for the cultivation of anything like the $800,000 required to free their nine comrades in the Queens House of Detention.

Moore and Tabor spent their days in the languors of Justice Murtagh's court and too many of their nights in the hysteria of a party whose meagerest detail of housekeeping had become a crisis. In September of 1969, Newton's command had dispatched Robert Bay and Thomas Jolly from Oakland to rebuild the ruins of its New York outpost. Bay and Jolly were large and heavy-footed men, more modest and flexible than was indicated by the almost lowering stare that seemed at first to be the entire range of their managerial presence. They were not malleable enough to surrender any of their conviction that they were ambassadors *in partibus infidelibus* and they were altogether proof to any workings of time and exposure upon their intolerance of alien custom. Bay's loyalty and Jolly's was to Huey Newton; but not even Tabor's apparent high standing there could bring him comity- with these proconsuls, to whom

172

he was still a New Yorker whose troubles were likely his own fault and were in any case a distraction from the more intimately important troubles of Huey Newton and Bobby Seale. Michael Tabor had been asked to write his autobiography. He still maintained a home of sorts with Rosalind Bennett, who was pregnant again; but, for state reasons, he had been married off elsewhere. When Huey Newton was released from prison, Constance Matthews, the party's international secretary, had been recalled from Algeria to serve as his confidential assistant. She had taken Algerian citizenship during her expatriation; and, as the terminal date of her visitor's privilege approached, Huey Newton thought to provide her with an American husband as a legal device against deportation. Michael Tabor was selected; and very soon, there intruded into the coldness of this marriage of state the special passion of a wife whose nature was less inclined to nesting than to the organization of the household as garrison. Michael Tabor had traded the soothingly passive for the drivingly febrile.

Less and less could he and Richard Moore pay attention to the trial that had been the meaning of their lives when they were in prison. Mr. Phillips opened and as the days went by, it became clearer and clearer how much less he was proving than he had once asserted. There was no sign that this weakness in Mr. Phillips had been noticed by the Michael Tabor who had been so alert to every incaution of the district attorney when he had seemed irresistible. All the defendants on bail except Joan Bird were so somnolent during Detective Eugene Roberts' testimony that their lawyers decided that it would be useless, and perhaps dangerous, to encourage either Michael Tabor or Afeni Shakur to cross-examine him; they were recognized as having withdrawn.

Reflecting on his book had set Michael Tabor to remembering the numbness of his childhood; and the pressures around him now reminded him of the exterior forces that had driven him to the escapes of the addicted. He had marked himself apart from the others with his clothes, the fly blue leatherette jacket with matching Lenin cap and the Metternich overcoat that seemed more impudently luxurious than they really were as they glistened among the rags that necessity had imposed upon those defendants still confined. He had come to be felt as a betrayer. "Get the money to get me out of here, even if you got to steal it," Lumumba Shakur exhorted him every other day. But circumstances would have been against him even if he could have functioned up to the promise of his presence. Even that had diminished as the Street more and more asserted its will; and there had been extracted from his countenance everything except a fundamental sadness too thinly masked by hauteur. He was being envied a freedom he did not feel.

Michael Tabor had begun to suffer illnesses of the kind we associate with giving up. He failed even to appear in court on December 22nd; and defense counsel explained that he had been taken from the subway with an asthma attack. When he appeared at the next sitting, Mr. Phillips, as guardian of all the tablets, confronted him with the declaration that the medical files of the transit authority recorded no case of a passenger removed from a train for illness on December 22nd. Justice Murtagh's bearing suggested that judicial notice had been taken of the indisputable reality of an imaginary world where no sparrow can fall without its due recording in some official file, and where if no such notation existed, this particular sparrow, in conspiracy with counsel, could only have invented a fictitious fall.

"All right," their judge said, giving up as so often before, "so much for that." But the suspicion of having been played with stayed upon him. As the business passed to a plea for Clark Squire's admittance to bail, the justice intervened to say that it was his present disposition to refuse bail to any defendant still in prison, although, in charity, he might consider applications to change that opinion "if and when counsel for the defendants begin to act in the courtroom as they properly should."

"You have," he declared, "clearly demonstrated that you are jointly undertaking to disrupt this trial and it is going to cease."

Mr. Katz replied that if the justice had uttered that state-

174

ment out of court, it would have been a delight to sue him for slander.

"All right," Justice Murtagh replied. 'I want to repeat that the continuance of the four defendants on bail is expressly made contingent on the collective good behavior of defendants and counsel."

The next day, Michael Tabor did not appear in court at all. After an hour, Mr. Lefcourt could only offer the surmise of another asthma attack. "All right," Justice Murtagh replied. "Bail forfeited. Warrant to issue."

Michael Tabor arrived that afternoon and was remanded at once to the Correction's Department. Mr. McKinney relayed his apologies, presented a medical diagnosis of acute asthma, and asked that bail be restored. Justice Murtagh denied the request and asked if Michael Tabor was now ready to go ahead with his trial.

First of all, Michael Tabor replied, "the omnipotent record that reflects everything should reflect that since the beginning of these proceedings, you have conducted yourself in the manner of a vile fascist swine pig and it comes as no surprise to me or to any of the other defendants that you are taking your present course of action.

"As far as your disbelief in my illness, that doesn't concern me in the least. We expect that. As far as proceeding to the hearings today, no, I don't want that, no, I don't want to proceed because I am sick."

Justice Murtagh was moving resignedly to adjourn for the day; but the rumble of Michael Tabor rolled over him in the passion of a contumely unable to conceive that its object could grant even this small grace:

"As a matter of fact, I'm not proceeding today, and I hold you responsible for whatever happens. That's not a threat. And let the record reflect that it's not a threat. It's simply stating the reality of the situation.

"Compassion we don't expect from you. Mercy we don't expect from you. As for your statement on charity, we don't want no charity. We don't want you to err on the side of charity. . . . And we don't expect any justice. That is just a typical example of your total disregard for any rights we are supposed to have. This is consistent with your whole thing."

JUSTICE MURTAGH: The defendant Tabor will be removed from the courtroom.

THE DEFENDANT TABOR: The defendant Tabor will walk out of the courtroom.

His departure had created a mixture of the suffering self with the unbending self that worked some of his old effect upon everyone who watched him except those fellow defendants whose sense of affront he must have aimed most to soothe. As it was, the sudden recovery of his presence did so little to dispose of their memory of the absence of his attention that he would come out from seven nights and five days on Riker's Island with the impression that no one of his fellows had spoken to him.

Still, while refusing him their comradeship, they seemed to have responded to his grievance. The next day, Justice Murtagh announced the holiday recess and extended to everyone present his wishes for a Happy New Year; and the defendants and many of the spectators gave way to laughter so derisive that their judge, aroused to being Sir Forcible, cited a young lady in the audience for contempt and declared that the bail of that most innocent bystander, Richard Moore, was henceforth forfeit too.

After an hour's argument at the bench, he had worked his way back to being Sir Feeble again; he would release Richard Moore and even consider the release of Michael Tabor as soon as he had gotten "an abject apology" for yesterday's display. Mr. Phillips scented one more of those moments of charity which were the single abuse of the court's authority that ever strained his fealty and interjected his opinion that Tabor's continued posture proved how worthless any apology of his would be:

176

MR. PHILLIPS: Mr. Tabor came back into this court today, after what he did yesterday, and then slept at the defense table here for numerous periods during the day, his head laying on the desk, paying no attention to the proceedings.

JUSTICE MURTAGH: I'm well aware of it. . . . [But] Mr. Tabor is most articulate and he may speak for himself if he wishes.

THE DEFENDANT TABOR: First of all, I will address myself to the accusation by the district attorney with regard to my sleeping. . . . The sleeping is a result of illness. . . . In order to alleviate that suffering, I rest.

MR. PHILLIPS: Your Honor, I would like to put on the record the fact that Mr. Tabor has been resting all through this trial. . . . Now, it's quite apparent to me, sir, that Mr. Tabor is taking some type of drugs which are effectively——

MR. CRAIN: Your Honor, is there no limit to the district attorney's remarks?

DEFENDANT TABOR: Your Honor, I demand an apology from the district attorney.

JUSTICE MURTAGH: All right, your request for an apology is denied. I have asked for an apology and I haven't received it.

Somewhere over the weekend, there was found a formula that suited the dignity of both this indicted felon and his judge. Michael Tabor conceded at Monday's luncheon recess that he had yielded to an anger "perhaps unjustified and unwarranted and unfortunate due to the circumstance."

"Do you express *profoundly* your apologies?" Justice Murtagh asked.

Michael Tabor paused, as though weighing the stipulation and noting the subtraction of that unacceptable modifier "abjectly," and, having thus underscored the fact of mutual concession, answered, "Yes." He was set free that afternoon.

But he came from Riker's Island as though from some after-hours club where he had first been carefully beaten and then

177

cast into the street; and he walked for the next month with a wound whose disablement was no easier to disguise than the occasion of its infliction was to discuss. He drew into himself. He had begun, at twenty-five, to remember almost the way an old man would what it had been like to be young. He had taken to talking about basketball to the exclusion of all other subjects; and those wild schoolyard boundings from the confinement of his childhood had come to seem to him far more persuasive in their illusory freedom than the leaps he no longer had the will to make in his manhood. He talked once about coming home and finding out that his mother was dead and, unable to feel anything, going to his room, putting on his basketball uniform, and just sitting there. After traveling all that way, he had come home to the remembered moment of entire deprivation.

There did, of course, still exist for him an underappreciated life with wider boundaries. Huey P. Newton had come East to stand with Bobby Seale in New Haven. Michael Tabor and Connie Matthews were welcome in Newton's train, and Richard Moore, if condescendingly, in theirs. Michael Tabor had become part of the nimbus of Oakland. That ascension so increased in the Others their sense of outrage at being deserted that they caucused and indited for *The East Village Other* a proclamation of the principles they had learned in their travails.

The language of that statement was unique among the utterances of long-beleaguered garrisons, less for its defiance of the enemy than for its resentment of the friend. Other outposts may have felt themselves abandoned; but very few can ever have had the pain of daily looking upon sights so suggestive of their isolation or so conducive to destroying the hope that somewhere a higher command is intent upon their rescue. They had dispatched couriers to the world outside their jail; yet every day they saw Moore and Tabor in clothes whose aspiration for splendid effect must come to seem not just a statement of difference from their own tatters but as cause to imagine diversions of funds that might more decently be used

178

to help their own women and children. They watched slumberous postures that suggested to them not exhausting duties to a common endeavor but instead a debilitating round of careless pleasures, among which these recreant messengers used the courtroom only as an interlude of rest and refreshment for further indulgence. The signs that Michael Tabor had achieved a special access to Huey P. Newton did not so much raise their hopes as deepen their mistrust. The illusion of its power that had drawn them toward that throne still persisted enough to make them think that if the Black Panther Party was doing so little for them, it was not from want of resources but from lack of feeling. They assumed that Michael Tabor's rise had been for his own sake and not for theirs, and that he served not to transmit their appeals up to Huey P. Newton but rather to subject them, through Michael Tabor, to edicts sent coldly downward that their troubles were altogether trivial beside Bobby Seale's.

Richard Moore's gaiety and Michael Tabor's hauteur, such comforts when both had been employed against judge and prosecutor, had become special afflictions to Lumumba Shakur and the Others now that these qualities seemed turned only against them. But the one man's gaiety and the other's hauteur were masks taken on a long while ago as each one's only shield. So, Richard Moore had confronted Justice Murtagh as Spirit Too Antic ever to conform, and Michael Tabor had faced Mr. Phillips as Pride Too Stern ever to yield. But those roles that can be so splendid on those large occasions when they defy their helplessness under oppression can seem no better than mean on those domestic ones when they are played only to cover embarrassment under reproach.

Those still in jail continued to expect more than the real world would provide them. If Tabor and Moore had been closer to the ideal revolutionary temperament than they were, they would have been as little able to achieve the hopes that had attended their release as Huey Newton was to help anyone outside his own small circle. The situation of the Panthers had made any one man's survival the only business he could sensibly tend to. But, by bad luck, the bearing that had made these two the focus of so many unrealizable visions would itself become the main point of outrage against them in their co-defendants' disillusion. What had seemed exhilarating about Richard Moore's refusal to care about the comfort of Justice Murtagh had begun to look like an incapacity to care about the discomfort of anyone at all; and what had been inspiring in Michael Tabor's pride before Mr. Phillips had begun to seem like disdain for everyone except himself. The very manner that had created the illusion became the more offensive for having survived it.

Lumumba Shakur and the Others sat down to compose their manifesto unable to remember a face or recognize a hand not turned against them. They felt that they had no choice except to address it as a salute to the Weathermen, those comrades of an identity so unfamiliar as to make them almost mythic—underground and blessedly out of sight and therefore exempt from test and failure in the experience of actual contact, unknowns preferable to anyone known because they were secure from being found wanting in a life where, whenever something was found, it ended being found wanting.

They praised the Weathermen for having learned that the Bomb was all that counted: "Revolution is violence," they affirmed. "Revolution is war. Revolution is bloodshed." They were insisting on paying honor to just the sort of deed imputed to them by their indictment, and they swore to emulate the Weathermen as soon as they were free to act as they chose. They were so anxious to attest a guilt that Mr. Phillips fell ever further short of proving against them and to show themselves entirely unrepentant of acts they had never performed that they modeled the intentions projected in their peroration so consciously upon Mr. Phillips' own statement of charges as to promise the shooting of policemen and the bombing of their precinct houses. In the defendants' beleaguerment this decree of no quarter to the besiegers had no effect except the impudent gallantry of refusing any quarter for themselves. Mr. Phillips, for whom their every contortion in torment was useful as

180

well as enjoyable, put their declaration in his files for bringing forth upon the day of sentence as evidence of a fixed obduracy in them that no mercy of the court could hope to temper.

The imprisoned defendants mingled defiance of those who had encompassed them with scorn for those whose standard they had followed into hazard and to their present conviction that they had been abandoned. In contrast to the commitment of the Weathermen, they arraigned what seemed to them the indifferent posturings of that "so-called vanguard," the Black Panther Party leadership, which was far away enough for its inadequacy to be imagined as deliberate, and their own two comrades, who were too close for their alienation to go unnoticed. The thick crowd of invidious appellations in this collective curse evoked the image of these prisoners in their common cell, each contending with the others to add another epithet— "tripping out, *pseudo-machismo*, arrogance, myrmidonism, dogmatism, regionalism, regimentation, and fear." The first three of these sins, since they produce the ruin of men, might be identified as belonging to Moore and Tabor; and the rest, since they produce the ruin of states and parties, as belonging, if not yet to Huey P. Newton, certainly to his cabinet.

Thereafter, whether from shame or affront it would never quite be possible to say, Richard Moore refused to enter the detention cells where their lawyers conferred each morning with the prisoners and the bailed defendants together.

On the last day of court in the week of February 1st, 1971, Moore and Michael Tabor sat at lunch with Diane Weems, Kuwasi's sister, who had established a place for herself in that Bronx command post of the Oakland expeditionary force where Richard Moore had lain about through the summer as unattended surplus baggage.

The urge to prophesy still worked in Michael Tabor even after the months had shrunk the range of his prophecy down to a dwindling corner of the Street; the manner had kept its grandeur through all the diminutions of the matter.

"That office ain't shit," he told Diane Weems. "What's it good for except selling the paper? The paper ain't shit. The

181

duty of the revolutionary is to tell the People things they need to know to survive."

"Do you know what survival is?" he asked. "Dharuba and I go in a bar. We got just enough in our pocket to buy one beer; but we know some nigger will come in and buy us another. That's survival.

"That's when you know the People. We can walk in a bar and the man there nods in the direction of another cat and says to you, 'Cool it; he's an agent.' Or someone you hardly know comes up and says, 'I can get you the stuff; I just got a shipment in.' That's survival. I see you in a bar and we rap; you can't do that until you get down to the People.

"But you think Bay and Jolly even know the hustlers on the Boston Post Road? They don't even know the after-hours places. When they want wine on a Sunday afternoon, they still got to call us up and ask where to get it."

"They don't have *style*," said Richard Moore. "Can they do what Iris can? We can send Iris to speak anywhere. Ain't nobody can raise money like Iris can."

"Yeah, Dharuba," Diane Weems answered. "But Iris was trained by you."

It was the last expression of intact faith that Richard Moore was likely to hear for a long while.

"Ain't nobody can train Iris," he said. He had lost her in his freedom after he had held her in prison with those letters that cried out his joy at being in a place where he could not be found wanting. Now, as he talked about her unreachable eminence, he described a finality of being found wanting; and his bowed head, his empty eyes, a never-before-noticed resignation in his voice, all witnessed together the justice of that judgment.

A visitor was overcome by the sense of social obligation which enjoins us all to try to raise the spirits, if not to fortify the spine, of the company. There was the promise of one more great scene to be played, he suggested: it would be only a few days before Michael Tabor would have his chance to cross-examine Detective Ralph White. "McKinney can do it," said Richard Moore in final dismissal of all redemption. They had already withdrawn; and every word they spoke was an employment of their old grand manner upon a grandiosity stuffed into pettier and pettier subjects until it seemed a deliberate parody that recognized how, somehow, things they could not even remember had made their persons trivial.

On February 6th, the next day, they were in New Haven with Huey Newton. The nature of their downfall and the term of their exile had already been appointed by Connie Matthews Tabor's conception of her own high destiny. She had quarreled with Newton or thought she had, since making Huey Newton quarrel would be a conquest beyond even so mettlesome a spirit as Mrs. Tabor's; his survival lay in his serenity. That afternoon, Mrs. Tabor may have made off with some of the Supreme Servant's cash and certainly took such of his private papers as seemed to her fuel for her passionate conviction that *he* had betrayed *her* and departed for Algeria to inflame Eldridge Cleaver's discontents.

After she packed, she went off with Moore and Tabor to a New Haven radio station where they broadcast their common secession. On Monday, just before they were to fly to Algeria, Connie Matthews Tabor informed Richard Moore that he could not go with them. He had again been judged an inadequate comrade; and, already late for court and knowing that Justice Murtagh would jail him if he went back there, he could only turn to the Street with no real company except Eddie Joseph, the orphan child who had taken to trailing after him as he had trailed after Michael Tabor. Huey Newton had not heard their radio interview; and, even after the undisguised outrage of Connie Matthews Tabor's departure, it does not seem to have occurred to him until Sunday that Michael Tabor was anywhere except faithfully employed at his stewardship as director of security for a Newton speech at Princeton University.

The same ignorance protected their lawyers through the weekend; but they had not been in the courtroom five minutes on Monday, February 8th, when the absence of Moore and Tabor told them to a certainty what had happened and cast

183

them into the self-reproach of having so altogether ceased to take seriously anything these two strays were saying as to have overlooked a hundred plain hints that it would happen. Shock so deprived them of their normal volubility as to present to the aroused sensibilities of Justice Murtagh the appearance of being accomplices in the flight. The judge already disliked these lawyers more than he did their clients; and now they had compounded their sins by having persuaded him to draw back from forfeiting the bail and remanding to prison two persons who had now abused what he knew to be his charity but others could well think his weakness. He ordered Joan Bird and Afeni Shakur to the Women's House of Detention. And when Mr. Lefcourt rallied what strength he had left him in his disaster to enter a formal request that the court reconsider, Justice Murtagh took the chance to suppress it with an unmerited reproach:

"Counselor, I was shocked, quite candidly, when you, the people who are representing the defendants, advised the court of the absence of these two people in a manner that conveyed to the court that you acquiesced in the fact that they were gone and so be it."

His immediate anger and his abiding sense of order forbade him to interpret these stricken expressions as anything but an entire absence of surprise. The defense attorneys had given him every evidence that they thought better of their clients than they did not only of judge and prosecutor but of every root and branch of the system conducting their trial. He had made the too-easy step from observing the identification to assuming the intimacy. Since lawyers and defendants seem to breathe together for his torment, he had come to be sure that no one of them could act without conspiring with the Others; and the unanticipated defection that had thrown Mr. Lefcourt and the others into a disordered silence could only seem to him the product of a common plan.

Mr. Phillips alone could feel immune to the sting of betrayal or the embarrassment of having overlooked the clues that preceded it. He triumphed in the certainty that Moore and Tabor

184

had fled before the massive tread of proof that he could still assure himself he had marched against them. The next day he was able to light up for the court so many shadowed places in their lives—the broadcast attack on the Black Panther leadership that even Huey Newton had not heard, the marriage of Michael Tabor that Rosalind Bennett could hardly have been told about, even the report of an undercover police agent in whom they had confided their plans to bolt—that the inference would not go down that he had become aware of their flight before their lawyers did and that, here as always, police and prosecution knew things about the Panthers which they did not even know about one another.

Mr. Phillips' self-absorption made him as untrustworthy a guide in general as his resources preserved him beyond challenge as authority about the particular. Richard Moore certainly and Michael Tabor very probably had fled from consciousness of guilt. But its origin could not be in the testimony that the district attorney was so laboriously mustering while they, in their distraction, were not paying enough attention to judge it light or heavy. "I guess Richard was just afraid of going back to jail," Iris Moore said afterward. "He was scared that any day Murtagh would put him back."

But what Richard Moore would have feared in that case was not prison itself but the company of comrades who had found him out. He had fled a guilt the exact opposite of the one Mr. Phillips was so confident had been brought home to him: the crime on his conscience was not of having pursued but of having neglected his commitment as a revolutionary.

Justice Murtagh listened to the district attorney's revelations, said again, "I am shocked," and recalled his conviction that defense counsel had treated the absence of these fugitives "in a manner that inescapably conveyed the message that they knew infinitely more than they represented." He rebuffed the protests of Mr. Lefcourt by demanding whether he would attest his own innocence under oath, and recommended that Mr. Phillips institute a grand jury investigation of the whole matter.

185

The shock of the event had impelled both belligerent powers to action. Downstairs in the pressroom, a representative of Huey P. Newton was distributing his decree that Moore and Tabor were enemies of the People and that they and all the other defendants, except Joan Bird and Afeni Shakur, were henceforth cast out from the Black Panther Party. The crime of the Others had been their letter to the Weathermen, an heretical outburst which overbore anyone who might have noticed that they had arraigned Moore and Tabor as enemies while Huey Newton still accepted them as loyal servants of the People. The party was punishing both the deserters and the deserted; and what was being said in Huey P. Newton's name sounded again, as so often, very little like Huey Newton.

The necessary victims of Justice Murtagh's action were Joan Bird and Afeni Shakur, whom he ordered back to prison as insurance against their also running away. Mr. Crain had described the pit into which they had been thrown as well as anyone never in prison can when he attempts to illuminate its conditions. Mrs. Shakur, he had observed, was six months pregnant and "to put her in that dungeon . . . and subject her to what we know she will be subjected to, in terms of incarceration, I think, your Honor, is something the court should reflect upon."

Justice Murtagh had heard him without even the condescension of a response; and then Afeni Shakur came back herself to remind him of what he had done:

"I would like to bring to the attention of the court what I am sure the court doesn't know about, and that's the situation that exists with Miss Bird and myself and for the other women that are being held in the house of detention. The boilers are broken there. There is no hot water. The conditions are not just abominable, as they were before; they are inhuman. The food that the women eat is cooked in one night. Like today's dinner was cooked last night and is sitting on the table waiting to be served tonight. There is no toilet paper. The facilities are not bad anymore; they are ridiculous. Women should not be put in there.

186

"Joan and myself are being held in a lockup simply because we refuse to be examined by those doctors who are not doctors, by those doctors who care very little about the structure of the female body. So we would request to have our own physicians come in and give us any examinations we need to have in the Women's House of Detention, and we would request that some facilities be provided so we can take hot showers. The showers are dirty enough as it is, but to be subjected to cold showers in that filth is ridiculous."

The court, Justice Murtagh unbent to reply, would request counsel to confer with the commissioner of corrections, and would hold itself available to exercise any authority it might have to correct any conditions that might exist. Mr. Crain intervened with an account of the wearisome round he had already endured with the commissioner of corrections and his sense of the futility of continuing with it.

"I would ask the court, since cooperation is not forthcoming," he concluded, "to issue the appropriate order."

JUSTICE MURTAGH: Unless the interest is in making a statement for the press—

MR. CRAIN: The interest is in assuring the rights of our clients, your Honor.

THE DEFENDANT AFENI SHAKUR: The interest, Mr. Murtagh, is in assuring the life of my child.

There had asserted itself, as the last shard of poetry among the ruins of that day, the superb effrontery of life insisting upon life. Afeni Shakur had weakened in the solitude of freedom as Moore and Tabor had. The lawyers had learned that she was pregnant some weeks before and with natural alarm for the rancors it would add to those already dividing their clients. ("Lumumba's going to look at her some morning and find out about her," said Mr. Lefcourt, "and then he's going to knock me halfway across the room.") Mr. Crain had even felt it necessary to inform Justice Murtagh of a condition that might require Mrs. Shakur's brief absence for an operation, the habitual subjugation of his good sense by his integrity having apparently left him indifferent to how an Irish judge of Puritan temperament might receive the news that a woman whose sentence he might soon come to measure out had been untrue to a husband who was incidentally not even her husband and that she now proposed to remedy her carelessness with the further trespass of an abortion.

Then it turned out that Afeni Shakur had never even entertained the thought of not having her child. After all, she said, she had been trying to have a baby for years. The present was dreadful; the future unpromising; the child was a wound to Lumumba, a wanton flourish before her judge, an uneasiness to everyone except herself. And yet there she stood between Lumumba Shakur and Joseph Phillips and spoke as though she were bearing a Prince. With Woman as with Man, the results of the flight from duty to private refuge have a way of turning out inconvenient; and yet there are inconveniences that have to do with the continuity of life as there are inconveniences that have to do only with its denial. The first are the inconveniences that most often fall upon Woman. Behind Afeni Shakur there could almost be seen the long scroll of birth and death and birth again, of pain and resurrection, the things women know; and it could be understood that the grandness of Afeni Shakur's impudence consisted in her capacity to appreciate the special opportunities of Woman.

Michael Tabor and Connie Matthews had joined Eldridge Cleaver in raising the standard of rebellion in Algeria. Lumumba Shakur and the Others would be known for the duration of their case as Cleaverites, not because they had decided to be but because the two rival captains chose to act as though they were. Persons in prison are so without power that when they were arrested, the license to describe their characters had passed to the district attorney and now the license to define their positions in a quarrel so little of their making as to have no real place in their consciousness had been assumed by Michael Tabor whose abandonment of them in no way in-

188

hibited his assurance that he continued to speak in their name.

Outside, in the Street, there had begun one of those wars where factions turn upon one another those murderous instincts they spared the enemy they had originally united against. Robert Weaver, a Cleaverite, was shot dead on a Harlem corner early in March. A month later persons unknown entered the Queens County office of the Black Panther Party, a Newtonite enclave, bound up Samuel Napier, circulation manager of *The Black Panther,* taped his eyes and mouth, laid him face down upon a cot, and shot off the back of his head. Napier had been an inoffensive man, with no ambitions except to sell his papers, as unquestioning in his loyalty to Newton as he was unaggressive in the feuds that had become its test. Napier had been Afeni Shakur's friend while she was out on bail; and his death ended any illusion still remaining to her that life is a thing of simple causes and enemies recognizable on sight.

Weeks afterward, out of prison, she was at lunch; and one of her companions, secure in the creed that could never again seem to her as certain as it had, began talking about such Negroes as had become policemen.

"What do you think of a brother who would be a pig?" he wondered aloud. "To take a brother into a station house and beat him. What do you think of that?"

"And what," Afeni Shakur answered, "do you think of a brother who will go to another brother and tie his hands and put plaster over his mouth and blindfold him and put three bullets in the back of his head? What do you think of that brother? Joan and I cried when we read about that," she said.

Nothing at all was heard from Richard Moore, and his lawyers were afforded very little news about Michael Tabor except what they might gain from a video tape cassette dispatched to the mainland by the Cleaverites. It brought back an image of the victim liberated from his oppressors, more than ever imprisoned in himself, the eyelids too heavy, the voice the monotone of the speech of somnolence, the message a peevish complaint about Huey P. Newton. The only access anyone

189

'would have to Michael Tabor, in any natural state, would turn out to belong to Mr. Phillips, that master, right up until the end, of all intimacies as he was controller of all intimations.

On March 31st, just before closing his case, the assistant district attorney told the court that he had a transcript of a telephone conversation with Michael Tabor in Algeria that he thought would be useful for the jury to hear.

"He threatens to kill me," he explained. Mr. Lefcourt had no trouble imagining the dimensions of this latest disaster. "You know what he must have thought," he said bitterly. " 'To hell with the other defendants. I'm clear. I can say anything I want.' "

And then, in his pride, Mr. Phillips played his tape.

MR. PHILLIPS: Mr. Tabor, this is ADA Phillips in New York County, and we have a number of problems that you have created as a result of your leaving New York.

MR. TABOR: Hello, motherfucker, who is this?

MR. PHILLIPS: This is ADA Phillips in New York County calling.

MR. TABOR: Not *the* Phillips?

MR. PHILLIPS: Yes, *the* Phillips, the one you refer to as "pig Phillips."

MR. TABOR: Yes, pig Phillips, yeah. Right on.

MR. PHILLIPS: How do you like Algiers, Mr. Tabor? [Pause ten seconds.] Mr. Tabor, hello, hello, Mr. Tabor.

ELDRIDGE CLEAVER: Hello.

MR. PHILLIPS: Mr. Tabor?

ELDRIDGE CLEAVER: No, this is Eldridge Cleaver, who is this?

MR. PHILLIPS: This is ADA Phillips in New York County. I was speaking to Mr. Tabor and I have to advise him of certain things . . . we had to advise him of his rights.

ELDRIDGE CLEAVER: Are you recording this?

MR. PHILLIPS: Yes, I am.

ELDRIDGE CLEAVER: So are we. . . . Well, here he is so he is going to talk to you about all that.

190

MR. PHILLIPS: Thank you very much.

MR. TABOR: Right on.

MR. PHILLIPS: Mr. Tabor, I wanted to talk to you about, uh, three things. Uh, one is that we have here in New York a tape recording of your voice and——

MR. TABOR: That don't sound like you now.

MR. PHILLIPS: I'm terribly sorry. It's me. I have a cold. I'm sorry it doesn't sound like me.

MR. TABOR: Well, you've always been very arrogant and nasty and how come you so nice now?

MR. PHILLIPS (laugh): I'm only getting a legal job done, Mr. Tabor, and that's, uh, the only purpose in my calling you.

MR. TABOR: Okay, what do you want to know?

MR. PHILLIPS: I wanted to know whether or not the tape recording we have here in New York is actually a tape recording of your particular voice and whether, uh, you, uh, posed for those photographs that we do have.

MR. TABOR: So far as any recording or anything is concerned, uh, the important thing that has to be stressed at this point right now is that you know this as well as I know it that this entire case that you, along with Murtagh, along with all the other individuals that you conspired with, that entire case is a cold-blooded farce. You know it's a frame-up, Joe, and I know it, . . . so there's really no sense for us to sit here going through any changes about that.

MR. PHILLIPS: Well, if that's your position, Mr. Tabor, uh, I think you should have stayed here and waited for the jury to return its verdict.

MR. TABOR: Your main concern is not the innocence or guilt of them brothers back there, but rather just getting them convicted so that you can get political mileage out of it.

MR. PHILLIPS: Well, that may be your view, Mr. Tabor. I didn't call you to debate the issue. I called to advise you of certain legal, uh, rights.

MR. TABOR: I am aware of my legal rights. . . . Now

191

you calling up over here to Algiers and you want to get some statement from me so you can go back in the mother-fuckin' courtroom and try to more effectively railroad those brothers some more the way you're doing. . . . I just want you to know that my position remains, is the same as it was when we were back in Babalone. The same allegations and charges I leveled against you back there, I still reiterate them: you still the same fascist, you still the same pig, you still the same vi-yall motherfucker that you always been. . . . I want you to play that in court.

MR. PHILLIPS: Well, uh, I expect to. . . . I certainly, uh, didn't expect you to authorize it.

ELDRIDGE CLEAVER: Joe?

MR. PHILLIPS: Excuse me, hello.

ELDRIDGE CLEAVER: Say, Joe Blow.

MR. PHILLIPS: Who is this?

ELDRIDGE CLEAVER: This is Eldridge Cleaver.

MR. PHILLIPS: Yes, Mr. Cleaver.

ELDRIDGE CLEAVER: I want to inform you of the charges against you.

MR. PHILLIPS (laughs): I don't want to be informed of any charges. I've got enough problems with my own case without getting any additional cases today, Mr. Cleaver.

ELDRIDGE CLEAVER: You are wanted for crimes against the People.

MR. PHILLIPS: Now wait a minute, I, uh, uh [laugh]. If you say so.

ELDRIDGE CLEAVER: We plan to see to it that you die for your crimes. . . . You know exactly what you doing and we gonna get you for that, Joe Blow.

MR. PHILLIPS: Mr. Cleaver, one other problem we have in relation to, uh, our case is . . . May I please speak to Mr. Moore?

ELDRIDGE CLEAVER: Take that shit off the calendar because we're through with your fuckin' courts. We're through with you from now on. It's war. Do you understand that?

• MR. PHILLIPS: I am aware of what you're saying, Mr. Cleaver, and, uh, I think if you would bear with me, I just have a, a——

ELDRIDGE CLEAVER: You have no jurisdiction. You can tell Murtagh to shove his law books up his ass and you can shove yours up your ass, because they're null and void . . .

MR. PHILLIPS: Mr. Cleaver, do you believe a man of your, uh, of your purported intellect and writing ability has to degenerate to that type of argument or vilification?

ELDRIDGE CLEAVER: You're no good, you're a snake and nothing is going to work out good for you, because we're not going to let it work out good for you, and death to all fascist pigs and that includes you.

MR. PHILLIPS: Well, I'm sure you feel that way.

ELDRIDGE CLEAVER: And all the other fascists you're hung up with.

MR. PHILLIPS: Mr. Cleaver, uh, I, I do have one other, uh, point I would like to make and that is with Mr. Moore and, if I could advise Mr. Moore that the trial has continued in his absence . . .

ELDRIDGE CLEAVER: You can't help Mr. Moore. You can't help anybody. You're just trying to become governor or something. . . . What are you—a Republican or a Democrat?

MR. PHILLIPS: Uh, Mr. Cleaver, our office is nonpolitical and we don't get involved in that kind of squabble.

ELDRIDGE CLEAVER: You're nothing but a fucking pig man.

MR. PHILLIPS: Well, I've been called that by your associates on a number of occasions and I, I don't really feel that it demeans me, I think it demeans the person who is articulating that kind of language. Mr. Cleaver if, if you would allow me to speak to Mr. Moore and so I can advise him that the trial has continued in his absence, uh, I'll leave you and won't bother you any further, sir.

ELDRIDGE CLEAVER: Here's somebody else.

MR. PHILLIPS: Hello.

193

CONNIE MATTHEWS TABOR: Hello, this is Connie Matthews Tabor.
MR. PHILLIPS: Yes, Mrs. Tabor.

. . . Could you tell me where I could reach Mr. Moore so I could advise him of——
CONNIE MATTHEWS TABOR: Why should I tell you where you can reach Mr. Moore? You can find him yourself.
MR. TABOR: What did you say, Joe?
MR. PHILLIPS: I thought you might since you are friends of his, I thought you'd be able to give us some assistance in finding him.
MR. TABOR: You know I wouldn't give you any assistance of any kind, Joe.
MR. PHILLIPS: My opinion, Mr. Tabor, is that in talking to me and, uh, authorizing us to tell the court about this conversation, you have rendered considerable assistance to us.

MR. TABOR: I'll be seeing you soon, Joe, and, uh, what has to be done is just something that has been decreed by the masses of the people. You see, you know and I know that you are guilty. That you been slimy and lying and throw all kinds of shit into the game. You made it very clear to us how we have to deal with you, and give Murtagh my regards too . . . and tell him we'll get back; I'll be knocking at your door one night . . . [Pause three seconds] "Power to the People" and death to the fascist pig.
MR. PHILLIPS: Uh, Mr. Tabor, uh, I'm surprised that after all that we have gone through you can still utter threats to kill people. It's rather remarkable; you think you would have learned that, uh, killing people is not the solution to any problem. [Pause five seconds.] Are you still there, Mr. Tabor? [Pause seven seconds.] Hello. Hello. [End.]

The recording ceased its scratch; and Mr. Phillips turned in triumph to look upon his victims laughing at him. Everything

194

Michael Tabor had been for them before he erased every memory of what he had seemed to be had returned for them in that moment. They could forget that he had abandoned them; they could forget they were in prison and alone; what they felt was beyond just relief and had become something like glory. The last word had been gotten; and, of all persons presumed fallen away beyond recovery, it was Michael Tabor who had done The Dozens for them.

Justice Murtagh thought awhile and then decided that no purpose would be served by playing this conversation to the jury. Mr. Phillips was disappointed. His insensitivity to everything around him had sunk at last into absolute insensitivity to himself. He had only been tone-deaf when he thought to impress a jury against a defendant by sponsoring his message: "You know it's a frame-up, Joe, and I know it." But it was simply uncomprehending for him to disregard all thought about how he himself must sound—insinuating to outcasts, deferential to pariahs, affirming that he had no reason to communicate with his targets except to inform them of their rights, being addressed by Eldridge Cleaver and stumbling at once into the revelation of how far above his station the occasion made him feel, allowing to beat unspoken but unmistakable behind his every syllable the sentence "Wait till I tell my wife," half-lackey, half-bully, a most unsavory concoction of the pious, the oily, and the vengeful. It was a conversation in which Mr. Phillips had been what he was at bottom and Michael Tabor had raised his fallen self to be for a while what he would like to think he was.

IX

The journey of these defendants toward the cell and the dock had been marked by a special trust in the policemen who were doing the most to send them there.

In November of 1969, Sanford Katz had gone to Columbus, Ohio, where William King and Lee Roper had been run to earth by the FBI. Katz was still wondering in the fog before trial just who Mr. Phillips' witnesses might be, and he was not at all sure that these unfamiliar recruits to his client list might not deserve his suspicions too. He found King masked with suspicion, clearly no more trusting his lawyer than trusted by him. Yes, King conceded, it could well be that the police had penetrated his security section; he could in fact think of no one under his command in whose fidelity he had complete confidence except Eugene Roberts, who would later appear testifying against him. Roberts had all along been a detective third-grade in the New York City Police Department's Bureau of Special Services.

Earlier, in the Manhattan Detention Center, while they were reviewing personages who had escaped indictment and then dropped from view, Mr. Lefcourt asked Lumumba Shakur whether one of the police agents might be Yedwa Sudan, whom he had met as Ralph Wyatt, and whose efforts were about to be crowned by Special Services with his promotion as Patrolman Ralph White to detective third-grade.

"Man, he *couldn't* be a cop," Lumumba Shakur answered. "You should have seen the shit he *did.*"

But all Ralph White had done was to smoke marijuana, to wave his shotgun and fire his pistol, and to rave about taking care of business by any means necessary. When it came to the deed, he had managed, in some fashion, to have Lumumba find out that he was one of those persons likely to fall short. But Lumumba Shakur could accept Yedwa Sudan's want of kidney because they so shared the sense of mischief, the common pleasure just in hanging out. They were men who grin.

The hunter had fit the quarry as neatly when Detective Roberts selected William King as the Panther closest to him. Each was a man of veiled and private thoughts. King had been a marine and the dream of commanding a military troop must have taken hold of him in the corps. He had so little in his nature that was political that he once told Mr. McKinney that he could not recall ever having so much as attended a demonstration.

He could be almost florid when he was conjuring up the terror in the streets let loose by some civil uprising of his imagination; yet, aground in a courtroom, he never seemed to know what to say. He was forward enough in the tumults of the pretrial hearings; but, alone among those of the defendants most actively intervening, his outcries were invariably inappropriate.

All the others were responding to some chance to wound the enemy offered by the enemy; Justice Murtagh and Mr. Phillips would lead and they would counterpunch. But William King had no device except rudely to shout the formula for prisoners of war: "Get my name down, pig. William King. Kwando

197

Kinshasa. Dig, pig?" He had never bothered to learn that game of running changes so habitual to a culture that learns by talking. The absence of its formulas in his style set him apart from the others and made him the outsider it took longest for his lawyers quite to trust.

So King had come to the Panthers as an engine might seek a vehicle and in Detective Roberts he had found the only wheel that he could count upon to remain steady on its axle. There was the past; they had played together as boys. And there was a present in which only Gene Roberts followed his leader. There were ten members of that security section which King preferred to call the Panther Guerilla Team. As evidence of its fanaticism, Mr. Phillips would offer Roberts' recollection of the chill night patrol on March 18th, 1969, when its members had waded waist-deep through a river in the Bronx Botanical Gardens. Yet only five of the ten members of the guerilla team had endured these, the most strenuous minutes of their basic training; and there had been no other drill when as many as half the members of the team had showed up to harden themselves for the Deed. Only William King and Eugene Roberts had made every formation.

Eugene Roberts was the oldest in service of the police witnesses. He had been in the Navy as a medical corpsman, come out to work first as an attendant in a nursing home, then as a shipping clerk in the garment district, and then at the Chase Manhattan Bank. He had elevated himself slightly with each new employment, until he passed his police examination and was called to the department in April of 1964. And there, after a two-hour conversation about his political philosophy—perhaps the longest he would ever have and, in his disciplined way, carefully forgotten by the time he came to witness—he was assigned to the Bureau of Special Services as an undercover patrolman.

Roberts would spend the next five years in close companionship with men who thought of themselves as black revolutionaries while he himself was in service to the only institution in their ambience that had a secrecy of structure and controlled

198

regularity of function that was to any degree like the hidden army of William King's imagination.

When he came to trial, Mr. Phillips would offer to the jury *The Battle of Algiers*, a film celebrating the Algerian terrorists, as a model not merely admired but brought to the point of execution by persons who would always seem to him even more awesome when bound together in conspiracy than they were contemptible to him as individuals. Still, to watch *The Battle of Algiers* was to be reminded, on all points save rhetoric, not of the Panthers but of the Bureau of Special Services. The Algerian Liberation Front was organized into closed cells; no member knew anyone outside his own cell, or anything about those above him or even about most of those beside him in the structure he served; he knew in fact only as much as he needed to know to function.

And precisely that, he could swear, had been the pattern of Eugene Roberts' career as a policeman. He had contact with no one in the department except the Bureau of Special Services' staff member assigned to transmit his reports up from and his orders down to him. He did not even know which object of his investigation might be himself a brother agent. Once he heard Patrolman Ralph White, known to him only as a Panther section leader, declare that Panthers in prison must be freed "by any means necessary"; and he faithfully reported that utterance as coming from "Ralph Wyatt, a militant" armed with a shotgun. He would learn that Ralph Wyatt was a Special Services agent only after the arrests.

Eugene Roberts had been first dispatched to penetrate Moslem Mosque Number One, the church that Malcolm X was attempting to rebuild after his excommunication by Elijah Muhammad. The history of revolutionary blackness is a thread that is always being broken and then tied together by strangers to its past. Mr. Malcolm had been dead three years; and everyone Gene Roberts met in the Panthers revered his name; but the only one among them to possess any private recollection of his presence was this police agent.

We have no secure way of knowing just what Mr. Malcolm

199

meant to Detective Roberts. He had been one of Mr. Malcolm's bodyguards and on duty at the death which a policeman less complicated would certainly have designated as "the homicide" but which Detective Roberts invariably called "the assassination" as though he, though plainly committed to the opposite of hyperbole in all references to other objects of his police work, would always set Mr. Malcolm apart from every other as someone whose person and whose fate deserved the language appointed to describe the violent end of heads of state.

"Isn't it a fact that you helped murder Malcolm X?" Mr. Lefcourt asked him.

"YES!" Afeni Shakur cried out from her chair, the soft accused becoming momentarily the hard accuser; with the defendants stirring and lowering like some revolutionary tribunal behind him, Mr. Lefcourt added, the scorn of the judge who had already judged infusing him too, "Yes, we would *all* like to know the truth about the truth about the assassination."

Gene Roberts remembered that he had been on security duty at Mr. Malcolm's last meeting and had been relieved for a few minutes and was sitting in the audience when there was a commotion and chairs were overthrown and shots were fired:

"As I turned, I saw Malcolm grasp his chest. I didn't see him fall. And I followed down one aisle and by the time I got to the back of the auditorium, the two individuals that was in the middle aisle, we arrived at the same time. One went by and at that particular time I grabbed a chair. The individual looked in my direction and pointed his—what looked like a .45—at which time I made a sidestep, and, as I stepped to the side he fired, missing but hitting my—hitting my jacket.

"I then threw the chair, knocking him down. After a couple of seconds elapsed, I turned around. . . . I came back to the ballroom, went to the stage, where I proceeded to give Malcolm X mouth-to-mouth resuscitation."

When Mrs. Malcolm reached the stage, it was Gene Roberts who, giving up, turned to her and said, "He's gone."

"What appeared to be twenty minutes later," he finished "the

200

police finally got there and took him over to the medical center."

Justice Murtagh would certainly have ruled Mr. Lefcourt's question objectionable if the district attorney had intervened. But Mr. Phillips had been most anxious to hear the answer. And Detective Roberts *had* met Mr. Lefcourt's insinuations with a reply triumphant for Mr. Phillips and persuasive even for persons more detached. Still it was one of those answers which complicates even as it persuades. Just by making clear the facts, Gene Roberts had stirred a cluster of unanswered questions, speculations hopeless to test in the only place where they could be tested, in the impenetrable corridors of his interior. For these speculations could only lose themselves in the puzzle of how Gene Roberts felt about Malcolm X.

Bayard Rustin, whose debates with Malcolm X were early steps toward the legend, said once that he learned very soon from those audiences that no one could be a Negro and not respond to something in Mr. Malcolm's message. What was more, Gene Roberts had been assigned to spy upon Mr. Malcolm at a time when he was more than ever attractive, being at once wounded, cast forth, and witty about it. The day after Mr. Malcolm's death, a Harlem photographer, whose business was among the other uneasy enterprises that surrounded the office of the relict Muslim Mosque Number One at the Hotel Theresa, could remember nothing of the victim except his good cheer in trouble:

"I'd see him every morning and he'd be pulling himself up the steps, so tired, and I'd say, 'How you doing, brother?' and he'd always answer, 'Struggling. Making it.' I knew he wasn't making it, but he was always cheerful."

It is unlikely that Gene Roberts could have been indifferent to the gallant dignity of someone who, however dimmed as a presence, shone brighter than he ever had as a person. Could anyone serving an army where nearly all his comrades were persons he did not even know and his superiors only shadows be more loyal to it in his heart than to a man as vivid as Mr. Malcolm? And, even if nothing so human intruded upon Pa-

201

trolman Roberts and even if he were only a machine, he was still a fine enough instrument to respond early to the manifold signs that Mr. Malcolm was someone more menaced than menacing. His conscience as a recorder could not have permitted him to conceal from the Bureau of Special Services the approach of death to Mr. Malcolm—those gangs of Mr. Elijah's whose point it was to be *seen,* to remind their enemy of their implacable patience; the darkness around him so oppressive that it would finally drive its object to leave Harlem by daylight and lodge himself at the downtown Statler Hilton the night before he died.

Gene Roberts had certainly reported all these forebodings to the Bureau of Special Services, and that certainty placed a most curious stamp upon the answers he gave to Mr. Lefcourt's further insinuations: "And you had been at various meetings that Malcolm spoke at—at the Audubon Ballroom where that happened?"

DETECTIVE ROBERTS: Yes.

MR. LEFCOURT: And at every time prior to that night that he spoke it was always large contingents of uniformed police there, were there not?

DETECTIVE ROBERTS: Yes.

MR. LEFCOURT: But that night there were none, right?

DETECTIVE ROBERTS: This afternoon, there were only a few on the outside.

And Detective Roberts allowed the inevitable inference to run with an impulse if anything to speed it on rather than turn it aside. The policeman had, in this case at least, foresworn his institutional duty to excuse the police. In the silence that followed his last answer, an earlier one commenced to resonate: "*What appeared to be twenty minutes later,* the police finally got there." Then his auditors could recognize that it remained the fixed impression of this police detective that his department had normally provided large complements of uniformed protectors to Mr. Malcolm's meetings, that it had with-

202

drawn them on the day of his liveliest peril and that the "very few" policemen he remembered seeing in the vicinity had taken an inexplicable twenty minutes to get from the street outside to a platform where the victim had passed beyond useful assistance. And yet these were recollections so little supported by official history as to contain no single fact not disputed by the record. The point had finally become less that Detective Roberts' version might be the correct one than that his testimony indicated a prejudice against his commanders that had endured intact through most of the years he had served them.

What he recollected could not reasonably have led him to belive that his own department had managed the assassination of Malcolm X. His only acquaintance with persons at all informed was with Mr. Malcolm's own circle, which, in the impact of the moment, had generally assumed that Mr. Elijah's was the directing hand. Mrs. Malcolm was sure it was; and Mr. Elijah all but boasted so. Credit for the deed was most serviceable to his image as Prophet favored by the God Who punishes apostates and would act as a deterrent to future temptations to faction in the nation of Islam.

There was, then, nothing in the ground about him to fructify any suspicion in Patrolman Roberts that the police department might have murdered Malcolm X. If such a speculation had occurred to him, he would have had no better way to test it than was possessed by anyone else in Mr. Malcolm's circle. Employers who did not trust him enough even to introduce themselves to him would hardly have made him privy to a project as deeply laid as this one would have to have been.

But still he had his own secret: he *knew* that his department had been told that Mr. Malcolm's fears for his life were not the pose of a demagogue calling attention to himself but an awareness of danger suffusing his private moments. Detective Roberts had reported to the Bureau of Special Services both Mr. Malcolm's state of mind and the threatening incidents that had brought it on; and, after that warning, his superiors had provided Mr. Malcolm's last meeting with no more protection

203

than the two-man patrol appointed for the most peaceable assemblages.

If he troubled himself with the mystery of his masters, Patrolman Roberts, given his impression of their casual response to his reports, could only have surmised that even if they had not thought Mr. Malcolm a menace deserving elimination by an act of their own, they had at least thought him a nuisance of the sort for whose sake they had very little passion to resist the course of events.

In any case, his life with Mr. Malcolm and its sudden breaking-off had marked Patrolman Roberts' character as a policeman with an ambivalence about, indeed a permanent wariness toward those strangers, his brother officers and his father commanders. He seems, for example, to have shared with entire seriousness the fears of police attack that the Panthers so often expressed:

MR. LEFCOURT: Were you afraid, being a Panther, that the police might attack?
DETECTIVE ROBERTS: Yes, because they didn't know who I was.

Before his enlistment in William King's cadre, he had made himself most useful to the party as charge of quarters in the Panther office. He was conspicuous there only for his regularity and his silences. The defendants could recall just one occasion when he seemed at all excited: on January 17th, 1969, Afeni and Lumumba Shakur came to relieve Gene Roberts at his post and he reported to them that there had been a number of suspect telephone calls and that parties unknown to him had been taking photographs of the office from the street outside. Such things, he said, made him certain that the police had begun a compeign to harass the Panthers. After they learned he was a policeman himself, the Shakurs assumed that he had invented all this as his own kind of harassment. And yet, provocation having turned out to be very little his professional style, it became much easier to believe that such incidents had

204

happened and that Detective Roberts had exaggerated their import and quite sincerely blamed them on his superiors, about whom he directly knew so little and whose good conduct when they sniffed the scent, he seems to have trusted very little more than would any Panther. And the Detective Roberts who was so susceptible to what sometimes gets itself thought of as the paranoia of Panthers about policemen was noticeably immune to what as often gets itself thought of as the paranoia of policemen about Panthers.

He had been under Mr. Phillips' direction ever since the arrest. In the service of the district attorney's office, he had undergone a forced draft upon his memory of the kind of things that Panthers say and that so plainly worked more forcibly upon Mr. Phillips' fancy than they ever had or yet could upon his. He could now recall, after such cultivation, a January, 1969, meeting where Afeni Shakur had grown angrier the more she talked about the recent arrest of a Panther's wife:

"She stated that there should be some retaliation for the arrest, and she stated the next time it happened that a pig should be kidnapped and held for ransom until they let the individual that was arrested, let him go."

"I then stated, 'By letting him go, the pig could identify us' and she says, 'Well, we really hadn't intended to let him go. He would be iced.'"

Detective Roberts would later concede to Mr. Bloom that his daily reports to Special Services nowhere reflected any such exchange. And yet it did not seem something he would need to invent, since there would have been no trouble getting such sentiments uttered by any of the bailed defendants in the trial corridors during any recess. Detective Roberts' recollection accorded entirely with what anyone must have come to accept as the nature of Panther meetings where reins upon the imagination were simply out of order, rather as they must have been at meetings in Mr. Phillips' office.

How much of Eugene Roberts' life since Mr. Malcolm must have been assemblages like these, where the abstract is everything, where Fancy advances Suggestion A, where Common

205

Sense may occasionally demur, and where Fancy ends the debate by leaping to Suggestion B, the issue being always not matter but manner. In such atmospheres, Common Sense must always have looked very much as Detective Roberts did sitting there now, with its meek body and its unintruding eyes, not as much timid as lonesome, so circumstanced as have known no employment except as servant to Fancy, conscripted squire to a succession of errant knights. If Common Sense, as embodied by Detective Roberts, had not bothered to report Afeni Shakur's Fancy, even though it was so perfectly tailored to the Fancy of his employers, the police officials, it was because Common Sense had not taken Fancy seriously enough to think it worth recording. Less and less was it easy to know just how Detective Roberts would have answered if he had been asked whether Mr. Phillips' grasp upon reality now was to any measurable extent stronger than William King's had been. Roberts was the chief witness to the plot that possessed Mr. Phillips' entire imagination; and who could say, listening to Gene Roberts, whether that plot had seemed to him made of matter or of moonshine?

All that had become entirely clear is that no secret agent ought to have begun his penetration of the Black Revolution with an assignment to investigate Malcolm X if the underground life was ever again to command his unmixed commitment and reward any sense of purpose he might have. An apprenticeship to Mr. Malcolm found and Mr. Malcolm lost could only make the journeyman too snobbish to give fair credit to such lesser personages as remained for him to spy upon. To compare was inevitably to become cynical.

After Malcolm X, Special Services promoted Patrolman Roberts to detective third-class and certified that place on the career ladder which makes secure the civil servant and exempts him from any compulsion to prove himself by conspicuous display. For a long while thereafter, his employers seem to have been satisfied to let him drift as he pleased. He made do awhile with the sweepings of the streets, hanging about first with Mr.

206

Malcolm's Organization of Afro-American Unity, a church whose light had been extinguished, and next with Charles Kenyatta's Mau Mau, where he listlessly learned and taught karate for battles about whose approach he could hardly have felt either confidence or alarm. The counterrevolutionary agent, to enjoy his work, would almost have to believe in the reality of the revolution. By every visible sign, Detective Roberts could not even then have been more disillusioned with the revolution than if he had ever authentically served it.

A few of his reports to Special Services from the time while he was in midpassage between Malcolm X and Huey P. Newton happened to be bound up in the sheaf of documents from his Panther period that Mr. Phillips had been required to show the defense. These fugitive scraps were chiefly remarkable for their condescension toward the objects of Detective Roberts' inquiry that was not only at variance with our conventional image of the secret agent who can only advance himself by exaggeration of the dimensions of his quarry but at odds too, in the unconcealed hauteur of their aesthetic standards, with the bearing of this witness himself, so clerkly, so automatic in the recitation of memories set forth as though they had been merely shoveled into his store with no distinction between what might be worth keeping and what might not.

Nothing was now visible of the critical intelligence that could so precisely judge the terrible Kenyatta as no more than a street hawker without even an appointed corner of his own, sharpening his urge for black revenge for no purpose except improving himself as article of sale to any instrument of state that might notice him enough to buy him. For Detective Roberts had been an agent who would report from the very heart of the secret—"Kenyatta is uptown telling the people to arm themselves; nothing significant; usual black power rhetoric"—or curtly dismiss the invitation of some Flaming Spear or other to enlist in some new battalion—"I told him I was tired of joining bullshit organizations." What could his superiors have made of such nuances except to overlook them and bring him here to court, to do his best with their conviction that his mission had been consequential in the absence of any such belief of his own?

The Panthers seem to have freshened Detective Roberts' spirit without quickening his interest. They were new to a place where he had long been; they were noisy and if he had ever been even noticeable, he had talked himself out. They were disorderly and he was so routine by habit that, even after his superiors had recommended that he miss a Panther meeting now and then "so I wouldn't be too conspicuous," he ended up having missed almost none. The one anecdote remembered by the defendants from his Panther tour suggested an almost compulsive obedience to any appointed round: he had been driving a car that Richard Moore was directing upon some directionless pilgrimage and had rendered so dumb a fidelity to each of Moore's successive whims for wandering without purpose that he either did not think about or dare to intrude with mention of the state of the fuel gauge until they just ran out of gasoline far from any familiar place. He would exist in the memory of most of the defendants as little more than an automaton; yet the Roberts who is audible in our only undisputed record of his bearing in the company of the Panthers turns out much more complicatedly human than that. Special Services had attached to him a transmitter that preserved the proceedings of the March 11th, 1969, meeting of William King's security section, a piece of the annals of revolution unique for those coughs that welcome the benign passage of the Good Brother Marijuana. And there and only there can Gene Roberts be recognized as someone who is set apart from the others not by his silences but by something close to the fluency of the pedagogue with his juniors.

He can be elder brother, solicitous: "Hey, what you doing, man?" (Sound of coughing heard.) "Hey, where you going?" (Sound of cougher heard departing.) "Hey, Baba, where are you going, man, with your pneumoniafied self?" He can be elder brother, teasing: if William King chooses to conjure up some combat patrol of his fantasy in the vacant darkness of the

Bronx Botanical Gardens, Eugene Roberts agrees to go with him there, "since you're playing super-mole and shit."

Most of all he is the lay brother among the acolytes, holding discourses whose every turn is by now habitual to him. The ideas that were at their dawn for the others had long ago passed toward twilight for Gene Roberts; there is no problem they begin to think about he has not already examined again and again; and he has stored up the keenest observations that he had heard in prior conversations exactly like these and serves them forth to these apprentices struggling to discover what he could already describe.

How, they wonder, can a man disguise himself?

Lee Roper has a glimmer: "Like, if the pig come up at night, by me having on this suit and the turtleneck makes me look like a college boy. They relate to the suit coat. But, if I had on blue jeans or something, [it'd] be a different thing."

"Yes," Detective Roberts answered, "they *do* have a Cinderella mentality."

"Learn to shrink yourself to the size of the company you are in; take their tone, whatever it is," Lord Chesterfield told his son. Since that is a lesson even more valuable for the secret agent than for the young gentleman making his way through more comfortable forms of insinuation, Eugene Roberts would not have been the model agent he was if he had not learned and rigorously practiced its rules. But, in these passages, there is an assertion of the self as above the company, the unmistakable intrusion of a mockery directed above as well as below him, as condescending to those superior officers whose bias can lead them to trust a man on his appearance alone as it is to these comrades he pretends are his whose want of sophistication drives them to enterprises as childish as the stalking of imagined enemies in deserted parks.

There seem to have been no other remembered occasions that brought the interior laughter buried so deep in Detective Roberts close enough to the surface as almost to be heard. But then there were no other occasions when he knew that the police department was listening. Might it not have occurred to him then that this being the only chance he might ever have to challenge the illusions of his unknown masters, he ought to suspend the caution that otherwise inhibited him from making fun of the illusions of his victims to their faces? For any such veiled and lonely struggle to instruct the higher policemen in the difference between what he saw and what they insisted on thinking he saw could, if made, only have been carried out in the style he brought to the part that he was playing this once for their ears. Those hints of derision toward the conspirator might have been designed to tell his auditors with how little seriousness they ought really to take the conspiracy and the soft and teasing reminder of how hard it is for policemen to tell appearance from reality could be an almost thunderous exhortation to them to commence to understand the difference.

In any case, his hauteur toward the Panthers had been made apparent, however gentled by an unexpected affection, and could only have been increased by the experience of doing business with persons so fitful of purpose.

On February 20th, King had ordered him to go with Walter Johnson to survey department stores and find the most practical locations for fire bombs and dynamite. Roberts met Johnson at the Harlem Panther office five days later and they went together to the Kaufman army surplus stores, where they asked where they could buy guns and the salesman suggested Abercrombie & Fitch.

"Johnson wanted to look," Detective Roberts later explained to Carol Lefcourt, "so we went over to take a look. . . . We had been told to go to several stores and we were going, so there was no sense for me waiting for him to come back to Kaufman's so I went with him."

At Abercrombie & Fitch they happened upon a find of the sort that only occasionally comes to explorers who wander without charts. "Wall to wall shotguns," Roberts reported to King, who knew enough of the tone required from Authority in the presence of Intelligence Information to respond, "Obviously a target of extreme importance." Roberts had also observed the rubber rafts on the first floor, a revelation that would later set King again to defining: "We could use that shit, man." Roberts' and Johnson went off to Macy's, where, as chief of mission, Roberts looked at toys for his child, tried on some gloves, speculated to Johnson about the efficacy of trying to steal them, and, rather by the way, convassed the premises for their vulnerability to an *attentat*.

"Johnson made the statement that around the clothes would be a good possibility for fire bombs, also around the stockroom would be a good place for fire bombs. The first floor, where they had a lot of jewelry, handbags, sweaters, and what-have-you, Johnson said would be a good place for some kind of explosive."

"From Macy's we went over to Korvette's and we went from the basement to the ninth floor of Korvette's. . . . The first place we went in [was] the basement where they had the motor oils, some butane containers, propane canisters, and Johnson said it would be agreeable to place fire bombs or explosives there."

They had decided to return to these sites on March 10th and fix the considerable amount of detail left vague in their first expedition. But Johnson failed to appear and Roberts felt no impulse to go alone. The next night, when they reported to King, they could only offer the inadequate gleanings of a single unsystematic patrol. Their summary of findings began in some confusion with Johnson locating the guns on the third floor of Korvette's instead of the ninth floor of Abercrombie & Fitch and being corrected by Roberts. They went on to make nothing very clear about their survey except its desultory nature. They had written down no notes, and sketched no plans, and had been most casual about checking the security systems in any of the stores.

They would, King said, have to return and bring back the essential details:

"Damned prime target, Abercrombie and Fitch. . . . Find out what sort of security personnel they have on the floor. . . . Time yourself, see how long it takes to get from the entrance to the room where the things are. . . . Then you find out the best time to draw attention away from that department. . . . Excluding the guns, the only thing we're interested in is a psychological thing of keeping a lot of people away from the stores. . . . Check out where all the stuff is flammable . . . stuff like rugs. . . . We're just interested in, you know, things that would cause a lot of confusion and slow people up; the thing of it is they're going to block exits and cause an awful lot of confusion, cause a lot of superficial injuries."

In the interval before yielding to his fantasy of destruction, King had given Johnson and Roberts a most sober schema of what they needed to find out to give any plan he might have any tinge of practicality. Yet neither of them seems ever to have gone back to the stores and carried out this further survey. Roberts was relieved of the assignment almost at once and set to playing super-mole with King in the Queens freight terminus of the New Haven railroad. He had assumed that while he was creeping and crawling so strenuously, Johnson would comfortably be cruising the stores. Still, more than two weeks later, when the security section talked about the subject again, Roberts was surprised to find that, far from Johnson having anything to add, King was still entirely dependent upon Roberts' own inadequate self for all details on these targets:

"King asked me to give Afeni Shakur a rundown on the department stores that Johnson had been doing. . . . I began to give Afeni Shakur a rundown on the stores that were being done and I told her that Johnson had stated that Macy's 34th Street and Alexander's 59th Street were prime targets, and that I agreed with Johnson."

King seems to have made no protest when he heard that Abercrombie & Fitch had disappeared from the battle plan, his prime target being just so easily forgotten. Afeni Shakur had made no reply worth remembering; and the vision of her as terrorist at the ready was thereupon dissolved by Gene Roberts' recollection of her stance the night before:

"King [had] told Afeni Shakur that he wanted her to pick two reliable sisters for our thing around Easter, and Afeni Shakur stated that she felt there were no such sisters available.

212

He stated that he still wanted the two sisters because the brothers would look less suspicious with two women."

The next night, after Detective Roberts had labored to put the nullity he remembered about Macy's into some efficient form, King had reminded Afeni Shakur, "I know what you said about the two sisters, but we want the two sisters anyway"; and, this time, she had made no reply at all.

This feckless conversation had run its changes just a week before April 2nd, 1969, the date that the district attorney had certified as marked out for a bombing assault upon "the midtown stores of Macy's, Alexanders, Bloomingdale's, Korvette's, and Abercrombie and Fitch." Here at last was the evidence for the lurid visions that had stalked through Mr. Phillips' head from the moment he had seen *The Battle of Algiers* and those women who filled its frames, moving alone through crowded places, leaving behind them pocketbooks filled with explosive devices intricately timed and then tripping away with death behind them. *The Battle of Algiers* was fading already as a model for any battle plan as incoherent as this one. And it had certainly faded rather soon from the consciousness of Walter Johnson, who seems to have drawn from it nothing except the notion that only pocketbooks were important. He had been conscientious only in searching out the pocketbook counters in each store; the symbol had gotten so mixed up with the cause in his mind that he was convinced that the deed could not be done at all unless each Panther woman could find herself a brand new pocketbook and leave her time bomb there.

Everything Detective Roberts had reported thereafter pointed to planning as inchoate as Johnson's part in the execution. William King had requisitioned only two women for an attack designed to strike five department stores at one and the same moment. Afeni Shakur, their recruiting officer, had been doubtful about her chances of finding even those two.

Such was the terror whose imminence Mr. Phillips had brandished in half a dozen courtrooms, faced down any doubts that might have troubled the judges before him, roused Justice Marks to set $100,000 bail on each defendant—"[because]

213

certain acts might be performed *today* . . . and result in the death of many hundreds of people in certain department stores"—and to the commissioner of corrections to provide that while he was holding them even before trial, "they be considered extremely dangerous . . . and kept separate and apart from each other at all times." No response this desperate could have been founded on anything except the conviction that an assault had been planned upon valuable property and respectable persons, and that its execution had been at hand. Even policemen and district attorneys could not have invoked such stringencies on a show of menace to nothing except station houses. Now the air could almost be felt going out of this horrid portent: whatever he might have contrived for Independence Day or Christmas, William King had been plainly unready for Easter.

And then, while defense counsel and perhaps even defendants too could for the first time abandon all belief in the Easter plot, it became clearer that, alone in the courtroom, Detective Roberts had never had a belief to give up. For, even if he had found in William King's troops the will such deeds would require, he had the best evidence that his captain did not remotely possess the means.

On March 30th, King telephoned Roberts and asked him to take some pills from the team's combat medicine supply and bring them to him at the Dyre Avenue subway station where he was struggling under the burden of a cold through his workday in the change booth. After the delivery, Roberts tarried by King's cage to say that he had, as instructed, found some aerosol cans which could be used for Molotov cocktails.

"King said, 'Good. Keep them at your pad until told what to do with them . . .' He said, 'We, the security section, may not hit the pig stations since we don't have any dynamite. If we get the dynamite, okay, but we're not relying on it.' He stated that one man will take one of the railroad stations and each man would do his own thing with Molotov cocktails."

Three days before what Mr. Phillips attested was to be the hour of its execution, the plot had no material resources except

214

those few aerosol cans. And Detective Roberts had small reason to suspect that King was concealing any store of armaments from him; King had known Roberts longer than any other member of the guerilla team; and, since no one else had been remotely as faithful to his duties, no one else could have been fitter to share any secret King might have. No promise impressed Roberts by now: on March 26th, with the dynamite already gone glimmering, King told him that Curtis Powell was going to New Jersey to buy materials to make gunpowder; and Roberts had judged that expedition so unlikely to be fruitful that he had not bothered even to report it to the police department.

On Monday morning April 1st, the day before the terror the police department had barely averted, Detective Roberts drove to Baltimore in the company of Richard Moore, Michael Tabor, and William King and was so lacking in any sense of his place in a conspiracy at the bursting point that he fell asleep and heard nothing that might have been said on the way down. They remained in Baltimore one hour, bought a rifle, and drove back home. Detective Roberts stayed awake on that part of the journey but to no useful purpose; he remembered no conversation that was of enough service for Mr. Roberts to include it in his evidence.

They reached New York around noon. The grand jury was sitting by then and Mr. Phillips had begun puzzling just where the best witness under the police department's command might be. Eugene Roberts was driving Richard Moore about, first to inquire about the automobile that the Panther Party wanted to buy and that the Ford Motor Company was most reluctant to finance, and then to the Freedom National Bank where "there was some discussion about a check," and then to deliver bundles of *The Black Panther*, and thereafter scurrying nowhere into the night while Mr. Phillips imagined them straining over the most meticulous and disciplined preparations for the next morning's deed. They, Moore and Roberts, finally wandered apart; and Detective Roberts went home, to be found there by Mr. Phillips and hastened before a grand jury

215

that could hardly have been any more alarmed than the witness was surprised by the weight of his evidence.

All that Eugene Roberts had observed would henceforth be defined by Mr. Phillips, the final receiving officer on his passage from hand to hand of stranger-porters, Roberts watching and listening and each of them bawling out what he had seen and heard in dimensions huge beyond any knowledge of his. That Roberts quite hated Mr. Phillips was the judgment of a psychologist enlisted by the defense to discover interior conflicts of that sort. Still, watching these two together, the relationship between them seemed afflicted less by dislike than by their simply not fitting together. There was something about Eugene Roberts that would not go into the box Mr. Phillips had built to hold him. It could not be said that he was resisting—he was indeed so accommodating in recitation as to seem if anything *too* mechanical—but there grew the sense that whole limbs of his were being not refused but, in ·some unfathomable but irreproachably correct fashion, held back from the package. Eugene Roberts' remembering did not even attempt to vault toward the heights of Mr. Phillips' imagining. The district attorney would hand him the paints and the brushes and he would study the design and then give it back unadorned and with its lines changed only by being blurred in the handling, with none of the wild reds of Mr. Phillips' vision, with, in fact, no tint of color at all. He seemed to say no more than that this was a fair representation of a subject he could hardly suggest was worth representing.

Looking back, long afterward, it could be said that Mr. Phillips lost his case in those moments when he was holding up this exhibit, all unconscious of the gap between what had been promised and what had now been delivered, and with each wavering line still a lurid splash to him. One could believe every fact in Detective Roberts' testimony without taking the smallest step toward accepting any of Mr. Phillips' inferences from it; Detective Roberts himself was the great wall against any such progression. He could not move us far enough toward

216

the official inference because he would so plainly never consider going there himself.

Those inadequate reconnaissances whose repair no one had bothered to attempt, the deficiency of explosives, the insistence of Afeni Shakur, their commander-designate, that there were no women to plant the bombs if there had been bombs to plant, and every other fact that stripped the department store plot of each condition necessary for belief had been displayed by Mr. Phillips' main witness on his direct testimony.

"I am shocked," Mr. Lefcourt said after Mr. Phillips had finished with Eugene Roberts. It was hard to know whether he was the more shocked because judges and district attorneys had been carried to so many cruelties by a peril this intangible or because the commitment of his clients was publicly being represented by conspiracies as incoherent as this evidence suggested. Most of Mr. Lefcourt was relieved—he could see that his case was no longer hopeless—but some small, romantic part of him had to blush for the pride of the Panthers in, and the admiration of white radicals for, the qualities expressed as their *badness*.

The evening after the next-to-the-last day of Detective Roberts' testimony for the people, Mr. Lefcourt returned to his office and got a telephone call from the bold Dharuba, unaccustomedly chastened. Yes, Dharuba said, the case was going well, but still . . . The regret in his tone made clear the suspicion that he might be being found out. As the talk went on, Mr. Lefcourt understood the wistful desire that Richard Moore could not bring himself to utter: it would be better for his pride if the defendants would all confess to having done what they had not done rather than let everyone see that they had done so little and, then, their reputation for *badness* restored, try to persuade the jury that it was a fine thing for them to have done what they had not done.

As for Mr. Lefcourt, however, the cheerful endurance of his clients had given him so many good reasons to respect them as persons that he had no need for further illusions about their dedication as terrorists. With an increase of comfort and no diminution of loyalty, he could thereafter profit from the great tactical advantage that belongs to the lawyer who has learned that he is not defending the Viet Cong and is opposed by judge and prosecutor who go on assuming that they are trying the Viet Cong. The most difficult task in any argument is to convince by hyperbole; and Mr. Lefcourt could feel himself relieved of that job even while Mr. Phillips gloried in it.

And Mr. Lefcourt had achieved with Detective Roberts at least the common ground of a sense of proportion; and that was enough to make the detective sound more like the defense's witness than the prosecutor's. Roberts had shrunk the case to a size where it better fit what Mr. Lefcourt had learned than what Mr. Phillips persisted in imagining.

After a while there settled upon the courtroom something almost like comity between the defendants and the cardinal witness against them. Afeni Shakur and Michael Tabor, commissioned to cast the outrage of the victims of the secret agent into his very face, slumbered across the defense table while he was testifying and drowsed through their turn to cross-examine. Even Detective Roberts, whose nights were so much tidier now, seemed to give way to a communal somnolence. His mustache began to droop; and even the sadness that had been the only expression in his large, brown eyes had faded away, leaving them so blank against the freshness of his light brown skin that his face seemed almost to have been made up for some party and to have stayed there too long. He withdrew further into himself and took to swaying back to await the question and forward to give the answer in the slow rocking of one who nods. He had started his motor at Mr. Phillips' touch; he had even run it faster at the stimulus of Mr. Lefcourt's mention of Malcolm X; but now he was idling. Nothing would provoke him; and it could be understood that, long before he came here, his private mind had measured out for him just how far he would go to damage these defendants and that now, having reached that stopping point, nothing, not even annoyance by hostile lawyers, would push him further.

218

The defense too had come to recognize this separate peace of Roberts' and all their lawyers but one began to treat him with unexpected gentleness as someone who, by some curious trick of the will, had made himself their witness. The exception, as ever in such exchanges, was Mr. Crain, whose preconceptions as instrument of revolutionary vengeance and son of a psychiatrist were proof to any evidence that the enemy could possibly be the friend and went burrowing relentlessly for the source of an imputed malign ambition that was probably never present and certainly long gone.

"Isn't it a fact," Mr. Crain insisted, "that you could never make it with the other guys in the neighborhood?"

"No," the witness answered.

"You weren't a very good ballplayer," Mr. Crain pursued.

"Average, yes," the witness answered.

"And you didn't feel that the jobs you had before becoming a policeman were jobs where you weren't getting any recognition?" Mr. Crain was closing in by now almost halloing his way from the view to the death.

"Not really," Detective Roberts answered. "They were, to my opinion, mediocre jobs, and I knew I could do a lot better. So I just went out and proved to myself that I could do a lot better."

Here was no game usefully to be hunted by innuendo. Eugene Roberts seemed the last of men to be tempted by the breath of Fame; and, such questionable susceptibility aside, every part of his body seemed now working to convey its conviction that Fame could hardly stoop to attend any victory over conspirators presenting so remote a danger as these did.

Mr. Bloom engaged the mystery in terms more kindly but not noticeably more successful:

MR. BLOOM: You had dinner at Richard Moore's, made by Iris Moore, isn't that right?

DETECTIVE ROBERTS: I believe so.

MR. BLOOM: Does that make you feel one way or another about testifying against Mr. Moore?

DETECTIVE ROBERTS: No.

219

MR. BLOOM: You don't care, is that correct?

DETECTIVE ROBERTS: It is not the point that I don't care.

The mystery of Eugene Roberts abided, but the mysterious menace of the Black Panthers had departed beyond recall, having been waved away by the detective who had been presented as knowing them best. Near the end, Mr. McKinney found himself moving so conveniently through Eugene Roberts' patent inability to believe in the serious portent of anything he had heard as to be emboldened to take the ultimate leap: "You really didn't think anything was going to happen, did you?"

Detective Roberts rocked forward, heard duty call from far away, and rallied to its summons to no further extent than to answer: "I personally believed something was going to be done, but I didn't know when."

Duty had become a voice audible only from a long distance for all parties, even for the defendants, who almost had to remind themselves that it was incumbent upon them to hate him for what he had done. "I guess," said Joan Bird, "he is what they told us about—just a tool of the ruling class." There was in this observation much less outrage than delight at coming upon a case of nature imitating doctrine so faithfully as to produce an instrument of class oppression who seemed himself so precoded, someone who, even when she had known him as a brother, could be remembered not as ever conversing but as always reciting.

The defendants attempted the forms of anger: when Mr. Katz announced the end of his cross-examination of Eugene Roberts by saying quite gently, "I'm through with this witness," Richard Moore roused his sleep-sunk self to a simulation of revolutionary dismissal and called out, "Get him away. Electronic nigger!" But there was an absence of animus in his tone; and some weeks later, when Mr. Phillips was well into the testimony of Ralph White, and Richard Moore well along toward his own private disaster, someone observed at lunch

220

that, in some curious way, Eugene Roberts had run his course most respectably and Moore answered, "Yeah, that Yedwah's another kind of cat. He's not the man Gene is."

He and Roberts had spent months together in a party so poor that what paltry chance to steal it could offer would so strain the thoughtless and almost innocent avidity of Richard Moore as to leave no room for anyone else to sweep up the petty cash and boldly proclaim its allotment to the brothers in the jails. But everyone had managed to eat; and it would have been tactless for one to ask the other how he did it. The Street assumes that everyone has his private something on the side. Eugene Roberts' something had been to be a policeman. Now after twenty months of what had been done to them by what he was doing on the side, there had gone to work for Roberts that inexplicable benediction of the Street, which understands what cannot be understood and pardons what ought not to be forgiven.

Ralph White took Eugene Roberts' place, on the stand, gave his name and rank as a detective third-grade, recited his badge number and established himself as the implement of ordered, bureaucratic procedures which could neither be recognized from his entrance with a walk so much like Dharuba's nor recollected through the long tenure on the witness chair that would follow for him. The mechanical had been succeeded by the spontaneous and all that had been solid became liquid.

Almost at once his official name and calling were displaced from the mind; Ralph White could be thought of only as Yedwah Sudan, as Anthony Costone had *become* Lumumba Shakur; Alice Williams, Afeni Shakur; Richard Moore, Dharuba; Michael Tabor, Cetewayo; and William King, Kinshasa, the last meaning Congo and appropriate to dark imaginings. For these are names for roles, and the Street is closest to being real when it is most a theatre, as Ralph White would be most authentic because he was so not-quite-trustworthy. Here could be recognized the man who is never secure from the doubts of sober persons: as he had told the grand jury, his police superiors had made him report to them in person twice

221

a week "to find out if I might be suspect"—just a joke of theirs and his, he was careful to explain. He was the gamester, to be enjoyed but always intently to be watched. Mr. Phillips owed to Yedwah such few gaieties as lit the dark of his brooding upon that ambience he was commissioned to destroy. When the district attorney observed that he had almost come to like Lumumba as someone who would give you the last puff off his reefer, it seemed certain that an image provided by Yedwah had lent this fugitive intrusion of affection to a doctrine otherwise so grimly punitive. But for Mr. Phillips to enjoy Yedwah was not to feel entirely safe with him. Otherwise, the district attorney would hardly have presented his proof of the events of March, 1969, before offering his best witness to the events of January, 1969. He took his witnesses out of the chronological order usual in the state's presentation of the facts alleged. But then, Roberts' manner suited the gravity of the case, while his story didn't; and White's story suited that gravity while his manner didn't; and manner took precedence over story.

Would the witness, Mr. Phillips opened, tell the jury about the events at the Ellsmere Tenants Council on January 14, 1969?

"I told Lumumba," Detective White began, "that Afeni had been telling people that I was a pig and that I didn't like it. He just grinned and said she was an emotional sister; and he says, 'Well, are you?' and he grinned. . . . I went into the backroom and shot a couple of shots into the tabletops. Lumumba, Mshina, and others who were there said, 'Take it easy' and he said he would talk to the sister, that she was just emotional."

And did he, Mr. Phillips went on, have a conversation with Lumumba Shakur later that afternoon?

"Yes," Ralph White answered, "he said there was dynamite hidden behind the refrigerator at the Ellsmere Tenants Council and I shouldn't do my thing."

Later, he would enlarge upon this scene at Mr. Lefcourt's urging:

"Lumumba . . . asked Mshina—should he tell me? 'Should

222

I tell Yedwah?' And they smiled and said something and Lumumba said, 'Hey, Yedwah, there is some dynamite hidden behind the refrigerator. So you should not do your thing.' It was kind of whispered. And then like he and Mshina kind of cracked up a little bit, laughed a little bit. I just said, 'Wow! Don't worry about that. Wow! Don't worry about that! Power.' "

With Yedwah, narrative had returned to its source as anecdote. This tale might not be true. But, if it were, it would have happened this way, as things happen on the Street where one man shows himself *bad* and the other cannot resist showing himself *badder* and consequences as terrible as two years in prison for eleven people can begin as often as not in a moment when someone is grinning at somebody else. If Yedwah was not the Truth, he was unmistakably the Life.

Mr. Phillips conducted him through the evening after Lumumba and Mshina had teased him with their secret—his return to the office by dark, his confirmation of the fact of the dynamite, and his report to his superiors. The next night, he had gone back, removed the dynamite in its attaché case, been driven to the bomb squad by a sergeant and a detective, and sat outside in their car for two hours until they brought back the attaché case filled with the counterfeit explosive that Detective Gleason had molded of clay and oatmeal.

As pieces of art, these sticks had seemed to him anything but persuasive; he told Mr. Phillips that "It looked horrible—soft and mushy—and the ends had to be tucked in and the wrapper kept unraveling itself. I tried to tuck it in and keep that wrapper from falling out."

At last, most uneasy, he had to give up and restore the attaché case to Lumumba's chosen hiding place. That afternoon, Lumumba Shakur pulled back the refrigerator, took out his treasure, sat himself down upon a milk crate, opened the case, and examined his dynamite.

"He was tucking the ends in and trying to make the wax paper stick," Ralph White later told Mr. Crain. "He was exam-

223

ining it and he looked—he was scratching his beard—indicating like he was curious or something; and he was tucking the ends and he turned up and examined it."

Yedwah remembered that he had endured the long doubts induced by this scrutiny with his hand in the desk drawer where he kept his .45 pistol. Finally, "Lumumba made five sticks per bundle. . . . He went to his desk and came back with a blasting cap and a cylinder and nonelectrical blasting cap and he came back with a fuse about a foot long and the fuse was orange with a very little light yellow in it. . . . He took the fuse and stuck it in the blasting cap and stuck the blasting cap in the fuse into the dynamite and then he starts throwing it up in the air, the dynamite, the fuse, and the blasting cap. . . . I told him he could blow the whole place up. He said not to worry about it, he knows what he is doing."

Mshina had taken away his two bundles in a paper bag that afternoon; and next day, William King had entered with Cheryl Spencer and his own attaché case. "I said, 'Power, sister, power, brother, what's happening?' Lumumba and he went back to the refrigerator and I saw Lumumba hand Kinshasa two bundles of dynamite . . . [and] Kinshasa hung around for about five minutes and he said 'power' and left."

When everyone else had gone, Yedwah reached behind the refrigerator, lifted the attaché case, judged it empty, and knew the event had passed from him onto its unknown track. He had been privy to a conspiracy for three days, the first and last of his term as a secret agent, and his experience of *knowing* had ended with the departure of these bundles. He would spend the rest of the night in a helpless, curiously passive effort to be knowing again. At the end of the afternoon, Lumumba Shakur had sealed the attaché case again and told Yedwah that "all the stuff is still in there." Yedwah knew that had been a lie, and an inexplicably useless one if Lumumba had let him watch Mshina carry off two bundles and had not even tried to conceal those gestures which had so powerfully suggested that Kinshasa had carried off the rest. Yet that statement, at once deliberately and ineffectually false, was enough to reawake in

224

Yedwah the sense of being untrusted and once again in danger of being found out. He called Lumumba Shakur ·with some story about needing to borrow some money: "He said he didn't have the money and was going to Rockland Palace." He hung up the telephone and tried no further. There had come back upon him one of those "sometimes" when, as he later remembered, he was afraid of Lumumba.

And yet that fear may have been in some ways a comfort. To have been found out as a policeman, awful though the consequences might be, would mean to be taken seriously while every other alternative that explained his exclusion from any part in the deed meant only that he had been found out as someone not to be taken seriously at all. For he was close to the Harlem Africans he conceived as the party's elite; they would drink and smoke with him; and in their company he talked with a *badness* very like theirs, if only because, as he explained to Mr. Bloom, "If someone said, 'What we got to do is start icing more pigs,' I'm going to say, 'Right on, yeah'; I'm not going to sit there and talk about Mrs. Pug's Bakery."

Even so, Yedwah must have drawn a more-than-ordinary zest from those aspects of the Life that are self-display. Just a few days after he joined the party, he made the acquaintance of Donald Weems, who would become his friend as Kuwasi Balagoon, when Kuwasi asked him the way to a party meeting at Long Island University. Yedwah's visibility as guidepost to the wayfarer shone through his recollection: "I was wearing my Black Panther garb—black clothing, black pants, black shirt, black beret with buttons—Free Huey buttons, Eldridge Cleaver buttons, Bobby Hutton buttons."

Still his talents and services were largely as hustler. These qualities made him the source of the only political patronage the Panther Party would ever get. In October of 1968, he had met Shirley Jones, director of the Bronx Action Group, a poverty agency. She had told him that the Ellsmere Tenants Council, one of its subsidiaries, was about to be funded, and offered to make him its director. He hired Lumumba Shakur as supervisor and six other Panthers as Ellsmere's staff. His only

225

subsequent explanation of that favor came from the divided self he struggled to keep in balance all through those months.

It had been, he insisted, his own idea and not his supervising detective's that he hire the Panthers:

"First of all, it would put me I thought beyond maybe suspicion. I had a cover job, number one. I thought it was a chance for me to keep an eye on, let's say, keep an eye on people in the party. I also thought there was a chance for us really to do something constructive for the community, I mean doing something constructive, you know."

The pursuit of his duties as Ellsmere's director spent itself in pushing its payroll through the stagnant conduits of New York's Human Resources Administration and in tending the garden of his friendship with Mrs. Jones. The burden of service to the poor fell upon Lumumba Shakur, who took it up with an energy unexpected in someone whose nature had seemed, from all previous testimony, subject only to the antic or the destructive impulse. "Lumumba was always first in the office," Yedwah remembered. Lumumba Shakur was so punctual that when he happened to be late on the morning of November 26th, that unaccustomed lapse could be offered as proof that he had been up late the night before bombing the Twenty-sixth Police Precinct.

Even Ralph White had caught some of this spirit of service; he had abstained, he later said, from reporting to the police on the efforts of the Panthers to help the Ellsmere Tenants except to observe to his supervisors "how depressed he was to see these conditions."

And yet Yedwah could never sustain any disposition for troublesome affairs; and by February, when the Ellsmere Tenants Council's budget came up for renewal, the inconvenience of it all decided him to let it die:

"Different little problems were coming up with the staff, and I didn't want to be bothered," he told Mr. Katz. "At the time, I didn't want the program to go into other hands. We were informed by the Human Relations Administration that we would be funded again if we submitted all our previous

226

vouchers. I just didn't want myself and that staff to operate the program."

It was that want of fixed purpose, for good works or bad ones, Yedwah's brothers seem to have discovered early in his mission.

"I supposed they trusted me to be a section leader," he confessed to Mr. Bloom. "But they never asked me to come with them. Different persons in the party might have told me they shot a pig, but they never gave particulars, and they never asked me to come with them."

What had directly happened to Yedwah in the party could then never quite support the terrors he assumed to exist in the shadows just beyond his sight. He could remember all the words, but their force kept being dissipated by recollections of scenes all else but purposeful:

"Lumumba said that they were going to set up a TCB squad; they were going to harass the pigs, they were going to put bombs in garbage cans and they were going to patrol the pigs. . . . It was one of those spontaneous meetings. Dharaba was saying that when the pig vamps on the brother, we're going to vamp on the pig. And Kuwasi was running around, jumping up and down ripping off some crazy poem."

Then there were those tests of the revolutionary, their proclamation so frequent, their existence so vague. ("Sekou and Lumumba said they had been tested and they had proved themselves; they had shot at cops.") Yedwah, for the sake of a pride that may have been even more personal than professional, wanted very much to assert that he too had been tested; his memory could transmute every occasion of mere intimation into the realized experience:

One summer night in Baltimore he and Lumumba Shakur had been drinking terrible bourbon and smoking reefers and wandering in a park.

"And he says, 'If we see a pig, we're going to deal with him.' So I said, 'Yes, sure, I don't care.' Then, we came to a little clearing [and] we saw a police car. I just told Lumumba that it was too far away and I probably couldn't reach it with that

227

gun. And we walked around a little more. And we didn't find any policeman by himself or alone.

"If that incident in Baltimore was supposed to be a test, then I was tested. That was making a move to kill someone."

Once, he and Kuwasi had gone smoking at Lumumba's and were making their way home on the subway. Kuwasi leaned over and said, " 'Hey, Yedwah,' did I want to go out with him tonight and shoot a pig and he would show me how to do it and he had done it before and he said it was easy, all we had to do was walk up behind him and shoot him in the back and then split. I said I don't know, I'd see him and let him know." But Kuwasi never returned to the subject.

And, work though he had at trying to seem bad, Yedwah Sudan seemed to have made his way as a serious man only with those women who, like himself, were separated from the center of authentic *badness*. He would sit and smoke with Shirley Jones and tell her stories of how he had drawn his shotgun on his landlord and how the holes in his walls had been left by its pellets. Sayeeda Shakur, Lumumba's first wife, used to tell him that he was a righteous brother underappreciated by the others; Rosemary Bird liked him; and he would report each such compliment to his superiors as the only attestations of the trust he wanted to think he had established for himself. Once Sayeeda sent him what he took to be a love letter. She had ended by asking him to destroy it unless it meant something to him; and he had torn the letter up and drawn a rebuke from his superiors for tampering with evidence.

And now he was sitting out the night of January 17th at home alone in that mood, one came to feel, which so often used to seize him at the Ellsmere Tenants Council when he would go back to his apartment and wear away the afternoon in immobile solitude, days when Lumumba would come looking for him and grin, "Hey, Yedwah, man, you looked stoned out" and when, as he remembered:

"I had just had it—Ellsmere Tenants Council, people there, the Panther Party, different things; I just was tired of doing the job I was doing. . . . In some ways, it bothered me."

Lumumba's whole bearing in the affair of the dynamite had been so final a dismissal: to tell him about it, almost as a joke, to let him watch its transfer to the posts and then never so much as suggest that there might be a place for Yedwah in any serious business. These were all successive demonstrations of contempt equally for his capacity to harm as to help. And Yedwah seems only to have sat fixed in the consciousness of having been judged and to have lacked even the will to go to Rockland Palace on the chance of finding the broken thread there.

Except for intermittent inquiries from his superintending policeman, the telephone rang only twice. The first time it was Sayeeda Shakur:

"She said she was angry with Lumumba, that Lumumba was going to do something that night. She said she was angry because Lumumba had taken Afeni with him to do whatever it was they were going to do, and that Lumumba wouldn't take her, because she didn't know how to use a gun."

They both had been found wanting. Two hours later, there was a call from Bayo Patterson, Ali Bey Hassan's woman, who had missed Yedwah at Rockland Palace:

"She called to say that two things were supposed to happen and one went okay and the other got effed up. She said something about somebody coming in limping."

The next day at Ellsmere "everybody was whispering and things were much different from what they ordinarily were." Lumumba took his grin to the Forty-fourth Precinct to offer his help to the captured Joan Bird and was promptly arrested himself. There were scurryings in the shadows; Kuwasi had shaved his beard and cut his hair and Sekou had vanished into New Jersey; Dharuba said that he and Michael Tabor were underground, and that it was up to Yedwah to keep the party together.

And yet none of those who had done the deed appear to have scurried as Yedwah did, in aimless, incessant imitation of the posture of a fugitive from punishment for his acts. The only picture of him in this fit comes from Robert Collier upon whom he descended on the night of January 18th pleading for shelter as a prime suspect in what had "gone down" uptown. Collier would decide afterward that Ralph White had come to entrap him; and White's version of their conversation *would* later serve as one of the more visible of the scanty scraps of whatever evidence was the excuse for Collier's being held in prison for two years at $100,000 bail. But whatever the effect of that expedition, Yedwah might well have been drawn to it less by any zeal for the hunt than by the need to exhibit himself. In that case Collier would be one auditor who, having avoided the play, might be induced to believe that here was one of the actors. All Collier remembered about the performance was its ambiguity. There was Yedwah standing on a corner and saying that he couldn't be caught, because he would break whenever the police put pressure on him. Even here on display there was some compulsion to signal that, if tested, he would come up short. Then Yedwah caught a cab and told its driver to take him to the Harlem River Drive, leaving Collier behind to puzzle over why someone in flight from pursuers uptown would go back uptown.

Lumumba Shakur came out of jail in February and he and Yedwah picked up again. But, with Ellsmere abandoned, Yedwah was drifting away from the Africans. He had taken up with Collier and Curtis Powell, whose images of action were grayer. Powell talked of raising bail for the Panthers in prison by selling Mao pamphlets or getting Art Blakey to record a Malcolm X album. They worked together in the Bronx Union of Concerned Parents; and, by March, Yedwah was so removed from the real action that his supervisors suggested that he stop hanging about with Curtis Powell and try to find out what was happening at the Harlem office. So he looked up Lumumba again so languidly that afterward he could barely remember that there had been a final evening when he waited while Afeni dressed Lumumba's children and then drove the family to Philadelphia; and he would be surprised to be told that this had happened on March 30th, only three days before the arrest. He had even stopped reporting to Special Services after March 24th.

"After speaking to my supervisors, I was under the impression that pretty soon I was coming from under. They would say, 'Just take it easy. It won't be too long now. Just watch yourself and be careful' and did I know of anything that was happening? And I said I didn't."

Near the end, Mr. Bloom asked Yedwah, "You had been a success, no more Klein's, Burns, TWA; you did what was expected of you; is that right?"

And Yedwah answered, "I just did a job, counselor."

And then there could almost be envisioned some moment when this would all be over, and Afeni and Lumumba would be together again with Lumumba's children and her own and a visitor would come upon Ralph White sitting with them, accepting the last puff off the last reefer, and Lumumba would be saying, "Hey, Yedwah, how come you did what you did to us?"

But Afeni would not be back with Lumumba. Their friendship had outlasted it all—the baby that was not his; the party quarrel where Huey Newton had cast out Lumumba and let her stay, without asking either of them; the murder of Sam Napier, who had been her close friend and the enemy of the Harlem faction. With all these shadows between them, they still sat side by side in a domestic concord that had survived their love and triumphed over the months that had made them so different from one another. For he was what he always was and she was no longer what she had been; she had become a mother; and the child was all. The sauciness was gone and the willed effrontery with it; and, in their absence, it could be understood that the Afeni of the words recalled by Roberts and White had not been the real Alice Williams but only a changeling child proving herself to Lumumba, the hard words only a mask for the terror that she might not have found a home.

She was back in prison; the whole burden of being face and voice for them all to the jury had, with Michael Tabor's flight, fallen upon her alone. Now she gathered herself and her child to herself and stood up to look upon Ralph White. The house of detention had stripped away the boots and the pants and the impudent bright skirts. She was left with the rag of a smock and the sweet, almost naked outline of the child growing, her body reduced to a single overwhelming reproach, "Why, Yedwah, have you done this to us?"

There followed the conversation that she and Yedwah and Lumumba would never have together. Her opening was uncertain, as though traces of her deference to the hunting male yet endured after the testing by Lumumba, the desertion by Dharuba, even the betrayal by Yedwah. She started as if Lumumba's troubles—indeed Lumumba's honor—were the only stake she had, and asked the witness about his relations with the first Mrs. Shakur, the one subject among Yedwah's trespasses upon their friendship about which she and Lumumba might be assumed as having forfeited any right to complain. That thought may have occurred to her too, because she let the matter trail off and asked:

"Were you afraid of Lumumba?"

"Sometimes," Ralph White answered. When she wondered aloud when those times might have been, Mr. Phillips hastened to the bench to warn, sidebar, that such inept questions might bring terrible harm to the defendants and that Mrs. Shakur was going to stumble into something about someone being shot in Brooklyn or all sorts of other things that ought not to be in this record.

So, her first path ruled improper, Mrs. Shakur turned to inquire why Detective White had expressed a poor opinion of the Black Panther Party to his superiors as early as November, 1968.

"There were some times," he replied, "when I thought the party was okay and there were some times when I thought the party wasn't moving progressively forward."

But, she recalled, he had reported to the Bureau of Special Services that "I am still under the impression that what the Panthers had put out for the people was zero."

232

He conceded that time had rendered that judgment more complicated:

"There were some things that the party was involved in that I thought was very beautiful. During the school decentralization issue, I thought that was beautiful and relating to the party program. There were people who tried, who emphasized the importance of getting out in the community and working more with people, and these people were never heard from. They were heard and then there was nothing else said. They were like set aside and somebody said we had to start offing the pigs, and these were the brothers that took over and they had these meetings and they still wouldn't let the community in these meetings."

AFENI SHAKUR: Was Lumumba Shakur involved in the struggle for decentralization?

DETECTIVE WHITE: Yes, he was.

AFENI SHAKUR: Were any of the other defendants involved in it?

DETECTIVE WHITE: Yes, they were.

AFENI SHAKUR: Then could you please tell us who were the people who pushed the other people aside?

"There were times when Tina Waites, Rosemary Bird, and other people were just talking about relating—about we should get some program and work the people in the community on some specific program. Then the party would go back into this *thing* about, okay, yeah that's good. Let's get together and have a meeting and we would start Mao again and reading from that Red Book."

The answers had commenced to be a little too long as the questions grew shorter and shorter. She had somehow reversed the ground; he was in the place where man is slightly desperate rather than she in the place where woman ought to be entirely so.

Abandoned, with no armor except her reproach, she had drawn him to that terrain where he would have to explain

233

himself. And so he explained as man so often has to woman—preaching over the corpse of his authority as though it were woman's destiny to tender it the respect due something still alive. And one began to understand that it is the particular pathos of the secret agent that he, who had only an assignment, has to describe it as an act of personal principle; and that Ralph White, after the deception that got him promoted and her imprisoned, still must assert himself the moral better of his victim, incapable of resisting the dare because unable to entertain the shame.

AFENI SHAKUR: Did you ever try to put a program into effect and be daunted by any of these defendants?

DETECTIVE WHITE: Well, I remember specifically—the Ellsmere Tenants Council was a program that could have worked. I can't remember offhand specifically what, but I know that there were different things that were happening, and I recall that the people—who—certain people who were trying to get, accomplish something specific where the party could go out and meet the community and actually talk about something relevant to the community.

He had begun to clutch for some moment in their lost time together that might remind her that she had been wrong then and that might distract her toward the recognition that he was what he had turned out to be, not because he had been paid to spy upon her, but because her conduct had destroyed the hope of serving the people he had brought to their comradeship. She had only to wait—having called up one-half of Ralph White's divided self for the discomfiture of the other.

"Do you remember those circulars, those throwaways, those questionnaires?" he went on. "They were pertaining to: What do you think about the Panther Party? What do you think about the police harassing the Panthers? There was nothing—well, one line was, can they—What can the Panther Party do for the community?"

"*No, I don't remember those,*" she answered, the tone now

234

hard and dry, the pace of her words quickening as his had. He had sounded as though he were running, and now she sounded as though she were pursuing, come down like the huntress upon the ground she had led him to be lost in.

AFENI SHAKUR: Do you remember telling this court and this jury that you didn't want the Ellsmere Tenants Council refunded?

DETECTIVE WHITE: Yes, I do.

AFENI SHAKUR: But you thought the Ellsmere Tenants Council was a good program?

DETECTIVE WHITE: There were times in which certain persons spoke about taking the money and buying guns. There were certain other times persons spoke about investing the money in pot—*true*—and then selling it again. There were certain times—there were times when Lumumba and them tried to oust me from the program. And I was afraid when the time came I might come from under, that Shirley Jones might be left holding the bag.

I was afraid that, without me being there and, if they could have carried out the program to do what they wanted to do—I think that maybe I was being a bit self-centered but I thought I had the program's heart in mind—and I didn't want, after I left the program, I didn't want the program to get started with me introducing the program, and then all of a sudden after I am out, something happens and whatever happens falls on Mrs. Jones' shoulders. I didn't want her left holding some bag.

AFENI SHAKUR: Whose bag would she be holding?

DETECTIVE WHITE: Is that a question?

That one false step toward her old sauciness had taken her into that street where women are men's to control. He had wheeled and almost caught her there. Warned, she drew back to those private places where she knew so much more about him than he could about her, back to her deposit of what she had heard in his cross-examination and of the confessions that

235

she had divined beneath the assertions. She could recover only by spending her capital and reminding him that she alone had always known even if she had not until now quite understood:

AFENI SHAKUR: Do you remember my telling you that I thought you were a cop because you shot the guns when it wasn't necessary and because you acted crazy and because you were always putting people's lives in danger; do you remember that?
DETECTIVE WHITE: No, I don't remember that. [Still with the advantage.]
AFENI SHAKUR: Do you remember my telling you that you were irrational?
DETECTIVE WHITE: I don't remember that. [The advantage shaken.]
AFENI SHAKUR: Do you remember my telling you that you were subjective?
DETECTIVE WHITE: You might have said it, but I don't recall. [The advantage slipping.] I really don't. [The advantage gone away beyond recovery.]

He was hers again, and she asked him if he thought he had done good work as a Panther:

DETECTIVE WHITE: As far as the Panther program, yes, I carried out the things I was assigned. As far as carrying out the ten-point program, I couldn't do that. Nobody could do just like that.
AFENI SHAKUR: Who assigned you?
DETECTIVE WHITE: Various members of the police department, various members of the Panther Party.

His divided self lay in pieces before her; and he went on explaining how well he had done what Dharuba had told him to. She drew him back to Ellsmere.

DETECTIVE WHITE: I think for the limited amount of resources we had, the money we worked on, the budget we

236

worked under, and the staff—we were understaffed—I believe
we did a pretty good job.

AFENI SHAKUR: When you say we, who is we?

DETECTIVE WHITE: The staff, the entire staff that was
there.

AFENI SHAKUR: Does that include Lumumba Shakur?

DETECTIVE WHITE: Lumumba Shakur, Oba Green,
Mshina. Yes, they did a fairly good job, yes, they did. I think I
did about as best a job as I could. I wasn't assigned to hire the
Panthers. Initially, during the summer, when the party first got
started and everybody was really trying to get involved and
talking about helping the community, I thought it would be a
good idea to hire the Panthers. I also thought it was a chance
for us really to do something constructive for the community, I
mean really doing something constructive, you know.

And then it could mysteriously be felt that they come together where no stranger could see them, all quarrel suspended, in a refuge that belonged alike to the girl who had
talked of bombing police stations and the policeman who spied
upon her; they had come to the ground of that idea of the
community for which she had searched and he had begun by
betraying. Consciously or not, by an act of queenly grace, she
accorded to this poor creature some right to the possession of
that idea too; her questions stayed harsh in form but henceforth curiously gentled in tone.

AFENI SHAKUR: Did you think that you were stealing
from the people when you were receiving your Ellsmere Tenants Council salary?

DETECTIVE WHITE: No, I don't think I was stealing from
the people. No, I do not.

AFENI SHAKUR: You think you worked for it? You earned
it?

DETECTIVE WHITE: Yes, I did.

AFENI SHAKUR: You think you earned your police salary?

DETECTIVE WHITE: Yes, I do.

She turned to his statement before the grand jury that the Panther Party had been carried off from better purposes by "a poor people's clique." She sounded as though these words had wounded her more than those months in prison; and he apologized for his having chosen them and pleaded that what he had meant was:

"There were those, like, you had the people on the political side of the party and then you had the people who were more or less like the military part of the party. And the people who were on the, like, political side of the party, they never really hung out with the type on the military side. Like the people in that military clique, like after we had left political education meetings—right?—and everybody said 'Power' and 'Right on' and 'Power to the People' and take the subway home; and, after that we go to somebody's house, and it was certain persons who was always there and we would smoke and we would drink and we talked about—then you go talking about different things, what we should do this and we should do that, and it's always some—I am finished. I am sorry."

She had no suggestion except that he go on.

DETECTIVE WHITE: *You* were even at those other little meetings—after the meetings—and other people. These people who were always talking about getting something together, genuinely getting involved in the street, or something like that—they were always pushed aside.

AFENI SHAKUR: They were pushed aside by this clique. Is that correct?

DETECTIVE WHITE: When I say clique, you are making it sound like some solid object. I don't mean like a solid object. I mean verbally they were pushed aside. Mentally they were pushed aside. I believe even morally they were pushed aside. I think after a while, people felt they couldn't get anything. You know how the party first got started and there was lots of— excuse me. I am sorry.

AFENI SHAKUR: Which side of the party did these defendants belong to?

238

Here was a question about which, Ralph White replied, he could only offer his personal thoughts which could not reflect those of the police department. For she had finally, by some process hopeless to detect, separated him from Mr. Phillips and converted the simple into the conflicted. Lumumba, Shaba Om, and King seemed to him more the military sort, he said; Curtis Powell, Robert Collier, Ali Bey Hassan, and Clark Squire more the political; Joan Bird and Baba Odinga he had never had a chance to know.

AFENI SHAKUR: And myself?

DETECTIVE WHITE: I . . . [he hesitated]. As far as your talking to—about what we had to do in the streets, I thought it was good you know. But, as far as your involvement, I thought you were more military than political.

AFENI SHAKUR: *What involvement?*

DETECTIVE WHITE: These were just my own thoughts, things I had observed about the different persons I was observing, things you say, things I saw you doing. . . . You would go into a thing about pigs, and offing pigs and different—things about offing pigs and this pig is this and this pig is that; and, if you find a pig, deal with him and everything. But you also spoke about the community. But I thought your military motivations were more so than your words. I can't remember everything you said or everything you had done or even all your actions; but I know—and I am only basing this upon—I was only basing my own opinion on what I saw about you or about anyone else.

AFENI SHAKUR: *I understand that. But you said there were things you saw me doing, I just want to hear one thing.*

DETECTIVE WHITE: I remember when—excuse me—I remember a meeting at the Panther office, you were real charged up about—you went into a thing about icing the pigs, along with that military thing, and very emotional. I remember that, plus other things I can't remember offhand. I am only saying what I based my opinions on, what I had seen. What I had seen and heard and I had forgotten most of them.

239

Near the end of their journey, she led him very quietly through his concessions that he had never seen her carry a gun or kill anyone or bomb anyplace or rob anybody.

AFENI SHAKUR: Did you ever see me at Lincoln Hospital working?
DETECTIVE WHITE: Yes, I have.
AFENI SHAKUR: Did you ever see me at the schools working?
DETECTIVE WHITE: Yes, I have.
AFENI SHAKUR: Ever see me in the street working?
DETECTIVE WHITE: Yes, I have.
AFENI SHAKUR: Are these some of the things that led you to think I was military minded?
DETECTIVE WHITE: No, it was not.
AFENI SHAKUR: You don't remember the other things.
DETECTIVE WHITE: At the time I remembered them then. I remember—you reminded me of the good things you were doing. If you reminded me of some of the things you said, I could answer that.

"*Yes,*" Afeni Shakur spoke her final word. "*I guess so.*" She asked for a recess and returned to say that she had no further questions. In those twenty minutes she had made Mr. Phillips' witness her own; and in their coupling, she had rescued herself and all the others. Yedwah had made his way by women; and here at last he had been beaten by Woman in a moment she had made so intimate that it might all have been performed in their own tiny room.

She would never reach such a moment again, perhaps because she would never need to. On those other occasions when she examined Patrolman Ashwood or made her last statement to the jury, her bearing had lost that fierce, calm concentration on necessity. That part of her that had carried her through this one essential engagement must have instructed that she had brought herself home free and need only wait now, drowsing with her child, the work of the hot noon done, and something like the peace of the twilight already soft upon her shoulders.

The second anniversary of the arrests came round to find Justice Murtagh sitting, more than he would have a year before, with his face between his hands, as though kept awake only by the last traces of his alertness to affront. Spring seemed to have begun faintly to melt his snows; he could detect the end of the journey. Mr. Katz and Mr. Lefcourt thought they could perceive signs of a slow, still distant, movement toward the comity that judges like to see as cases draw down to their resolution.

The justice had taken now and again, most frequently when Mr Crain was cross-examining, to turning about his chair from the courtroom until only the back of his head and his robed shoulders were visible, as though the duty to maintain the unblinking stare of office was too heavy for him to bear. Occasionally in such withdrawals, Robert Collier would call him to attention. The interventions of the defendants expressed more and more their annoyance at having been thrown among the ill brought up. "You are very rude," Afeni Shakur commented once when Mr. Phillips was plunging ahead careless of her priority to pass through first, "I was trying to object. . . . Will the district attorney please stop acting like a nine-year-old child?" When Justice Murtagh rebuked Mr. Bloom for inciting his clients, Robert Collier spoke up for his counsel: "Say it to me, judge. I'm responsible for my actions, not my lawyer." They drew closer and closer about themselves the aristocratic tone of reproach, as though cast back to a time years before rebellion and imprisonment, as though the whole experience had reminded them most of all that they had grown up in homes not just old-fashioned like Justice Murtagh's but by now obsolete, where the servant had the same claim to grace as the master and where the difference was recognized between what are good manners and what no better than correct ones. But then the powerless have an advantage when it comes to cherishing outworn courtesies, since nothing makes them seem worth more to the one who is being used or less to the one who is using.

Justice Murtagh and Assistant District Attorney Phillips were less capable than the defendants of the deportment that can confound our prejudices toward its bearer.

They had, to be sure, failed no easy test. The Shakurs held the chairs closest to Mrs. Phillips'. Lumumba Shakur's exuberance had preserved itself well enough from chastening recollections of the manners his aunt had taught him to show itself in regular asides that were by now more teasing than angry. Once Justice Murtagh announced that he despaired of ever making a trial lawyer of Mr. Phillips; and, as that paltering, suffering victim of the judge's momentary distemper about everyone tried to apologize, Lumumba Shakur said to him, "Speak up, Joe; don't be a bootlicker." A while later, he leaned back taking his ease, looked upon Mr. Phillips in full cry, and observed to young Mr. Weinstein, "Jeff, the man's messing up your case so bad, he's ruining your career." Afeni Shakur, however firmly her troubles had reminded her that her mother's strictures on her conduct had been wise as well as tedious, could not abstain from now and then crooning, "Your cheating

242

heart will tell on you" for the prosecutor's ears alone, and then, when he would turn in his outrage, favoring him with a smile so brazen and so beautiful that he could only puff up to the bench and dilate upon his torments at sidebar.

As for Justice Murtagh, his old wounds were yet so fresh as to make every pinprick fall upon him like a sword. He could not often let pass the opportunity of the jury's absence to lecture defense counsel in terms barely this side of revilement: "You, Mr. Bloom, are a man of more words than wisdom." "I regret [to Mr. Crain] that you are privileged to appear in a court in this state because of your lack of courtesy." "The conduct of Mr. Lefcourt, Mr. Katz, Mr. Bloom, and Mr. Crain is an utter disgrace."

"The court would never admonish the district attorney about anything," Mr. Lefcourt once protested.

"Because he acts like a gentleman," Justice Murtagh replied.

He could not, of course, steadily enough conceal from the jury all evidence of a rancor this vehement. His failure was understandable when it came to Mr. Crain whose examination of Ralph White, especially, descended in its desperation to hectoring of the least attractive sort. ("Didn't you just make all that up?") Yet Justice Murtagh was not visibly more patient with Mr. Bloom. ("Proceed, Mr. Bloom, and take that snicker off your face.") And Mr. Bloom was, if not altogether to be absolved from the sin of garrulity, so gentle and free either of guile or aggression that it was impossible to find for the impulse to disparage him any excuse but the itch to bully him.

Mr. Bloom was worrying over the surface of Ralph White in minute exploration for any scar that might turn up when Mr. Phillips interjected:

"Can't we get on to something relevant?"

MR. BLOOM: I object to the comments of the district attorney.

JUSTICE MURTAGH: Your objection is ignored. If you want a ruling on it, it is overruled.

"Judge," Mr. Katz wondered at one point, "wouldn't this be an appropriate time to cease the rather petulant personal remarks against defense counsel which have gone on now for several months and which are becoming quite offensive?"

"Would it not be high time," Justice Murtagh replied, "when defense counsel acted like gentlemen?"

Near the end of March, the justice became enough aware of an atmosphere where the jurors could hardly not know his feelings; and his sense of fairness directed an addendum to the admonitions with which he daily dismissed them:

"The guilt or innocence of the accused is purely personal with them, and they are not to be charged in any way with the conduct of counsel . . . if counsel act in a manner that in any manner displeases you, or if you think the court is displeased, kindly bear in mind that this aspect of the case is to be completely disregarded in determining the guilt or innocence of the accused."

For all the propriety of that formula, there had been about the winter a chilling air of nastiness in too much of what was official about the business; and it would be frozen to a degree almost repugnant with the introduction of the undercover Patrolman Carlos Ashwood, Mr. Phillips' last major witness.

Ashwood, while he had seen less of substance than either Roberts or White, could tell of things heard whose atmosphere ought in many ways to have made him a more persuasive witness than they. But there would appear to be merit systems that govern advancement in organizations whose purpose is society's overthrow just as there are in institutions designed to protect it. The standards turn out unexpectedly similar; the useful claims are those of charm or proven experience. Patrolman Ashwood was deficient in both. As a policeman he was still immobilized in the grade of patrolman while White and Roberts were already detectives; and as a secret policeman in the Panthers, he had never been able to penetrate, by engaging social presence as had Ralph White, or by prior revolutionary experience as had Eugene Roberts, those private places where the higher conspirators, whether they are relaxing in the one

244

case or contemplating the care of business in the other, let slip their schemes. Ashwood had been trusted to party duties no more covert than literature distribution. Still he had been unwearying enough about the fringes to be able to claim that he had been standing by the Panther literature table at Rockland Palace on January 17th when elements of Lumumba Shakur's strike force returned and had heard their mingled discomfiture and amusement over its miscarriage. Here was a scene that, if it hardly proved guilt, might well be a plausible pointer to it. A juror who believed Patrolman Ashwood could hardly avoid the suspicion that these persons had done something, however inconsequential. But his was a tale whose effect depended on some measure of disinterested moral conviction in the telling; and from the outset, Ashwood's sullen demeanor suggested a character most ambiguous. It would not be clarified to his advantage since, under cross-examination, he would demonstrate a spite especially unappetizing because its main foundation seemed to be the resentment of someone passed over for promotion in every enterprise he joins. He treated the inquiries of defense counsel with a disdain and ill-temper that made Justice Murtagh's occasional displeasures seem as gentle as the reproofs of a bishop. He was a rock the illusion of whose safety was in losing contention with the too obviously sulphurous nature of its fumes. Afeni Shakur invoked him into the dangerous dance she had executed with Ralph White. He proved his immunity to such seductions at the cost of appearing more repellent than was helpful to the impression his sponsors must have wanted to create.

AFENI SHAKUR: Did you ever see me kill anyone?
PATROLMAN ASHWOOD: I never *saw* you kill anyone.
AFENI SHAKUR: Did you ever see me blow up anything?
PATROLMAN ASHWOOD: I never *saw* you blow up anything.

These underscorings suggested a malice the witness was more anxious to show than careful to disguise; and Patrolman Ashwood had a visage so sourly ill-favored as to need only be

245

caught shading the truth in a slight something to start the suspicion that he might lie about everything.

He stumbled into the mischance of some such disabling small falsehood when Mr. Katz asked him the names of the supervisors who had guided his undercover travelings for the Bureau of Special Services, and he replied that he could not remember any of them.

MR. KATZ: You can't remember the name of any supervisor?

PATROLMAN ASHWOOD: Well, that was some time ago. The supervisor's name at that time was not of interest to me.

Mr. Phillips hastened to the bench to explain that the witness "is obviously reluctant to reveal certain things he probably feels are still of an undercover nature" and suggested a conference where the district attorney could tell him that these were subjects about which it was proper to tell the truth. "He is lying," Mr. Crain said, for once both precise and laconic. "He is simply misadvised," Justice Murtagh amended. "The court can sense that we have a problem of security that is bothering the witness."

And with that extraordinary expression of judicial notice that a policeman under oath may misstate the truth if he thinks it his duty to, the justice recessed the trial to give Mr. Phillips a chance to straighten out Patrolman Ashwood over luncheon.

Justice Murtagh's rule would have needed to run to a province more docile than the ghetto of the defense attorneys for him to expect this passage to slip by unnoticed. On March 22nd, Mr. Lefcourt revived it in front of the jury and asked Patrolman Ashwood:

"Is it not a fact that you were trying to protect your supervisors by not having their names revealed in the trial, and that, when you said, 'I don't remember their names,' you were lying to protect them?"

"That's not a fact, counselor," Patrolman Ashwood answered.

246

Mr. Phillips was on his feet and there was played out this scene:

"Counsel. Your Honor. This is asked in bad faith. Are you trying to mislead the witness?"

MR. BLOOM: Objection to the speech, your Honor.

AFENI SHAKUR: Objection to the continual speechmaking of the district attorney in this courtroom.

JUSTICE MURTAGH: Objection overruled.

MR. LEFCOURT: Your Honor, I object to the comments of the district attorney, because he tells an entirely different story sidebar than he tells here in open court.

MR. PHILLIPS: He told us—

JUSTICE MURTAGH: You are guilty of very bad faith.

MR. LEFCOURT: Well, your Honor, the court knows what he said sidebar.

JUSTICE MURTAGH: Please, Mr. Lefcourt. Now I will say to counsel as a whole, I want them strictly to refrain from objections, except when they are questioning a witness. This is Mr. Lefcourt's questioning and I don't want interruptions from counsel whether they represent themselves or whether they are members of the bar.

AFENI SHAKUR: May I state for the record that, whether you are demanding that I refrain from making objections or not, Mr. Murtagh, what you are in effect doing is denying me my right to defend myself. If you are going to demand that I not make objections, then I ask you to demand that the district attorney stop standing up in open court and telling continuous lies.

JUSTICE MURTAGH: Request denied.

MR. KATZ: Judge, I may just add or wish to add that counsel may be obliged from time to time to rise and make objections. . . . I think you are placing an undue restriction which rises to due process level, your Honor, by restraining counsel.

JUSTICE MURTAGH: I am fundamentally asking counsel to cooperate in having an orderly trial, and I ask you again to cooperate. Please be seated.

MR. KATZ: Your Honor, you may feel that rising to make an objection is disorderly. We find it necessary and constitutionally required.

AFENI SHAKUR: And may we ask the district attorney to cooperate in having a just trial?

JUSTICE MURTAGH: Request denied.

[Here, the stenographer records, "laughter emanated from the defendants."]

THE DEFENDANT WILLIAM KING: How do you like that one, Phillips?

JUSTICE MURTAGH: I admonish counsel that they have a responsibility for insuring that their clients do not misbehave during this trial and I see no evidence that I am getting support.

MR. BLOOM: Perhaps if you looked at us, you would see it.

MR. MCKINNEY: I admonished my client not to shout out. I would ask the court to make observations with his eyes rather than his mouth before he speaks.

JUSTICE MURTAGH: Counselor, your language is out of order.

MR. MCKINNEY: Your Honor, it's shocking that you should make that observation when I very specifically and immediately turned to my client and admonished him, and I feel that I must rise and protest the manner in which the court made the observation and the statement.

JUSTICE MURTAGH: Counselor, in the main, you have been a gentleman throughout this trial. There are such occasions as this when your conduct leaves a little to be desired.

MR. MCKINNEY: I consider that I am being a gentleman if I protest with vigor.

JUSTICE MURTAGH: You may protest with vigor, but counsel generally are admonished to conform with proper conduct. And your conduct is not proper.

MR. MCKINNEY: I think it was quite proper. The court made an inaccurate observation and I rose to make the record straight.

248

JUSTICE MURTAGH: I regret that you resorted to it.

MR. MCKINNEY: Your Honor——

AFENI SHAKUR: May we state for the record also . . . that the justice or judge in this case has failed to act like a gentleman.

JUSTICE MURTAGH: Mr. Lefcourt, will you kindly resume your questioning?

Until that brief and open quarrel, all the varieties of injured pride that struggled on the scene—the judge's in his prerogatives, the prosecutor's in the insolence of his office, the defendants' in their disdained humanity, their lawyers' in their own despised proficiency—the grievance of every actor that he was being rated too low had been felt by the jury as isolated emanations of the poisoned gases underneath. Occasionally a defendant would protest, more than occasionally the judge would reprove or Mr. Phillips badger or defense counsel flourish their impenitence. But these had been fragmentary discharges until now when all parties were seen to cry out together and in despite of one another. And, in that short while, Mr. Phillips, if he could not yet be said to have lost his case, had placed himself irrevocably distant from any point where he could hope to win it. The official party had created its crisis with entire indifference to the perils of its chosen ground.

Patrolman Ashwood was being cross-examined on his earlier affirmation that he had forgotten the name of any supervisor he had served in the Bureau of Special Services. No one who had been paying attention could doubt that this had been an untruth, least of all Justice Murtagh and Mr. Phillips who had each recognized and excused it as founded on the patrolman's perfect, if transiently uncomprehending, sense of duty. Mr. Lefcourt had been reminding the witness of this small sin when the district attorney broke in to say that any such question could only be asked in bad faith. The judge adopted this term of abuse as his own, only compounding its force into "very bad faith." A defendant wrapped in every claim that sentiment

249

can invoke—youth, womanhood, the fragility of impending motherhood, the loneliness of the cell—had risen to ask that the district attorney "cooperate in having a just trial" and the judge had rebuked her with his short "Request denied." The defendants had laughed aloud; and the judge had chosen to blame this disturbance upon Mr. McKinney, by no means the only one of counsel with an attractive but certainly the only one with a courtly mien. Mr. McKinney had responded from a dignity so outraged as to make plausible the most extreme imaginings of what prior torments this court must have placed upon manners like his to bring them to this final breach.

The full damage done by this spectacle to the expectations of Mr. Phillips and the assurances of Justice Murtagh was revealed first to the jurors and remained their property alone for the next seven weeks. Long durance had, to be sure, made them each other's familiars. But, if anyone of them had been so wanting in sensibility as to discuss the evidence they were listening to, he would have been inhibited by the Anglican stringencies which Mr. Fox, their foreman, had carried with him from British Guiana. Mr. Fox had all the authority that belongs to perfect manners when they keep company with an intactness of mystery. No one knew how he felt; and his mere presence made it an embarrassment for any other juror to say how he felt.

But that day, when lunch came and they passed to the solitude of the jury room, Benjamin Giles, juror number nine, could contain himself no longer. He was the only member of the panel older than Mr. Fox. He was a Negro of the thirties, a longshoreman who had been at once stubborn and accepting enough to keep his place in a labor force where the struggle between the Irish and the Italians abated only in their compact to expel the blacks from the docks. Mr. Giles had then his mask as Mr. Fox did; and that day he tore it off. Had they heard, Mr. Giles asked them all, what that judge said when that girl asked him for justice? Mr. Giles had had his fill; he "was going back into that courtroom and tell Murtagh that this is not Mississippi." But then he recalled all the circumstances that had

250

made his generation so proudly enduring yet eventually so resigned; he contemplated all the conditions about which nothing could be done and gave this one its appointed place among them, and, for a moment, yielded to the ancient fact of power, and said that he had decided to tell the court that he was ill and ask to be relieved.

"Mr. Giles," Mr. Fox responded, "this is not the time to leave. If you feel as you do, the time to show it is when we vote." Authority is in its very occasional bending; power is in grace; and the weight of the mystery is in its momentary lightening. At that moment, without knowing that it had happened, Justice Murtagh gave over the robes of office to Mr. Joseph Ingram Fox. Benjamin Giles would stay the course and henceforth would be what he was by nature, a man who would watch hell freeze over and write "Not guilty" across the ice.

It is unlikely that Mr. Fox had been entirely sure what he intended when he chose to stay home and reveal his artistic sensibilities in this courtroom where the audience was so small rather than go to Europe where he had been promised, after so long a wait, an audience large enough to be worthy of them. Still there were hints in his subsequent recollections: after the first day of his examination as a juror nominee, he had come home to tell his wife that he seemed to have the option whether to serve or not. He supposed to Mrs. Fox that he sensibly ought to go to Europe and try the long-deferred great chance of his career; but then he had come into the courtroom through squads of policemen and looked upon prisoners barely visible among their guards; he was troubled by being reminded of things in America that need correcting. "Don't worry," Mrs. Fox answered. "Stay if you think you have to. I'll keep you."

By March, this early, the score was complete in his head; Mr. Fox was thinking of its orchestration. He recalled what his father, a bailiff in a colony, had told him about the cadences of British judges, and he was devising, on that model never heard, the changes he would need if he were pleasingly to vary the sound of the words "Not guilty" pronounced 156 times. So he had come, and he stayed now, for nothing more or less than to show the very few persons who might hear him the way a judge should act.

What had descended upon Mr. Phillips was a disaster so unexpected as to be quite beyond his imagination. Ultimately he would be beaten because his larynx had so much more force than his case. But the first indication of his defeat would come after just two minutes when, of all persons, eleven Black Panthers would show themselves in possession of better manners than their judge and their prosecutor.

No more than their judge and their prosecutor could defense counsel have suspected what effects of this exchange were resounding through their jury. The scene had been most pallid against the gaudy splashings of the year before when they had suffered and, in truth, inflicted wounds far worse. Time had blunted most of the swords in this arena, and its warriors had come to think of these persistent rancors almost as the normal order of a courtroom's rounds. They had stopped even noticing, in what had become their home, that habitual ill-temper that could still appall the visitor. There were few interruptions these days and fewer intrusions. The noise in the streets had faded, to sound in force only once and with a different voice. The largest assemblage in the vicinity had been called together to protest anti-Semitism in the Soviet Union; and Mr. Lefcourt could further develop the education in irony these months had aged like a wrinkle upon the original innocence of his surface while standing at its fringes and hearing the mayor of the city of New York arraign the Communists for employing conspiracy laws to punish the politically objectionable.

The trial had been interrupted twice by the rhythmical tumults of a city with a populace whose insistence upon defying its rulers can embrace not just the prisoner in his jail but the policeman who sent him there. Proceedings had been suspended four days in October when the inmates of the Queens House of Detention seized their prison and withheld its raw material from the processes of justice; and they broke off again for two days in January when the police witnesses stayed home pretending to

252

illness from loyalty to a disguised salary strike by the Patrolman's Benevolent Association.

The Queens jail uprising may have been distantly inspired
but could not have been directly aroused by the preachments
of the Black Panthers. The insurgents had already subdued
their keepers and secured their garrison by the time they
unlocked Kuwasi Balagoon and the nine imprisoned male defendants from the fifth floor compound where they had been
isolated to keep their contagion from the other detainees. Even
so, innocent as they were of commencing the disturbance, they
were given a commanding place in its management thereafter;
and a citizenry generally at a loss for constructive leadership
and continually surprised at the odd places where it makes its
infrequent appearances could watch on television while William King, the terrible Kinshasa, hooded to protect his identity,
read aloud a statement most unexpected beginning with the
complaint that a number of black prison guards were being
denied promotion because of suspicious goodwill toward the
inmates. Afterward the district attorney of Queens publicly
thanked Lumumba Shakur and the others for their moderating
influence throughout the troubles, and then indicted King
and Shakur for kidnapping and mayhem, in deference to the
demands of a corrections commissioner, who, having made it
impossible for them to talk to the other prisoners, thereupon
blamed the Panthers for inciting them.

The judicial process seemed otherwise to have been restored, if not to a gentle at least to its crudely normal tenor.
Defense counsel had no reason to think that the atmosphere
would seem to these jurors any worse than it did to any other
set of respectable citizens. His opponents knew, of course, that
Mr. Phillips' case appeared rather better for them than he
thought, if only because they had come there expecting it to
look much worse; even so, it was with a lively appreciation of
remaining hazard that they set about deciding what witnesses
they might safely call for their clients.

Mr. McKinney, being the most experienced head on the

panel, thought that to call anyone at all would be to invite trouble. He was, however, prepared to make one tentative try for innocence by association and call Clark Squire's employer to attest that there were no dangerous chemicals around his computer company's offices. Mr. Lefcourt proposed to summon Shirley Jones, who had once supervised the operations of the Ellsmere Tenants Council and could testify that if Ralph White had fired his pistol into the tabletops there, he would have been shooting in a direction opposite from any dynamite hidden behind its refrigerator. Mr. Katz thought it would be helpful if Joan Bird's mother would testify about what she remembered about her daughter's treatment under arrest through the night of January 17th. Mr. Bloom thought it would have been delinquent in him not to have put forward two or three of Robert Collier's friends to rebut, in details niggling where they were relevant, the already niggling evidence against him.

It was a sparse battery and its testimony would be of negligible value. Even so, just to confront any defense witnesses at all so enraged Mr. Phillips that, while providing the defendants with very little useful evidence, the appearance of even these few was enough to set him off into the wildest fits of self-injury.

Mr. Bloom's first witness was Colin Connery, a volunteer handyman at Robert Collier's Tompkins Square Community Center. Connery was very like Mr. Bloom, a gentle young man slipped from the middle class into company thought disreputable and consequently, like Mr. Bloom, of a species considered fair game for bullies. Connery came to explain away the pipes that had been seized in Robert Collier's apartment. These could well, he swore, have been left over from some scrap plumbing he had pieced together to install a shower for Collier. As for the can of gunpowder that was the closest approach to a high explosive in Mr. Phillips' arsenal of evidence, Connery had been in and out of Collier's bathroom until a few days before the arrest and had never seen it.

Mr. Bloom had hoped to raise somewhere in the jury an

254

inference that the arresting policemen had brought the gunpowder along on their raid to plant it on Collier's premises. It was not a large prospect; a policeman zealous enough to contrive evidence could certainly concoct an exhibit more terrible than this paltry thing. Connery's memory indeed suggested a more plausible inference quite damaging to the defense; if he hadn't seen the gunpowder can three days before the arrest, then Collier had but recently acquired it and could thus be thought of as collecting explosives just a day or two before the one set for the act of terror the prosecution charged him with plotting.

Mr. Phillips could very well have moved from such a surmise to make the witness Connery his own. But the affront offered by someone who looked so like his own image of inoffensive conduct and who had yet betrayed every advantage that ought to have barred him from affection for Robert Collier so consumed the district attorney as quite to displace any appreciation of how useful this witness, delicately handled, might be to him.

Here was a young man, growing up in Queens, educated at Swarthmore, subsidized by Presbyterians, who had turned from his ascending path to plunge downward into the East Village, the company of Robert Collier, and no vocation except existence for two dollars an hour as plumber and carpenter to certified freaks and putative conspirators.

Mr. Phillips might have been warned by a modesty and earnestness in this quest that was enough like the demeanor of at least three of his jurors to suggest that, however curious they might think Connery's commitment, they were unlikely to view its motives as so much more malign than their own. But he reasoned not; it was his taste to bludgeon Connery back across the road that had led to the infamies he now exhaled—the college degree in physics whose attraction he had abandoned, the turning to the church, the casting about in the East Village for work at once dignified and useful. Even under assault the witness clung to his unspeakable affection for Robert Collier. "Bob," he explained once, "is very accessible." Mr. Phillips did his utmost to make Connery's pilgrimage, not always inerrant but in sum quite affecting, sound as much as he could like a course in criminal conduct, and he crowned his morning with the question, "Did you come here with the intent to tell the truth or just to tell some lies?"

Mr. Crain had, to be sure, pursued this unattractive line with Detective White—and rather more extensively—until he had driven Justice Murtagh to precipitate one of the few exchanges in a generally dreary quarrel that might have been called handsome:

JUSTICE MURTAGH: Ask questions respectfully of the witness.

MR. CRAIN: I don't have to be respectful of the witness. [Pause.] I'm sorry, Mr. White.

DETECTIVE WHITE: That's all right, counselor. You are forgiven.

But Justice Murtagh showed no distaste while the hatred in Mr. Phillips' tone rose higher and higher until Mr. Bloom was impelled to object and the judge limited his reply to the observation that "you gentlemen have been guilty of worse."

Mr. Phillips spent the luncheon recess employing those powers of information that are the singular resource of prosecuting attorneys. His delight in their exercise was unaffected by any caution that their display could well stir in jurors concerned about the privacy of the citizen more alarm about himself and his office than about the witness. His first exhibit from this store was Connery's employment record with the Department of Social Services. He gnawed at that awhile with no useful nutriment and then came to his grandest morsel.

Colin Connery had affirmed that he had never been convicted of a crime.

"What then," Mr. Phillips asked, "were you convicted of in Chester, Pennsylvania?"

The witness recalled that he had been arrested in connection with a civil rights demonstration as one of three hundred

256

others taken into custody that day, and had never even paid a fine.

"Did you," Mr. Phillips plunged on, "plead guilty of unlawful assembly and were the charges conspiracy as well?"

His examination of Connery had brought Mr. Phillips' urge to punish anyone whose private loyalties conflicted with his own prescription of public duty into full flow when he came to look upon Mrs. Shirley Jones, who had been overseer of Ralph White's stewardship of the Ellsmere Tenants Council. Mrs. Jones had resisted being called most strenuously; she had already suffered embarrassment as a mother and a career woman from Ralph White's candor about their friendship; and she had in the interim advanced from the loose disciplines of poverty politics to the stiffer ones of the city's Department of Human Resources and the risk of offending a public employer. Mr. Lefcourt had finally resorted to a subpoena to extract her trivial witness.

He yielded her to the district attorney as soon as she had disputed Ralph White's memory of the location of the table-tops into which he had fired the shots that impelled Lumumba Shakur to caution him to be careful of the dynamite in the future.

To Mr. Phillips, Mrs. Jones represented a depravity worse than normal even in a witness for the defense. Mr. Crain had cross-examined Detective White about transactions between Mrs. Jones and himself that only she could have told the defense. She was, then, not just testifying for these persons; she had actively assisted them.

Long minutes of savagery wrung from her a confession he might easily have had with a few seconds of civility. Mrs. Jones remembered that she had first met Mr. Lefcourt a year or so before when she visited his office.

MR. PHILLIPS: And they asked you to come down and help with the case. Is that correct?
MRS. JONES: Yes, they did.

MR. PHILLIPS: And did you go voluntarily down to help with the case?

MRS. JONES: Yes, I did.

MR. PHILLIPS: Now, isn't it a fact during this trial that Mr. Lefcourt has called you on a number of occasions to discuss the testimony as it developed?

MRS. JONES: I don't know what he called me for, but he's called me more than once. I've only spoken to him on the phone about twice.

MR. PHILLIPS: How many phone calls have you received in the last five months in relation to this case?

MRS. JONES: I don't recall.

MR. PHILLIPS: *Weren't there over fifty?*

MRS. JONES: I receive, during the course of the week, maybe eighty phone calls, so you couldn't possibly expect me to remember who called me, where, when, and how.

MR. PHILLIPS: I'd expect you to tell me how many——

MRS. JONES: I don't recall. I don't recall.

MR. PHILLIPS: Well, is it fair that you had over fifty phone calls in the last six months with relation to this case?

MRS. JONES: I spoke to Mr. Lefcourt twice. I don't recall how many phone calls came from his office.

MR. PHILLIPS: How many phone calls did you receive?

MRS. JONES: I don't recall.

MR. PHILLIPS: Are you just saying that because you don't want to answer my questions?

MRS. JONES: I'm saying it because I don't remember.

MR. PHILLIPS: Well, when I asked you what day you went to Mr. Lefcourt's office this week——

MRS. JONES: I said I couldn't recall.

MR. PHILLIPS: You couldn't recall. Were you just answering that way or did you really not recall?

MRS. JONES: I don't recall the day that Mr. Lefcourt was at my office. I was at his office Monday night.

MR. PHILLIPS: When I asked you first about that, you wouldn't tell me, would you?

MRS. JONES: I didn't recall.

258

MR. PHILLIPS: And you didn't recall any phone calls. How many times did you go to Mr. Lefcourt's office over a year ago?

MRS. JONES: I went one time a year ago and I went once last week.

MR. PHILLIPS: All right, is it fair to say that you went once last week?

MRS. JONES: What are you asking me is it fair to say?

MR. PHILLIPS: Because you just testified that you went once this week.

He had grown quite incoherent in his wrath and, as it swelled, the substance of his questions shrank until it was no longer possible to credit them with any purpose except to overbear. Mrs. Jones was a young woman who had arrived at a position in life with a fair claim to respectability; and she had come here with the uneasiness of anyone whose privacies have already been too much aired and might, for all she knew, be further waved about now. In small matters, she had exhibited an insecure memory not unnatural to feelings like hers; but she had been completely open in conceding that she had supplied the defense with information and thus answering the only substantial question Mr. Phillips had asked her. Sinful as her action may have been, even the district attorney might have been expected to forgive her adherence to Ralph White's enemies after her experience with his friendship. Instead Mr. Phillips used her as few Cossacks would a woman of the town. And, of a sudden, juror number ten, Charles Bowser, commenced to glare at Mr. Phillips' neck, swelling in the fullness of its cry and unconscious of a force of anger upon it that anyone who could still feel anything would almost have to feel. The eyes of Charles Bowser, supervisor of welfare caseworkers, were basilisks behind his glasses, his lips were white, and his fingers pressed against them as though to hold back their anathema until some proper time to hurl it forth, enraged black professional man enduring for a while but implacably engraving upon his memory the sight of violated professional woman.

259

And one came to see that Mr. Phillips had gone beyond the limits of a singular personal identity, had become an archetype, the epitome of a malevolent idea. His brutality toward those few outcasts in the dock might have been taken as a sign that he was only narrow. But now, seen just as brutal toward persons so nearly like the ordinary run of mankind, his great breadth could be recognized as encompassing everyone within its hatred. Somehow, then, one knew him defeated; and there was a terminal coldness, as if the one thing more unpardonable than coldness would be an instinct of sympathy for someone whose incompetence was in the integrity of his malice. There is a way of thought in America, embracing most of what is respectable and even more of what is official, that would reproach Colin Connery for trusting Robert Collier while it esteems judges who trust Joseph Phillips; and on that stage and for those few minutes, everything Lumumba Shakur and the others had said about that way of thought seemed homely truth.

Mr. McKinney moved at last to ask the judge "to request Mr. Phillips to address the young lady with a little more decorum."

JUSTICE MURTAGH: Yes, I will grant that request.
MR. PHILLIPS: Yes, sir.

Still he could not let do.

"How many phone calls did you have during this period?" he asked.

"I don't recall," she answered.

"If you did recall, would you tell me?" he asked, his tone of threat dutifully moderated into one of scorn.

"I think I would," Mrs. Jones replied. Justice Murtagh suggested that the subject be changed to something more worthwhile; and Mr. Phillips conceded that he had no more questions, being finally debarred from that delight at degrading which was most of what he had found worthwhile in the encounter.

260

Then there were no witnesses left and no voices to be heard except those of defense counsel, prosecutor, and judge. The defense witnesses had been significant to Mr. Phillips not for any story they told but for the offence to authority of their appearance in a cause this infamous. And having so exercised himself to avenge their affront, he did not bother with rebuttal testimony, the injury they offered him having been to his dignity and not to his case and what they said seeming as trivial as the impudence of their saying anything at all was unbearable. He had done his worst and had spent his last secret. The property title to all mystery had passed to the jurors, who remained no easier for the defense to fathom than their prosecutor had once been.

It was around that time that Mr. Phillips is said to have observed that he had conquered all the jurors except Mr. Giles. Mr. Lefcourt had begun the trial with his highest hopes in Mr. Chaberski, the graduate student, and Mr. Butters, the vocational teacher; but now he thought he had detected a fatal disdain in Mr. Chaberski and as dangerous a want of attention in Mr. Butters. Being wrong was an advantage to Mr. Lefcourt, who was better off the longer he thought he was in serious trouble; and being wrong was the final disadvantage to Mr. Phillips, who was especially bad off the longer he refused to recognize how much worse trouble he was in. The condition that they were both wrong suggests that if most politicians are lawyers, surprisingly few lawyers are politicians, and therefore get themselves led astray by models more abstract than serve more worldly professions.

There were eleven defendants left on trial; matters had lasted seven months; the jury had come to inhabit their world and had made individual judgments about this one's merits and that one's deficiencies. If there were disagreements, blocs would form; logic would not be perfect; and the soundest guide to the process would not be those judges until now so unanimous for Mr. Phillips and against Mr. Lefcourt but a quite different institution, responding to prejudices as judges do, but to prejudices less carefully prescribed, since they would arise out of existence rather than precedent. A jury is in fact not an institution at all, but an occasion like what a political convention might be if the delegates assembled without contracts or even commitments.

Such frames of reference were beyond Mr. Phillips, of course, not because he was without cynicism but because his cynicism was hierarchical in foundation; he was incapable of allowing for disorderly feelings in persons who led orderly lives. He overrated habit as men will whose lives exemplify good habits as a substitute for inspiration. For example, insensitive as he was, he had taken note of the decreasingly concealed diffidence of Mr. Giles while remaining unconscious of the unmasked hostility of Mr. Bowser. His class sense obscured his vision. Mr. Giles was a retired longshoreman, while Mr. Bowser was an active executive in the Department of Social Welfare, the same agency that would provide a district attorney with anything it knew that might assist the harrying of Colin Connery, who was not even a criminal but just a witness for criminals. Mr. Bowser worked for what was almost a police agency, since its function, like Mr. Phillips' own, was the management of unsatisfactory persons. Thus, Mr. Bowser was almost a policeman too; and his having made it so plain at the voir dire that he hated being one in no way troubled Mr. Phillips' confidence that in all affairs men act according to the habits of their lives. Mr. Lefcourt, while much shrewder, might be excused a similar mistake. He read *The New York Times* every morning and came to court to suffer the contempt of the presiding judge. That experience was bound to carry him part way through the rite of passage from the illusion of the young that everyone thinks as they do to the illusion of the mature that no one possibly could. It was Mr. McKinney, the best established of counsel at the bar, who had looked at Mr. Bowser and guessed earliest that Mr. Phillips could not win, having recognized in that brooding presence across from him the feelings that had survived his own improvement in his social station and had surprised Justice Murtagh with increasingly unpleasant frequency.

262

In any case Mr. Bowser's somber glower seemed so fixed against Mr. Phillips as to evoke the promise of at least one juryman who would stand forever against conviction. And, if Mr. Giles could be taken as standing with him, Mr. Lefcourt had two hard delegates; and the puzzle became where Mr. Phillips would find a bloc this granite for his side.

The mind was running across the balance as it might have at a political convention. Mr. Hills, Mr. Rasmussen, and Mr. Kennebeck, all being editors, might be taken as the largest collective at the convention, having in its hands the quarter of the votes that New York and California can usually contrive between themselves and their satellites. One might take them as the embodiment of the white liberal mind, and, giving Mr. Phillips the best of it, assign to their modes of reasoning the severest definitions according to Lumumba Shakur. Still the white liberal mind is stubborn mainly in the assurance of its own virtue and one cannot expect to find in it the enduring kidney that could outwear a black caucus turned hard. Mr. Phillips, even if he had these big states, would need other bridges to the rest. There might, of course, be Mr. Chaberski, assuming that Mr. Lefcourt was correct in being depressed by his apparent cynicism about the arguments of the defense. But then it would be like Mr. Chaberski to make it manifest that, sympathetic though he might be, he was no man's gull. Still, accepting Mr. Lefcourt's worst fears, Mr. Chaberski did not seem yet to have acquired that bottom which carries authority when a man has to bargain; he seemed cunning enough to guide but not quite yet weighty enough to lead by himself. He was not the campaign manager but rather the young man who comes to the convention to learn how to be a campaign manager, just as Mr. Butters looked more and more like the young man who comes to the convention and ends up moving to make the nomination unanimous in hopes of getting a no-show job out of it. Mr. Beiser, the history teacher, was like some old friend one met in the Americans for Democratic Action, whom one remembered as moving to South Dakota and who then reappears as a member of that state's delegation, bafflingly

263

uncommitted. Mrs. Yanes, the civil servant, seemed the type of the national committeewoman, a person of some force but unknown contracts.

To cast over these puzzles was to come to the truly consequential mystery of the foreman, Mr. Fox. It had grown to be noticed that every day he would arrive with Mr. Irizzary, the maintenance man, and Mr. Garry, the post-office worker; he had then, without even trying to, established his caucus, a bloc like the one which congressional leaders manage to assemble at every political convention, not usually commanding but most seriously to be taken if matters come to haggling.

Now perhaps Mr. Phillips, having *The New York Times* as he did, might, by stretching the imagination, be thought of as having the Hill-Kennebeck-Rasmussen delegation too. Mr. Beiser could well take cognizance of the indisputable verdict of history that Lumumba Shakur at least had done something. Mr. Chaberski might well turn out to be the sort of careerist who would take a job with President Johnson but would be too smart to work for President Nixon, and would thus fit well enough within the liberal spectrum to go along with some middle course. Mr. Butters might drift in; and together they might provide Mr. Phillips with a far better scenario than he had any visible right to expect. That would still leave him with only six delegates and still desperately dependent on Mr. Fox's caucus which, with the addition of Mrs. Yanes, might amount to as many as four votes by now. Now reason would govern Mr. Fox if he voted to acquit or to convict; but his presence suggested everything but the sort of man whose passion would accompany his reason if he decided to convict. So there did not exist a juror, even granting Mr. Phillips everyone else, who gave promise of digging in, as Mr. Bowser so plainly and Mr. Giles, more and more apparently, were about to. The prosecution was in the most serious trouble; yet so heavy are the chains the tradition of order binds about us all that Mr. Phillips sat down to prepare his summation in absolute confidence and most of defense counsel in barely diminished alarm.

The natural condition of the lawyers, with each one's

strengths and weaknesses, had survived intact through their hammering by Justice Murtagh, and each one went at his final business in the style he had first brought to the courtroom. Mr. Katz was elegant and scornful, cunningly gentle with Detectives White and Roberts, aiming his summation at Mr. Chaberski as his own opposite number, affectionate and respectful toward the defendants but carefully reducing the real danger from them to proportions acceptable to men of the world. Mr. Bloom was more daring, reaching for hyperbole—"John Mitchell and his charming wife Martha, J. Edgar Hoover, Spiro Agnew"—identifying the prosecution's witnesses with "the trusted slave who would whip the other slaves when required," somehow, thanks to some saving grace of milk in his sinews, escaping every risk a white man runs when he speaks in the name of the young and the black to persons who have been there in both cases.

Mr. Crain was at once the proclamation of historical vengeance—"these secret agents . . . black men and women who have been forced to sell their souls and forfeit their manhood . . . the lying, the distortions, the exaggeration, and the degradation"—and the most painful display of nerves, because being above all a responsible man, he knew that his was a style that might harm his client by annoying the jury. Manfully he sought to replace it with an agreeability that, from lack of custom, occasionally broke too far in the direction of the forcedly jocular and even so was rather charming for being so earnest. The day after his summation, Mr. Crain shaved off the beard that had made him look so like an assistant revolutionary prosecutor and revealed an everything-but-self-assertive face toward which even Justice Murtagh could not feel unkind. Mr. Crain must, one thought, have considered this sacrifice awhile and delayed it until his last full-scale appearance before the jurors, being too honest not to let them see him as he wasn't.

For Mrs. Lefcourt the case had covered more hours than her whole trial career. She must have endured her own long night of preparation with a weight of familial concerns heavier upon her than her years deserved, almost a child responsible for elder brothers. Her client Walter Johnson was called "Baba" ("Little Boy" in Swahili) by the others and was not much younger than she. He had been a most tangential conspirator in a conspiracy that had long ago lost much show of cohesion. The sum of what he had done was contained in two afternoons visiting department stores and it is unlikely that he would have done even that little if the steadfast Detective Roberts had not kept him at the task. Mrs. Lefcourt began her preparations by collecting all the testimony against Walter Johnson and, when she had assembled these bits and recognized how meager they were, she understood, with entire domestic economy, that the best she could do for the family was just to recite and dispose of them. The process was brief; at its end she told the jury that this was all she had to say.

And then before her mind's eye there fell the terrible shadow of Mr. Phillips. "He goes last," she said, "and will be able to say whatever he finds in the evidence. Now perhaps I haven't been able to answer everything that he might come up with. So it's a little frightening to stop."

Was it, she could almost be felt as wondering, for nothing except these trifles that Walter Johnson had been in prison for two years? And could she, after saying no more than what she had, leave him safe against the uncooled imagination that had put him there? For just that moment she looked into the abyss of masculine rhetorical abstraction, seemed tempted to plunge, and shrewdly modest drew back. "I leave you," she concluded, "with the life of Baba Odinga."

For Lumumba Shakur, no accounting could be so simple. Even Mr. McKinney, far more certain than his colleagues that Mr. Phillips' case was a ruin, was as certain as they that Lumumba Shakur was still trapped there. The puny evidence against the others worked even upon their lawyers to magnify the weight of the case against him. Something *had* happened on the night of January 17th; there was the physical fact of a substance like dynamite and the artistic persuasion of Ralph White's portrait of Lumumba Shakur tossing it about the office; all the weight left to Mr. Phillips' case sat squarely upon

Mr. Lefcourt's client. Mr. Lefcourt fell back, in this isolation, to the struggle of hand to hand on narrow ground; he would concentrate upon the destruction of Ralph White.

He went at it with unexpected softness, cautious about judgment as to how any Negro lives his life, almost sympathetic to the pain of Ralph White's decision to become a police operative, to the pressures upon him, to his anxiety to please his superiors even while his affections kept binding him closer to his quarry until these insupportable conflicts drove him to counterfeit the image of an evil Lumumba Shakur to justify the fact of a betrayed Lumumba Shakur. It was a drama suited to the actors, being one of those psychological romances of the nineteenth century. Mr. Lefcourt's single analogy to its circumstances was the treason of the agency Indian to the plains Indian; each party to it was, he was saying, a sort of victim. The defect of Mr. Lefcourt's tale was that it could not quite explain away the evidence; for all Mr. Lefcourt could say, Ralph White could as well have put that disabled nature of his to the destruction of a guilty man as an innocent one. But there was no defect at all in this telling, because Mr. Lefcourt was creating a very old-fashioned story about two friends, one true, one false; and the moral choice in all such narratives has a way of ceasing to be which one is the policeman and which one is the criminal but only which one is false. He finished his story and went even further back in time for his analogies:

"We have heard a lot about power in this courtroom—the power of the district attorney, the power of the courts, power to the people we have heard. But now it is all yours, all your power. You know, perhaps, some of your power directly flows .from a case that started three hundred years ago, almost to the day before ours in 1670, September 3rd, 1670. That case was the Panther of that time in England, William Penn.

"He was accused of conspiracy, conspiring with one William Meade in Gracechurch Street. The jury was asked six times to come in with the verdict the court wanted of guilty. And they refused six times. The seventh time they came in and said, 'Not guilty.' And all of them were immediately imprisoned for contempt of court. And that started the process that developed your power. Your power is supreme at this point. You have all the power. The government here owns the building, pays the salary of all the witnesses for the prosecution—save two—the judge, the court officers——"

JUSTICE MURTAGH: Counselor, the court has great patience, but will you please deliver a proper charge?
MR. LEFCOURT: I am finished, your Honor.

"You have the ultimate power and nobody—nobody—can review it. I ask you to reject the spying as unreliable on the basis of what you have heard, and turn them loose and strike a blow for the hope of movements everywhere."

Afeni Shakur had been selected to speak next to last, just before Mr. McKinney. What had been expected of her, in that time when to think of the case was to be desperate, had been a showing of the face of the party, a review of those centuries of suffering from which its savage creed had now burst forth, an incarnation of the judge whose time awaits but will certainly come. But now all had changed and become vulnerable, softened, pleading, with anger and with dignity to be sure, but pleading all the same, all that was symbol fallen away, nothing that was not personal remaining; here, at the last, the face of the party was revealed, in its final refinement, only as the face of the victim.

Afeni Shakur's first attempt was with the formalities. She read aloud snatches of the record, and then she abandoned them and every trace of an intention of grand, general remonstrance and looked at Mr. Fox as though suppliant before some king at whose feet she had arrived across snows and through thorns, past guards and through mocking courtiers, and simply said:

"I don't know what I'm supposed to say. I don't know how I'm supposed to justify the charges that Mr. Phillips has brought before the court against me. But I do know that none of these charges has been proven and I'm not talking about proven beyond a reasonable doubt. I'm saying that none of the charges have been proven, period. That nothing has been proven in this courtroom, that I or any of the defendants did any of these things that Mr. Phillips insists we did do.

"So why are we here? Why are any of us here?

"I don't know. But I would appreciate it if you would end this nightmare, because I'm tired of it and I can't justify it in my mind. There's no logical reason for us to have gone through the last two years as we have, to be threatened with imprisonment because somebody somewhere is watching and waiting to justify being a spy.

"So do what you have to do. But please don't forget what you saw and heard in this courtroom. . . . Let history record you as a jury that would not kneel to the outrageous bidding of the state. Show us that we were not wrong in assuming that you would judge us fairly. And remember that that's all we're asking of you. All we ask of you is that you judge us fairly. Please judge us according to the way that you want to be judged."

It was the more curious, for being so obviously uncontrived, that of all parties, Mrs. Shakur, the Panther, and Mr. Lefcourt, the most radical of lawyers, should have been the voices for the defense that relied most on the Old Whiggery and on the concept of a justice, proof against the winds of doctrine and deaf to the urgings of kings.

It was the revolutionaries who had been driven back to the conservative memories. When Mr. Bloom and Mr. Crain talked about what had been done to Negroes, they were speaking, if to anyone at all, to the white jurors; and, when Mrs. Shakur invoked the Old Cause against the state and Mr. Lefcourt remembered the lonely resistance of other jurors in other centuries, they described not the reality but the promise of America, its primitive, native illusion, and they were, of course, speaking mainly to the Negroes.

As for Mr. McKinney, he simply ran across the rooftops. He alone had read the jury and guessed the result and understood, that, having begun being condescended to and passed to being humiliated, his hour was now at hand and that all affairs would conclude with Mr. Phillips, of all persons, finally abased and Justice Murtagh confounded by the whims and moods of the judicial process. When Mr. Lefcourt returned to the defense tables after embroidering his romance, Mr. McKinney leaned over to him and said, "That does it. It's over. I'm going for all of it." There had not existed for him Mr. Katz's wearying craft, or Mr. Lefcourt's struggle with his novel, or Mr. Crain's agonies over how to be true to himself and inoffensive enough to do his clients no damage, or Mr. Bloom's heroic burrowings for this straw or that. Without their exertions, Mr. McKinney could not have felt as safe as he now did; but, the job having been done, he knew that argument was no longer needed. The field was clear; all key and cadence left for him belonged to triumphal marches.

He was possessed by a perfect assurance that must have seemed terminal desperate effrontery to Mr. Phillips. Mr. McKinney was supercilious toward nothing there except the evidence, and whenever he noticed that, it was with the most genteel pity for something that, found wanting, was already forgotten. His purpose was in his elegance, the highest gift to his clients in his keeping; and they, who had leaned forward so pleadingly through the other summations, sat erect and secure of their futures through his until he came to his peroration:

"And I say to you, ladies and gentlemen, when you retire to the jury room, you will be accompanied by whatever power customarily guides you in arriving at important decisions, and I respectfully submit that, if you are so assisted, you will arrive at a verdict that cries out loud and far as to each of these defendants 'NOT GUILTY, NOT GUILTY, NOT GUILTY.' "

Such was the precise and familiar *envoi* of Lloyd Paul Stryker in the cause of rich, respectable, and criminal clients and here it was being handed over in all its splendor for persons all else but rich, anything but respectable, and hardly criminal.

There remained only Mr. Phillips to accumulate all his disasters in his summation. He began with and maintained a facetious tone—"There is sort of a humorous entry here" or "I

270

really enjoy defendants' exhibits" or "A bit of humor might be helpful to our mood"—as though his were a mind so impenetrable to normal sensibilities as not to conceive the existence of auditors to whom the prospect of deciding that a defendant ought to go twenty years to prison was no light subject at all.

Then having unsettled those jurors he thought his equals in education by want of regard for their gravity, he approached those he thought his inferiors with no respect for their intelligence. Nine times he told the jury that he knew it could not remember this piece of evidence or that; and at last, when the sense of being laborious overcame even his self-esteem, he said:

"I look at twelve faces and I say, 'Well, gee, maybe I had better make that point. Maybe Mr. Irizzary has forgotten this, or Mrs. Yanes forgot that, or Mr. Giles has forgotten something else.'"

He had managed to look at twelve faces and select one who was a Puerto Rican and two who were Negroes as those least likely to negotiate the course without his guiding hand at each one's elbow all the way. He was unconscious that he had become only a bitter thought; once, as crashing proof that Sekou had taken his station to fire upon the Forty-fourth Precinct, he held up a photograph taken of that site in clear view across the Harlem River Drive. Mr. Giles turned his head; Mr. Bowser kept his angry eyes fixed only upon Mr. Phillips' stomach. He was condescending to granite.

There ran through his descriptions of the defendants that almost benign indifference of spirit he had shown once offstage when he said that the only remedy for persons like them was their improvement by the penal system. Their difficulty, he said to the jury now, with intention kinder than not, was they had heads too empty to withstand intrusion by the fantasies of *The Battle of Algiers:*

"[That film] explains that there is a philosophy, a theory of revolution, of terrorism, that is productive, that you should and can put bombs in public places, and that it is desirable. Now that to me is undesirable under any circumstances. But, to an

271

uneducated mind, to people who really aren't that terribly well educated—and you saw the tapes and you can appreciate the intelligence of the defendants in this particular case. . . . That's not going to make a terrorist out of anyone who is sophisticated. . . . But you can appreciate the effect that this film is going to have on uneducated minds."

He had already dismissed his prisoners to some remedial reading course under conditions of maximum security; and all that was human with teeth left to gnaw upon him was their counsel. Near the close of his second day of summation, he began enlarging upon the tortures Detectives White and Roberts had endured from the defense table:

"And that was the questioning—it was Mr. Crain who was questioning and, in Mr. Crain's usual manner, he was calling the witness a liar in the form of a question."

Such were the strictures on manners thought deserved by Mr. Crain from a prosecutor who had himself called three witnesses liars in the form of questions; and such was the sympathy thought deserved by Ralph White, whose police career, by his own witness, had included several consummated violations of the public law while this record showed none at all for, say, Walter Johnson, whose two years in prison were all the same a matter for a frigidity in Mr. Phillips as marked as his compassion for Ralph White's six weeks under cross-examination. But then badness of character is a question of function: Mr. Phillips' sins and Ralph White's were in pursuit of their social duties, while Mr. Crain's and what Walter Johnson's might have been were in their despite.

Mr. Phillips went on to say how hard it was "to think of the most asinine thing that was said here." He entertained himself with the fancied crudities and infelicities of counsel until he came to the one that he savored most; it was, of course, Mr. Crain's:

"You recall Detective White was contradicted by, I think, Shirley Jones. Shirley Jones—that's another one of Mr. Crain's great episodes. That one is worth thinking about. Do you recall Detective White testifying about Shirley Jones?"

He paused. Pleasure played about his lips, even faintly kindling his slate blue eyes. "It was a spicy bit of testimony there." Mr. Bowser, long enough granite, had turned to flint.

"But in any event," Mr. Phillips went on, "Mr. Crain repeatedly asked Detective White, 'Isn't it a fact that you told Shirley Jones that it would be cool to kill pigs and that you were really playing the role of super-Panther with Shirley Jones?'

"All those questions Mr. Crain put. Do you remember those questions? Now there is a rule of law which says those questions have to be put in good faith. Shirley Jones came. Shirley Jones testified. And she, Shirley Jones, wasn't asked about any of that.

"What did Mr. Crain do, invent it? Did he make it all up?

"He made it all up out of his own head. Not a shred of truth to support it."

Mr. Crain arose, least to be anticipated of all guardians of good manners.

"Your Honor," he most precisely pointed out, "[Detective White] answered all those questions in the affirmative himself."

JUSTICE MURTAGH: Kindly be seated and allow the district attorney to argue his case.

MR. CRAIN: He's not arguing from the evidence, your Honor.

JUSTICE MURTAGH: *Apparently he is doing too well for you. Be seated.*

That would be the last of all the moments in those months when the character of this party or that one was henceforward a closed question. Every excuse of how Justice Murtagh had been tried dissolved in this one blinding revelation of how wanting he was. That he would endure Mr. Phillips' rant was understandable—he had endured a deal of rant from opposite quarters—but that he would approve of it was atrocious. Unfortunately for illusion there are, if one waits long enough,

273

flashes of a true, too ugly self, that burn away every memory of respect and even sympathy, that abolish every good opinion that form has implanted, that illuminate and even define the institution this officer embodies. Thereafter one could look upon Justice Murtagh and see him give a little here, suffer quite manfully there, even indulge the kindness of letting Afeni Shakur out on bail again and still find oneself unable to detect there any trace of generosity. Nothing was left in one's thought of him except the almost nasty particularity of what all the old words of honor had come to hold for somebody reduced to a lexicon where dignity is not a general right but a private property, where the bully was the prisoner who protested and not the prosecutor who mocked him, where the only gentleman he recognized in the courtroom was this prosecutor who called him "Sir" and badgered women. He was the guardian not of manners but of customs of humiliation, not of equity but of habit.

And yet, by this very animus, he had become the fairest of judges, having in its final display lost all command of the jury. He may not especially have regretted that sacrifice; whatever malice he may have had for the defendants—and his general contempt for their parts would have always kept that small— had been swept away by his resentment of their lawyers. If by now he really much cared how things turned out, calculation would have urged him to temper Mr. Phillips in his flights since they clearly were more damaging to his case than to any of its targets.

Mr. Phillips abated his intemperance to suggest that it was the hour for the day's recess, and Justice Murtagh agreed. Conversation had already begun at the defense table, and their judge asked the defendants and their counsel to please have manners:

"To what you doing to us we supposed to have manners," Robert Collier answered. "You're kidding me?"

Mr. Phillips finished halfway through the morning of May 11th on a note not memorable for excess of license with either

274

his manners or his passions. Even he had commenced to run down; and Justice Murtagh went at once into his charge to the jury. He was by now restored to a vanity about himself in the eyes of history as against those of Mr. Crain. His concerns had all turned to the ceremonial, and he finished his charge on the morning of May 13th, certain that he had achieved a model of fairness to both sides. To the defendants and their counsel his charge seemed naturally, in the words of Mr. Lefcourt, "prejudicial, highly inflammatory, and aimed and desired to achieve conviction."

A lawyer might or might not find those epithets accurate; but a lawyer's ear was no longer relevant. What counted was how the charge sounded to a jury of laymen; and, listened to that way, Justice Murtagh's instructions on the law were unexpectedly useful to any juror minded to acquit. They provided not just chinks but quite capacious exits to escape through without concern that one might be avoiding one's duty to the criminal code.

The panel was adjured to disregard Joan Bird's January 17th statement to the police—the closest thing to a confession Mr. Phillips possessed—if it felt that there had been unnecessary delay in her arraignment or deceit, trickery, or violence in her questioning. These were all suspicions not easy to dismiss in the circumstances of a young woman held in close custody by one hundred policemen for fifteen hours in a station house. The disappearance of Moore and Tabor would, the justice said, ordinarily be of slight value as evidence of their guilt; and anyone who can find an innocent construction for the flight of an accused felon "has a duty to adopt it." Justice Murtagh chose to define the doctrine of conspiracy to that utmost limit of its logic where it could well dispose a reasonable man to more distaste than reverence for any such law: "It may be that the conspirators have never seen one another and have never corresponded. One may never have heard the name of the other, and yet by law they may be parties to the same conspiracy to commit the crime." No such conditions obtained in the instant case, and their invocation so fit the conspiracy doctrine to the most extreme among the alarms of those it disturbs as to constitute more an invitation to nullify than a prompting to follow it.

His charge completed, Justice Murtagh met the protests of the defense team with the reflection that he had been most "charitable," to which Ali Bey Hassan gave reply, "Nobody asked for your charity." They wrangled on through motion after motion and Justice Murtagh disposed of each and all until he came to one of Mr. Crain's and said, "I'm not going to entertain it. I don't think it has merit."

CURTIS POWELL: Naturally, you racist fascist pig.
JUSTICE MURTAGH: Have that man removed from the courtroom.

After eighteen months, they were just the same, unvanquished and unforgiving; and Justice Murtagh, in this interval between the rigor of deportment with which he had managed their trial and the severity with which he would appoint their sentence, had to suffer the displacement of the security of his kindness by the intrusion of the untamed impudence on which he had wasted it a little while. It was Mr. Phillips, too late aware of appearances, who took alarm at how the absence of a defendant might look to the jury at its last sight of the courtroom before it would begin to deliberate. He opened in his accustomed office as recorder of demerits by hoping that the stenographer had noted "the numerous other outbreaks of noise and demonstrations by the defendants," then fairly pled with Mr. Bloom to apply for Curtis Powell's restoration to his seat in the dock and, being rather casually rebuffed, had the humiliation, just before the jury returned, of having himself to ask "if we may have the defendant Powell back to avoid any problem." The defendant Powell was escorted back, grinning and swinging his arms. Justice Murtagh had nothing left for the jury except formal submission of the case. He suggested that they relax, have lunch, and then proceed to consider the evidence in that atmosphere of "cool, calm deliberation" which, if he had not often enough achieved he felt most competent to counsel.

And Mr. Phillips could free himself from the delicatessen sandwiches Mr. Weinstein used to trot out and fetch him so that they could review the morning and watch over the afternoon at work in the office. He appeared for lunch at last at Forlinis Restaurant where defense counsel had long before established their table and where they indulged the frivolity of occasional conversation about other subjects that made one part of his assurance of their moral disadvantage to him.

They had been elevated to their own table in the back room by now, and Mr. Phillips, as an irregular, had to begin with a table at the bar. All risks of confrontation were incorporated in the figure of Mr. Crain who, shorn of his beard, had been restored to small boyhood and, having tried the spumante, was small-boy-tiddly and wandered among his seated colleagues exulting, "Did you hear Phillips at the end, like school wasn't in, him telling teacher that Lumumba was talking?" But Mr. Phillips' huge back was unhearing and indeed unrecognized; in some way he had already sunk beneath the notice of these persons over whom he had so long trod in triumph. It had been noticed that, during his summation, more jurors than not had carefully not looked at Mr. Phillips, as condemning jurors are thought not to look at the defendant once they have made up their minds. Afeni Shakur was laughing in another room and even his victims did not see Mr. Phillips any longer.

In their own room, the jurors had already finished their lunch. Mr. Fox suggested that it might be useful to have everyone present make some general observations on how the case looked to him. "I think," he said, "we might begin with *Mr. Bowser.*" It was over with that sentence; every delegate knows how the national chairman feels the moment he announces the name of the keynote speaker. Mr. Bowser spoke the thoughts he had been looking for well over two weeks; and, one by one, every other juryman said the same thing. Within twenty minutes, the judgment to acquit was unanimous. There were left a

277

few details of housekeeping: Mr. Chaberski observed that since he could not have voted to convict Michael Tabor and Richard Moore in their absence, he was not sure about acquitting them now. There was a brief hesitation over this sound but minor demurrer; but no one of them, including its proposer, felt any disposition to stand on what seemed to them a point of ceremony, the habitual elevation of the ceremonial over the human having been one of the offenses most vivid in their memory of the last eight months. Beyond that, the largest portion of each one's time seems to have been spent writing "Not guilty" 156 times on their verdict sheets.

Persons sensitive to forms would later criticize them for having listened to evidence from October to May and then disposed of it between two o'clock and four o'clock of a single afternoon; but the swiftness of their course was itself an insistence on form, its speed being one point of its affirmation.

Justice Murtagh was informed that the jury had reached a verdict around four o'clock; defense counsel, being unable to grant him even the slight virtue of realism, were certain he thought it was guilty on all charges. The security precautions he spent thirty-five minutes taking would in truth have been sufficient to repel any imaginable assault by persons incensed at the verdict and aroused to liberate its victims from the chains that would follow their conviction.

So Mr. Fox and the jurors filed in at 4:35 to what was now a fortress, and the ragged band outside its walls had been made smaller than it had ever been by a suddenness of event that had caught so many of the faithful unaware that Joan Bird's mother, the most regular of attendants, could not be found in time.

William Wallace, as clerk of court, asked Mr. Fox please to rise, and Mr. Fox did, the verdict sheets held between his hands and below his belt in a position overwhelmingly suggestive of their use only for form and in no case ever for reference. Black clerk, black foreman, black obliteration of Mr. Phillips and suddenly with banners every imagination of Lumumba Shakur's secret army, its transient hour come at last.

278

"Members of the jury," William Wallace intoned, "Have you agreed upon a verdict?"

"Yes," Mr. Fox answered, and who could really be sure what fugitive echo of Joe Turner singing that it's your dollar now but it's gonna be mine some sweet day had entered with so many other intricacies into the orchestration of this single syllable that compressed, not within so much as a bar as within just one note, every reminder of the forgotten, every mandate of the unfranchised, all the pride of the overlooked, every merit of the undervalued.

As to the defendant Lumumba Shakur, on the first count charging the crime of conspiracy in the first degree, how do you find, sir, guilty or not guilty?"

"Not guilty" came back the voice of Mr. Fox's father, that British bailiff, whose life was the knowledge that a gentleman models himself on the nearest aristocrat.

"As to the second count, charging attempt to commit the crime of murder, how do you find, sir?"

"Not guilty." The register had been altered, the modulation had commenced, the art of the variation was, with infinite care, being watched over; and it could be understood how little Mr. Fox had given up when he decided to abandon the promise of Europe for the occasion of being here. One's audience, small though it be, is one's own.

"The third count, the charge of an attempt to commit the crime of murder, how do you find, sir?"

"Not guilty," Mr. Fox said.

And then Afeni Shakur began to cry and Lumumba Shakur to shout and, after all that time, sundered first by Mr. Phillips and then by the distractions of the Street, they came together rocking and crooning in one another's arms. In the jury box the shoulders of Mr. Frederick Hills began to shake and he lowered his eyes, the white liberal mind, so long inscrutable, now unashamedly melting. Mr. Fox rang his changes 153 more times; Mr. Wallace pronounced his "So say you all"; and Justice Murtagh, entirely contained, thanked Mr. Fox and the others for their dedicated service and bade them farewell. A few minutes passed while the judge engaged the unprepared formalities of an acquittal, found out from Mr. Phillips which defendants could go now and which still had warrants against them on other charges, sifted out those who had to remain, and sent the others forth. Alex McKiever and Curtis Powell were the first out of the courtroom. They had not slept or sat upon any article of furniture that was not the property of the state for twenty-five months and now they perched on a table the court officers had set up as a barrier in the hall outside and looked up and down the corridors as though they had only been spectators all along. Downstairs the jurors waited to congratulate them; and after a while defendants and jurors went to the law offices of Mr. Crain and Mr. Lefcourt and drank champagne together. "Where'd you find out how to talk like that, child?" Mr. Giles asked Afeni Shakur. "Fear, Mr. Giles, plain fear," she answered.

All that was official and respectable ordered itself almost at once and without apology. Justice Murtagh composed an exposition of the virtues of the jury system for the Jesuit magazine, *America*. District Attorney Hogan's observations seemed to suggest that the grand jury might have been carried away. "[This verdict] should put to rest the unfounded but frequently heard comment that it is impossible for a black militant to get a fair trial in the United States," said the *Times*. "The jurors punctured the balloon of the Panthers' radical supporters." The institutions that had kept Lumumba Shakur and the others in prison more than two years had watched these defendants acquitted in two hours and could, without reflection, cherish this judgment upon their vices as an ultimate proof of their virtues.

The only protagonist in these events to rise immediately in the world was Joseph Phillips. The chairman of the committee on crime of the House of Representatives was looking for a general counsel and sought Mr. Hogan's advice. The district attorney must have felt that his best man was replaceable. Mr. Phillips was recommended and by that fall was directing an investigation of the Attica prison rebellion. Mr. Chaberski had

280

observed that when he read of the forty-one persons killed there, his first thought was that if the Panthers had been convicted, they would have gone to Attica and most of them would now be dead.

Afeni Shakur had her son and named him Parrish. Lumumba Shakur came out of jail and, quite soon, when he was walking the streets, a police patrol car paused beside him and its driver said, "Well, Lumumba, you've had your last trial." His reply could hardly have been much more attractive; still his life-affirming side would not down and by summer he was back harrying landlords and threatening pushers.

Three weeks after the verdict, Richard Moore and Eddie Joseph were captured while holding up a black social club in the Bronx. The police said that Moore had found an off-duty patrolman's badge while he was forcing his victims to empty their pockets and had beaten its owner brutally with his machine gun. He had fallen upon an assemblage of the sort his father must have most enjoyed; he had arrived, it appeared, at that place where the need to survive is at once intense and disregarded; and there was about this final shame something like a compulsion to be caught.

Detective Ralph White was dispatched to identify the prisoners and reveled in his moral advantage. "You're nothing but a punk," he remembers telling Dharuba. "I'm a man. I risked my life for two years, And you, what are you good for? Just stuff like this."

Lumumba Shakur and William King traveled to Bronx Supreme Court to observe Richard Moore and Eddie Joseph return, once more in handcuffs, for their first trial hearing. Mr. Lefcourt could follow this last turn no further; Mr. Bloom faithfully took his place. Lumumba and Kinshasa sat unforgiving in their seats, prepared to cast a cold eye on the fallen; and then the door opened and Richard Moore was brought in, as always on such scenes, Dharuba, even now, with thirty-four witnesses against him, with that smile half-wise and half-foolish, still the leader of the reel with every partner gone except Eddie Joseph behind him, so lost and so earnestly trying

281

to be gallant. And that sight and all its memories wiped everything out; Lumumba leaned back and laughed. "Arrogant niggers." The presiding judge was asking the prisoner if he would like a court-appointed attorney. "Spare me," Dharuba replied; and Lumumba Shakur laughed again.

Afterward outside he began organizing the defense.

"We got to tell the community, get the literature out to explain why he did it. That was a skag joint. All he was doing was fighting the pimps and the pushers."

Suddenly there before him was the wagon carrying Dharuba back to the county jail. From it there came a glad cry of "Power to the People"; and, as it went off, Lumumba and Kinshasa raced down the steps calling, "Hey, boy, what you doing in that truck? Get out of that truck. Get out of that truck and come right back here."

They were, in their fashion, all together again.